Capital Formation in Canada
1896-1930

Capital Formation in Canada
1896-1930

By
KENNETH BUCKLEY

With an Introduction by M. C. Urquhart

The Carleton Library No. 77
McClelland and Stewart Limited

Capital Formation in Canada, 1896-1930
was first published in 1955 as the
second volume in the series Canadian
Studies in Economics published by
the University of Toronto Press.

Table of Contents

Introduction to the Carleton Library Edition

It is a great pleasure for me to write the introduction to this republication of Kenneth Buckley's *Capital Formation in Canada, 1896-1930*. In doing it, I have acceded gladly to the request of the managers of the series that I include some biographical material about Ken Buckley. I first met him in the summer of 1944, worked quite closely with him at that time and again fifteen years later, and kept fairly well in touch with him until his death in 1970.

Kenneth Buckley's *Capital Formation in Canada, 1896-1930* is the best original work on Canadian economic history of the post World War II period. Its capital formation estimates for 1896 to 1930 – the first such data available for the years before 1926 – continue to be the standard estimates for that period; and its still relevant analysis of the part played by capital formation in the economic history of the time remains a model of clarity and elegance.

This book emerged from Ken Buckley's Ph.D. thesis, which was presented at the London School of Economics and Political Science in 1950. Whilst it represents his first work in economics, it established both the subject matter of his lifetime work – the growth of the Canadian economy – and the conceptual design of the analytical model which shaped nearly all his work. I shall say more on these matters, but first I believe it worthwhile to turn briefly to the formative forces of his earlier years, which besides being of interest in themselves, throw light on the direction of his work.

First, there was his background in and his deep attachment to the Prairies; he was born in Saskatchewan in 1918 and aside from relatively short periods of absence, mainly connected with furthering his education, spent his entire life in that province. The settlement of Saskatchewan and Alberta had taken place sufficiently recently that he personally knew many of the original settlers – his own parents were among them. He knew from them, first hand, the conditions of early settlement, much of the course of settlement and many of the problems of settlement. The period covered by the life of these settlers was to be the early focus of his studies of Canadian growth; it was the period during which the developing wheat economy provided the force that merged the segregated parts of Canada into an integrated economy.

Second, Kenneth Buckley's age group contained those who reached their teens at the onset of the Depression and who spent the next twenty years of this formative period of life in the depression of the 1930's and in the wartime years and their immediate aftermath in the 1940's. The years of depression in Saskatchewan were dreadful. Net income received by farm operators from farm production in that province was negative in five of the ten years from 1930 to 1939. Personal income per capita in Saskatchewan fell from $465.00 in 1928 to $124.00 in 1933; it was still only $161.00 in 1937. In many municipalities, both rural and urban, the proportion of families on relief varied from a fifth of all families upward. It was not an easy period in which to grow up. How Ken Buckley managed to get to University – he was the only member of a family comprising four brothers and four sisters to do so – I do not know, for his family was among those that were hard hit by the depression. Whether it was this experience that made him the rebel in spirit he was is open to question – I should guess not entirely. But I have not much doubt that it helped shape the direction of the research work that he did later.

Third, as a graduate student he spent the summers of 1944 and 1945 in Ottawa in the public service, where, more or less by accident, he was assigned to a position in which he participated in the preparation of the first estimates of capital formation in Canada, a topic related to his major interest in his later life on which point I will elaborate shortly. He had graduated from the University of Saskatchewan, having specialised in English, in 1942, had then spent some months in the R.C.A.F. but had been mustered out for reasons of health in 1943, and was taking an M.A. in economics at the University of Toronto in 1943 to 1945 where he was a student of Harold Innis. His experience in Ottawa, at this time, complemented his studies at the University of Toronto.

My own contact with Ken Buckley began when he joined the government unit to which I belonged, in Ottawa, in 1944. At that time I was with an economic research unit – its director was Dr. W. A. Mackintosh – in the Department of Reconstruction (later Reconstruction and Supply). Its purpose was to do research related to problems of post-war reconstruction and post-war adjustment. One of the projects being undertaken within this unit at that time was the preparation of the first estimates of capital formation in Canada, covering the period 1926 to 1941, estimates which ultimately appeared in a document prepared for the Dominion-

Provincial Conference on Reconstruction which was held in August, 1945. O. J. Firestone was in charge of the preparation of estimates of direct government expenditure – that is, expenditure by Government departments – in capital formation. I was in charge of estimation of private and commercially-oriented public capital formation including capital formation in both privately-owned and publicly-owned public utilities.

Ken Buckley worked with me in the summers of 1944 and 1945 on the part of the capital formation estimates for which I was responsible. How far it is fair to say that his experience in Ottawa at this time shaped his later work is conjectural. However, it is pertinent, I believe, that he was, on this occasion, immersed in the preparation of these estimates of capital formation and saw their emergence with the information that they provided for a period of time which had spanned prosperity, depression and then the onset of war. Further, the Keynesian Revolution was widely accepted by then and the importance of the critical role of capital formation in determining levels of economic activity was better understood than ever before. The unemployment of the 1930's had disappeared with the war but there was concern that it might reappear afterward. The Federal Government had pledged itself to the goal of maintaining full employment and was preparing bold proposals to be made to the Provinces for the maintenance of high levels of economic activity and the improvement of social well-being at the Dominion Provincial Conference of 1945. I think it probably fair to say that much of Ken Buckley's interest in capital formation, which plays a major part in his research through the rest of his life, came from this time.

My other main experience of working in direct collaboration with Ken Buckley occurred when the Historical Statistics project, which culminated in the publication of the volume *Historical Statistics of Canada* in 1965, was under way. I should like to record here his contribution to it. I believe that it was Ken Buckley who first suggested looking into the possibility of a historical statistics volume for Canada at the first meeting of the Committee on Statistics of the Canadian Political Science Association, in 1958, under Gideon Rosenbluth's chairmanship. In any event, he was asked to see if there appeared to be enough material for a volume of historical statistics in Canada and to report back on the matter. After his report that there were adequate statistics, the project then proceeded and he became Assistant Editor. He and I laid out a design of the volume and did the necessary collation of the work planned for each of the sections at the time that the contents of the various sections were decided upon. This collation work had to be repeated, of course, at the time the final editing was done. Ken Buckley himself did three of the sections in the volume for all of which he was eminently the most suitable person. In addition to the work on his own sections, he did a very considerable amount of work in editing the introductory write-ups in other sections. In this last regard he did a substantial amount of work on the sections on the Balance of International Payments, etc., on Agriculture, and on Minerals and Fuel. But in addition he helped with the editing of much of the rest of the volume. As well as the substantial amounts of time devoted to the project in Saskatoon, he spent a summer in Ottawa on it and the major parts of two other summers in Kingston.

Before touching more directly on his work in economics, I shall make brief allusions to his other contributions as an academic. First, he did a substantial amount of work in trying to further the well-being of academia itself. He was strongly committed to his own university (even although, at times, he was critical of what was being done with it). And, especially in his early years, he put a good deal of effort into trying to maintain and strengthen it as an academic institution. Related in part to the foregoing, he put a substantial amount of effort in the 1950's into trying to improve salaries and other staff amenities mainly through his local faculty association but also through national bodies by way of contribution of material to the C.A.U.T. Bulletin and the N.C.C.U. Proceedings in 1954-55. At that time academic salaries were relatively very low as they had been from the end of the war. Ken Buckley worked up much of the data to provide the background for the presentation of the case for salary improvement. In the first instance, it was, I believe, for use at his own institution. But it became more widely available and used more widely than in the University of Saskatchewan itself. And it was an important element in the presentation of a brief by the Canadian Association of University Teachers to the Royal Commission on Canada's Economic Prospects of which Walter Gordon was chairman, which marked, at least in time and I believe also as a causal factor a turning point toward improvement in University salaries. It is well known also that he did considerable amounts of work in trying to arrange improved pension plans for academics. While an imaginative plan proposed by him and a colleague in the Department of Mathematics in his University was not accepted, their efforts helped to draw attention to pension problems and indirectly contributed to improvement in pension plans. Ken Buckley contributed to these activities in the 1950's through his local faculty association which he helped to develop, in which he played an important part for a number of years, and of which he was at one time the President.

Second, he made a quite substantial contribution in a number of ways through public service. Without elaborating these points, I shall just mention that at varying times he was Consultant of the Continuing Committee of Local Government in Regina; Chairman of the Local Placement Advisory Committee; on the staff of the Royal Commission on the South Saskatchewan River Project in 1952; Consultant, Restrictive Trade Practices Commission, Department of Justice, Ottawa; Member of the National Conference for Research on Cooperatives; Member, Advisory Committee on Census Monographs, Dominion Bureau of Statistics, Ottawa; Member, Canadian Council on Urban and Regional Research. In addition, the Prairie universities in their earlier years did a substantial amount of extension work and, indeed, still do; Ken Buckley contributed very considerably to this work of his University.

I turn now to a brief consideration of Ken Buckley's work in economics and especially that part of it to be found in this volume. Most of it was centred about the historical development of the Canadian economy which he saw as taking place in long swings of 15 to 20 years duration; it dealt most deeply with the period from 1900 onward but there was also a good deal of work on Canadian development in the 19th century. In form his work was quantitative analytic although not econometric.

I suspect that Ken Buckley is known best for the estimates of new quantitative data which he prepared. The most commonly used of these are his estimates of capital formation in Canada for the period 1896-1930 which appear in this volume: but he also prepared a good deal of other original material. This material includes data such as: estimates, for the period before 1896, of railway and canal investment in Canada and of direct Federal Government investment; estimates of interprovincial migration of population from 1871)1951; estimates of swings in the number of births of the Catholic population of Quebec from 1820 to 1918 and of total number of Quebec births from 1926 onward; and estimates of rural-urban movements of population.

It would be a great injustice to Ken Buckley, however, to think of him as primarily a producer of estimates of quantitative magnitudes for Canada even if it is these for which he is most remembered. He could not be accused of "measurement without theory": he had a quite clearly stated conceptual analytical framework of the nature of growth in the Canadian economy, quite beautiful in its simplicity, elegance and power, that guided him in the quantitative estimates that he chose to make. This framework appears quite explicitly in his first work, his Ph.D. thesis, which appeared in print as this book in 1955. Although he adjusted the analytical model somewhat from time to time it was not basically changed in his later work.

The model was relatively simple. The initiation of a period of growth depended on the emergence of a basic economic opportunity. In his Ph.D. thesis he regarded the development of the external market for Western wheat as the initiating factor in Canadian growth following the turn of the century. But having noted this fact, he does not dwell upon it. Rather he directs his attention to what he thought was the big driving force in development. This driving force was domestic capital formation – hence the emphasis throughout his life on trying to get improved estimates of such capital formation.

Capital formation might be stimulated directly by the economic opportunity provided by changes in technology and/or the development of new products and markets. But in Buckley's view it was of critical importance that the new opportunities opened up by new commercial markets (or for that matter stimulated by such things as Government expenditure) led to movements of population. These movements of population might be international or they might be internal. Both such movements in Buckley's view contributed directly to stimulating much of the capital formation of high growth periods. This stimulus came in a number of ways. Until the end of the 1920's, expenditure on railroads, much of it coming from the completion of networks of lines as settlement progressed, was extremely important. During the settlement of the Prairies large amounts of investment outlay were made in the Prairie farms and in the facilities for marketing wheat. The movements of population stimulated urban housing expenditure. And much of direct Government expenditure, which became increasingly important, was related to the movement of population and the need for city services and for roads. Ken Buckley makes a good deal of the fact that from 1900 right through to the time of his last published work of any significance, prepared for a conference in Banff in 1963, approximately two-thirds of investment expenditure on construction had been on transport or urban housing or direct government expenditure, that is, on population-sensitive investment. Investment and movement and growth of population interacted one with the other. These points are best illustrated by two quotations taken from his first and his last major work. His theme is made quite clear in his words on page 4 of this volume:

The production of wheat on the Canadian prairie provided the basic economic opportunity in the economic development of

Canada from 1896 to 1930. This opportunity attracted labour and capital to the direct exploitation of virgin land resources and induced investment throughout the economy in major secondary and tertiary industries and, through these, in housing and other community facilities greater by many times than the investment on the agricultural frontier itself. This leverage effect, the most significant aspect of the frontier, was a determining factor in the development of Canada's economic structure and to a large extent, of its political structure as well.

It is illuminated further by the following quotation from the Banff study.

At this point it must be clear that I am impressed by the importance of population movements. I do believe that these movements are induced by the initiation of some other opportunities, and that once they begin they in their own turn induce further movements of population and this process accumulates, and the long swing comes to an end when the demands of growing populations for social capital goods [railways and housing as well as other social capital] is finally saturated.

Thus investment and population movements are the great themes of his work. Both entered in an important way into his *Capital Formation in Canada, 1896-1930* although in this work more effort was put into making investment estimates than in preparing new data on population movements. Investment appears also in his "Growth and Housing Requirements," a report on the economic and social aspects of the housing problem in Saskatoon (1958). His published work in the Report of the Royal Commission on the South Saskatchewan River Project (1952) deals with investment as does his article on "Capital Formation in Canada" in National Bureau of Economic Research, *Studies in Income and Wealth,* Vol. xix, (1956). Population movements are the core of his *Historical Estimates of Internal Migration in Canada* given at the first CPSA Conference on Statistics (1960); and the title of his Banff paper (1963) is "Population, Labour Force and Economic Growth." As might be expected, the three sections of *Historical Statistics of Canada* which he prepared himself for the volume were on population and migration; on the labour force; and on construction and housing.

I have not dealt with Ken Buckley's article "The Role of Staple Industries in Canada's Economic Development" which appeared in the *Journal of Economic History, December, 1958.* It may be regarded as his one major excursion into discussion of the basic initiating force – the basic economic opportunity – which sets off periods of high growth rates. Nor have I dealt with his book *Economics for Canadians*, written with his wife Helen, and some of his other writings that were outside the mainstream of his own work.

It may be proper for me to conclude with one more quotation from his Banff study. "It is the nature of economics and of political economy to set up conceptual schemes of economic growth and theoretical interpretations and then to test them quantitatively and, in Canada, this process of detailed study has barely begun." Ken Buckley's own work is, by a considerable margin, the outstanding work of the post-war period in moving towards this goal.

M. C. Urquhart
Queen's University
July 27, 1973

Author's Preface

This study concentrates upon a single aspect of the growth of Canada's productive capacity. The method of the study is quantitative and the chief results are statistical series which establish the trend and pattern of real investment in Canada in the years from 1896 to 1930 during which an integrated national economy emerged.

The first six chapters are an historical account of capital development from 1896 to 1930 written within the framework of the staple approach. As a result of the approach and the concentration upon the role of investment, the account may be regarded as a footnote to V. C. Fowke's thesis with respect to the function of agriculture from 1850 to 1930, as developed in his studies of federal agricultural policies. I have also used A. H. Hansen's concepts of extensive and intensive investment and N. J. Silberling's theory of urban building and real estate cycles.

An account of the concepts, sources, and procedures used to measure investment is given in the last five chapters of the book. The estimates are presented in the appendix. The conceptual relation between these estimates and the official estimates, which begin with the year 1926, and procedures to be followed to obtain consistent historical series from 1896 to the present are described in "Capital Formation in Canada," *Studies in Income and Wealth*, Volume XIX, National Bureau of Economic Research, which is in press at the present time.

I have been assisted in this study by many friends and colleagues, among whom I should like particularly to mention R. C. Tress, M. C. Urquhart, D. C. MacGregor, O. J. Firestone, and H. L. Buckley. Professor Tress supervised the study at the London School of Economics and Political Science where it was accepted as a doctoral thesis in 1950. I should also like to thank Professor V. W. Bladen and Miss B. Plewman of the University of Toronto Press for their assistance in preparing the manuscript for publication and to acknowledge the generous assistance of the Canadian Social Science Research Council which financed a year of pre-doctoral research as well as the publication of this volume.

Two of the four sections in Chapter IV appeared as an article in the *Canadian Journal of Economics and Political Science* and I am obliged to the Editors for permission to reprint them here.

K. A. H. B.

1.
Introduction

I. Concepts

THE TERMS "capital" and "investment" are always related to each other in the same way: capital is a stock of some thing or things; investment is a flow of additions to the stock. Capital is defined in this study as the stocks of goods of all kinds in the hands of producers, housing in the hands of consumers, durable physical assets – excluding war goods – held by governments, and the net stock of international financial claims.[1] By this definition gross investment includes four major components:

(1) industrial, commercial, institutional, and residential construction, major repairs and alterations, valued at final cost;
(2) the total flow of finished durable machinery and equipment to producers, valued at the cost to them;
(3) the net additions of finished and unfinished goods to producers' stocks or inventories, valued at current prices; and
(4) the net change in financial claims against foreign countries as measured by the net balance on current transactions in the foreign trade account.

Real capital[2] may be defined without regard to legal ownership, whereas financial capital, such as stocks, bonds, and money claims can only be defined in terms of a relation between a creditor and a debtor. In the case of internal financial capital, where the creditor and debtor are both within the country, the stock of claims may be ignored. However, international financial capital, which arises with movements of claims between countries, must be taken into account because the stock and flow of such assets will affect the size of the commodity flow available for use by members of the community. Accordingly a distinction is drawn between gross domestic capital formation, which includes the first three components listed above, and gross investment, which includes all four.

The value of the productive capacity of natural resources is determined by capitalizing the yield in the same way as the value of other durable physical assets is determined, and in practice the line between the two is drawn arbitrarily, if at all. It is relatively simple, however, to separate current additions to these analytically distinct forms of capital. A wide range of explorative and experimental activities is specifically related to the discovery of new resources, especially in new countries.[3] These activities and activities undertaken to improve existing resources raise the total stock of productive capacity. But in an important sense natural resources are given, and it is therefore convenient to distinguish resource development from the expansion of the purely commodity elements in the structure of production, and restrict the term investment to the latter. Only those expenditures on resource development that do not involve outlays on structures or machinery and equipment are excluded. As a result of this restriction, the estimates of gross investment developed in this study differ slightly from official estimates prepared in recent years.[4]

Gross investment is the value of the total flow of additions to the stock of capital during a given period; net investment is obtained by subtracting from the gross flow the value of capital consumption during the same period. The concept and measurement of capital consumption present difficulties which have not yet been solved for the Canadian National Accounts. Normal depreciation and obsolescence charges – that is, the loss of value in durable physical assets which is, or should be, charged to income account under customary business practices – may be taken as an approximate measure of actual capital consumption, and hence of the level of replacement investment required to maintain the stock of capital intact.[5] This method of passing from gross to net investment is employed in the present study in the one section where an approximation of net investment is required.

II. Background of the Capital Development from 1896 to 1930

The production of wheat on the Canadian prairie provided the basic economic opportunity in the economic development of Canada from 1896 to 1930. This opportunity attracted labour and capital to the direct exploitation of virgin land resources and induced investment throughout the economy in major secondary and tertiary industries and, through these, in housing and other community facilities greater by many times than the investment on the agricultural frontier itself. This leverage effect, the most significant aspect of the frontier, was a determining factor in the development of Canada's economic structure and, to a large extent, of its political structure as well. Political and economic behaviour were influenced by the prairie, even in advance of its emergence as a wheat economy, through the anticipations of its impact when it should emerge. Other factors, such as the past experience and failures of the isolated colonies in British North America, the availability of capital funds, the pattern of American experience, and, especially, the geography of the country, were important in the development; but the crucial determinant was the opportunity anticipated and finally realized on the prairie frontier.

The British colonies in North America were joined in political union by the British North America Act, 1867, but it was not until after the turn of the century that a significant degree of economic integration was achieved. Meanwhile the powerful anticipations underlying Confederation determined the policies of the new federal government. The nature of these anticipations was frequently expressed: "Coming further east still, let us but have our canal system completed, our connection with the Pacific Railway at the head of Lake Superior, the Northwest becoming rapidly settled, the exports of the settlers passing through our canals and the whole system of the Ontario railways complete, and the result will be that the trade of the city of Toronto which has doubled in five years will be quadrupled, and the case will be the same with Hamilton, London, and other cities in the West (Ontario). Such will be the direct and indirect results of these facilities. . . . [6] The potential frontier, Rupert's Land and the Northwest Territories, was acquired with imperial aid in 1870. The Intercolonial Railway to the Maritimes was completed in 1876 and the Canadian Pacific Railway, from Montreal to the west coast, in 1885. The national policy of protective tariffs was introduced in 1879 to promote industrialization and, along with the uneconomic, all-Canadian transportation system, to ensure that the impact of the leverage effects of the new frontier be contained, so far as possible, within the territorial bounds of the new political unit.

In the difficult physical environment of British North America, the essential capital formation needed to bring potential resources within the scope of the market passed beyond private means in the early part of the nineteenth century, as durable structures replaced inventories as the major component in the structure of productive capital. Governments were compelled to assume an active role in the investment field and the fulfillment of this role became their major function. A comparison of the period from the mid-seventies to the mid-nineties in Canada with the periods before and after reveals marked contrasts in the efficacy of government intervention in the field of investment. In the three periods governments supported the extension of railways, canals, roads, and other transportation equipment. In the earlier and in the later period, that is from 1840 to about 1870, and 1900 to 1930, large external economies were apparently created by these government activities and large-scale booms induced. In both periods basic opportunities were present in the form of an accessible agricultural frontier. Actual resources were linked to markets by the new equipment, and these resources attracted a large inflow of settlers whose pioneer efforts eventually converted wilderness into prosperous settlement. Secondary opportunities flowed from the basic production: trade and local manufacturing grew to supply the growing production and consumption needs of the pioneer and other marketing facilities were further improved to market his surplus products; demands of the people exploiting these secondary opportunities provided the new opportunities to be exploited by others at third and fourth remove from the initial development, and so on.

From about 1870 to 1895, government efforts were on a larger scale than in the earlier period (1840 to 1870), but the repercussions were brief interruptions in a secular depression extending over twenty-five years. Explosive building and real estate booms were induced, but these were not general, and had a very short life in those localities where they did occur.[7] The absence of basic opportunities in this period accounts for the disappointing results of government action on a large scale. The whole effect, during the period, was virtually limited to the initial impact of each government act.

The prairie frontier finally passed the critical margin separating potential from actual resources when the opportunity it afforded became definitely superior to alternative opportunities open to migrants. This shift in the character of the frontier occurred quite suddenly in the mid-nineties. The determination of the timing of this major turning point in Canadian economic development has been attributed to many factors and the importance of some of these is assessed in the following chapter. Two factors were fundamental. The interior of the continent is a single, continuous plain and the movement into western Canada was a natural extension of the American frontier after the occupation of more accessible free land in the United States. This natural movement of population was accelerated by a sharp upturn in the price of wheat in the mid-nineties. At the outset investment was largely the expenditure of personal effort and savings upon opportunities recognized by those close at hand. Most of the first arrivals on the frontier were North Americans. Their expenditures embodied knowledge gained from experience in a similar environment. Outside capital was not attracted on a significant scale until the boom was well under way.

At the turn of the century, from 1896 to 1901-2, the United Kingdom was experiencing an investment boom on a scale that provided ample domestic opportunities for labour and capital and at the same time affected favourably, from Canada's point of view, the price of wheat.[8] When the domestic cycle in the United Kingdom had run its course, and after the nature of new frontier opportunities in Canada had been thoroughly demonstrated and the rising trend in the economic activity of the dominion was well advanced, the flow of British labour and capital to Canada began.

The sudden shift in real opportunity in Canada is reflected in the real exports per capita which are shown in Figure 1. The rate of Canada's economic growth has varied with the availability of virgin resources and the relative ease of converting these into cash sales in the world markets. Expanding exports of primary commodities were the means of acquiring manufactures essential to the further expansion of domestic production and consumption, and they generated the profits necessary to attract and service foreign investment. Only when conditions conductive to the expansion of the rate of exports prevailed, could the expansion of the productive capacity of the country, in terms of its capital, human, and natural resources, proceed over an extended period beyond the rate fixed by domestic savings and domestic population growth. In their relation to exports, natural resources were the lever inducing rapid growth in the other (human and capital) dimensions of productive capacity.

Real exports per capita, as shown in Figure 1, followed a flat trend from 1875 to 1896 and then began to rise.[9] This shift in trend after 1896 indicates an expansion in opportunities that accelerated for some time at a faster rate than the spectacular growth of population which it induced. The change took place before the flow of foreign capital began and was, in fact, a cause of that flow. The terms of trade over the years when the shift in opportunity occurred are also shown in the figure; they reflect favourable price trends which served to reinforce the change in real opportunity. But the terms of trade, like the cheapening of transportation and the decline in interest rates, had been more or less steadily improving Canada's position since the eighteen-seventies and, like them, was a contributing rather than a causal factor in the turning point.[10]

Variations in the rate of growth of population in a new country like Canada were largely the net product of movements into and out of the country.[11] Whatever may be the explanation of the worldwide migrations that occurred, the experience of each new country was determined to a large extent by the nature of the economic opportunities available for individual migrants relative to opportunities available among its competitors in the field of immi-

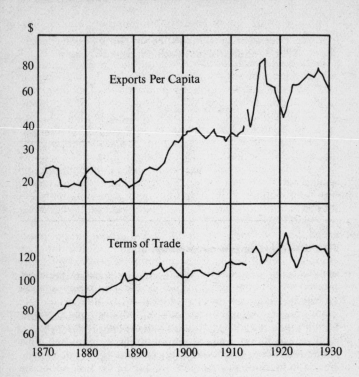

FIG. 1. Real exports per capita and the terms of trade, 1870-1930. (Source: Taylor and Mitchell, *Statistical Contributions,* and Dominion Bureau of Statistics.)

gration. In Canada, from 1870 to the mid-nineties, these opportunities were directly related to government actions of various kinds, and their short-lived character was reflected in the flows of immigrants and emigrants during the period. In spite of large numbers of arrivals in the decades from 1870 to 1900, net migration was negative in each. After the change in the opportunities in 1896, net migration became positive and contributed almost 40 percent of the 100 per cent increase in the population that occurred in the following thirty-five years.[12]

TABLE I
**Gross Domestic Capital Formation and Gross Construction,
1901-30 Expressed as Annual Averages Per Capita**

	1	2	3
	Gross domestic capital formation (current dollars)	Gross construction (current dollars)	(constant dollars)
1901-5	45	24	33
1906-10	70	44	51
1911-15	86	53	55
1916-20	98	52	35
1921-25	81	50	30
1926-30	119	63	39

III. Summary of the Investment Boom

The rate of expansion of the capital equipment of the country which occurred from 1901 to 1930 is shown in Table I. Global estimates of domestic capital formation per capita expressed as annual averages for each quinquennium are shown in the first column. Reducing the expenditures to a per capita basis brings out the high rates of investment activity achieved before 1915 during the period of the first heavy movement of population into the West. The true intensity of the process in this period is masked by the upward drift in prices. An indication of the bias introduced by price changes may be seen in columns 2 and 3 of the table, where the annual average gross investment in structures – the largest of the three major components of domestic capital formation – is shown in current and constant prices. The highest rate was achieved from 1911 to 1915. During this period the all-time peak, that of 1912-13, sustained the average despite the sharp recession and depression of 1914-15. The average for the preceding quinquennium was almost as high because annual expenditures, although lower than those later achieved, were better maintained. A mild depression in 1908 had little effect on construction. The rate during the war and post-war boom compared favourably with that of the following period of agricultural depression and was not a great deal lower than the rate from 1926 to 1930 when the final large scale movement into the West occurred.

Direct investment on prairie farms absorbed large absolute

expenditures. The size of these and their relation to gross domestic capital formation from 1900 to 1930 are shown in the first three columns of Table II. The capital formation that accompanied the development of the wheat economy as a highly specialized export region – its form, its pattern, its size, and the shift in its relative importance as part of national investment over the period – are examined in Chapter II.

It is apparent from the last four columns of Table II, which show the absolute and relative size of investment in transportation, that railway investment did not reach the same level of intensity as prairie farm investment until after 1905. The lag is suggestive. Following the initial burst of activity in the West, investment in the railway field rose to a remarkable level and high rates of investment were maintained until 1915. After 1915 a downward trend set in. Investment in other transport – canals, harbour work, etc., highways and bridges, trucks and automobiles for business use – continued to grow as a result of the innovation of the automobile. However this growth was not great enough to offset the decline in railway expansion. The relative importance of the whole transport group declined after 1915. Prairie farm investment was at its relative peak from 1901 to 1905 (column 3), continued at a slightly lower level until 1915, and then declined. Relatively speaking, transport rose after 1905 (column 7), remained at remarkable levels until 1915, then declined.

The expansion of steam railways was directly related to wheat. The prairie offered little resistance to the construction of the network of lines which were built within the region. Mileage grew from 3,300 in 1897 to 4,000 miles in 1901, 6,000 in 1906, 8,000 in 1911, and 14,000 in 1916. In post-war years when extensive railway construction was quiescent elsewhere in the dominion, the construction of branch lines continued on the prairies, raising the total mileage to nearly 18,000 by 1929. This construction would have been induced in the normal course of events. But unfortunately prairie expansion also induced the construction of two complete transcontinental systems and these, built like the Canadian Pacific within the framework of national policy, traversed the barren wilderness of the Canadian Shield at very great cost.

Early prairie roads were mere trails following the square pattern laid down by the survey system, sufficient for the moving of grain to loading platforms and elevators along the railroad and of supplies from the villages back to the farms; but the automobile revolutionized local demands, not only on the prairie but throughout the country, and as a result road construction became a major field of investment. This development is treated in Chapter III

TABLE II

Prairie Farm and Transport Investment Compared with Gross Domestic Capital Formation[a]
(millions of dollars)

	1 Gross domestic capital formation	2 Prairie farm investment[13]	3 Percentage 2 is of 1	4 Transport Railway	5 investment Other	6 Total	7 Percentage 6 is of 1
1901-5	1,283	221	17.2	165	36	201	15.7
1906-10	2,287	319	13.9	473	66	539	23.6
1911-15	3,279	463	14.1	682	166	848	25.9
1916-20	4,033	370	9.2	423	238	661	16.4
1921-25	3,641	245	6.7	386	367	753	20.7
1926-30	5,831	454	7.8	583	642	1,225	21.0

(a) *Sources:* Appendix tables H, J, and K, and Chapter XI.

along with the pattern and trends in the investment in railways, canals, harbour work, and other transportation equipment.

Had the expanding export region exchanged the proceeds of its sales directly for imports as it would largely have done in the absence of a nationally planned transport system and tariff, the economic prosperity of the eastern provinces would have been dependent on local developments. But the expenditures of the new region were chanelled to the east, and protected manufacturing industries expanded greatly to meet the demands. British Columbia, on the west, redirected the lumber products of its forests from exports to the prairie market which absorbed up to 70 per cent of the total. The Maritime provinces in the far east shared in the boom so long as the extensive phase of railway construction which accompanied prairie expansion persisted on a national scale. Its iron and steel industry was unable to compete effectively with firms located in the central provinces when the peak demands for railway equipment subsided. The central provinces were the chief beneficiaries of national policy. Capital invested in their manufacturing industries increased from $357 million in 1900 to $4,091 million at the peak

TABLE III
National Manufacturing Output in the Central Provinces in 1929(a)

Industrial group	1	2	3
	Percentages of net national production		
	In Ontario	In Quebec	1+2
Automobiles	96	–	96
Rubber tires	95	4	99
Machinery	72	25	97
Castings and forgings	69	21	90
Railway rolling stock	23	53	76
Hardware and tools	68	29	97
Agricultural implements	95	3	98
Cotton yarn and cloth	18	75	93
Boots and shoes	36	60	96
Rubber footwear	38	62	100
Clothing, men's	36	61	97
Clothing, women's	56	40	96
Hosiery and knit goods	72	22	94
Electric apparatus and supplies	77	22	99

(a) *Source*: Mackintosh, *Economic Background of Dominion-provincial Relations*, 50.

in 1929. The greatest relative expansion occurred in iron and steel and textiles under a tariff designed to give maximum protection to finished goods, with the materials, equipment, and other items affecting the costs of production of the finished commodities entering free or at a nominal duty.[14] The concentration of production of manufactured goods in the central provinces and its distribution between Ontario and Quebec are indicated in Table III. The selected items shown cover about one-third of the national production, and the geographical pattern reflected is representative of the total.

Opportunities for capital and labour in manufacturing were considerable, but the most spectacular increase in opportunities came in the tertiary industries. Transportation has already been mentioned. The high degree of capital intensity in the transportation industry and the geographical extent of the country implied very large investment outlays. Apart from certain other utilities the degree of capital intensity among the remaining service industries were relatively low; but in absolute and relative terms the largest job opportunities were opened up in these service fields. The total labour force increased by 120.2 per cent from 1901 to 1931. The farm labour force increased by only 57.9 per cent. (The process of mechanization in agriculture was relevant here.) Other primary occupations increased by 113 per cent. The labour force in manufacturing rose by 65 per cent, and in construction by 128.1 per cent. Thus primary plus secondary occupations increased by less than the national average. A 218 per cent increase (on the average) occurred amojng workers reporting the following occupations: transportation (252 per cent), trade (253 per cent), clerical (339 per cent), other service (161.4 per cent).[15] It is apparent that the expansion of job opportunities in the service industries contributed more than other industrial fields to the expansion of non-farm population and, through the accompanying process of urbanization, to the demand for housing – the largest single component of the volume of construction – and to roads, streets, sidewalks, schools, hospitals, public utilities, and other community facilities. The importance of this relation of the service industries to the expansion and pattern of investment expenditures is sometimes overlooked.

Table IV compares the investment in railway structures in value and percentage terms with the investment in housing. The value of direct government construction (excluding railway construction) is also shown in the table. In the whole field of construction during the period under review housing was the only component to rival transportation in fundamental importance and to surpass it in size. In absolute value terms, investment in residential housing over the

TABLE IV
Major Components of Gross Construction, 1901-30[a]
(millions of dollars)

	1 Gross constr.	2 Railway constr.	3 Percentage 2 is of 1	4 Housing constr.	5 Percentage 4 is of 1	6 Government constr.
1901-5	681	124	18.2	222	32.6	79
1906-10	1,439	381	26.5	468	32.5	149
1911-15	2,007	537	26.8	568	28.3	342
1916-20	2,122	253	11.9	641	30.2	256
1921-25	2,271	253	11.1	742	32.7	436
1926-30	3,109	389	12.5	1,060	34.1	578

(a) *Sources*: Appendix tables B, J, L, and N.
(b) Direct railway construction by the federal government is included in column 2 and excluded from column 6. The total federal railway investments for the six quinquennia in millions of dollars were: 15, 99, 98, 36, 3, 24.

whole period was almost as large as the total investment in all transport structure and equipment (see Table II). In addition, the relative stability of the housing component, reflected in column 5 of the table, contrasts markedly with the railway component. The latter rose from 18.2 per cent of gross construction in 1901-5 to over 26 per cent in 1906-10 and 1911-15, and then fell off to average about 12 per cent of gross construction in the following three quinquennia. Meanwhile housing was fairly close to 30 per cent of gross construction in each quinquennium.

The relation between tertiary occupations and basic production in western Canada was obvious and direct. The bulky character of wheat held the producing units within a short road haul of the railways.[16] Stations were erected at intervals of approximately eight miles along the track,[17] and around these clustered the local distributive agencies adapted to the needs of the prairie wheat economy. Three to six grain elevators, a loading platform, and, at some points, a small stockyard lined the track.[18] Terminal elevators were built at Fort William and Port Arthur at the head of Lake Superior at an early date. The bulk of the grain was moved by water to lower lake terminals and then to New York by the Erie Barge Canal or to Montreal. A small capacity was provided on the Canadian Atlantic seaboad to handle winter shipments. Interior terminals were built on the prairie after 1912. Pacific terminals were built following the completion of the Panama Canal.[19]

The high degree of specialization of prairie agriculture and the character of local resources implied dependence on primary and secondary producers in other regions and an extensive marketing structure to facilitate supply. In addition to the assemblers each small market centre supported a variety of merchandising and service establishments, professional men, and financial institutions.[20] The cities that emerged in the three provinces displayed the same general pattern as the towns and villages with the addition of many wholesale institutions and, substituting for the country general store, a somewhat more specialized structure of retail outlets. In short, the cities, towns, and villages were centres of tertiary producers. Among secondary producers, building and construction workers were the more numerous, with manufacturing virtually limited to processing of farm products, particularly the production of flour.

Winnipeg became the wholesale centre for the prairie provinces and was the only large city in the West until the opening of the Panama Canal enlarged Vancouver's opportunities. But Winnipeg was subsidiary to Montreal and Toronto. The two eastern cities became national metropolitan centres with the whole economy shared as a hinterland between them. The concentration of the wholesale trade of Canada was reflected in the first full census of merchandising which was taken in 1931: 69.7 per cent of all whole-sale sales in Canada in 1930 were made in the four largest cities, with 23.1 per cent in Montreal, 20.1 per cent in Toronto, 19.1 per cent in Winnipeg, and 6.4 per cent in Vancouver. Head offices of national wholesalers, of large department and chain store retailers, and of the various financial services were concentrated in Montreal and Toronto. The two cities also attracted manufacturing industries with the result that a large part of the secondary industries was located within or near their boundaries. The rapid growth of these and other urban centres in Canada from 1896 to 1915 was largely the result of prairie expansion. The accident of war, which added a stimulus of its own, the gradual emergence of important new staple exports, and the substitution of capital for labour in agriculture were among the major factors contributing to urban growth after 1915. The fluctuations in urban building and real estate activity that accompanied the growth of cities and the relation between popula-tion growth and movements and urban residential construction are examined in Chapter IV.

The role of government in Canadian capital development has already been mentioned. The pattern and trends in public invest-ment are described in Chapter V.

Table V emphasizes in a different way the investment oppor-tunities that accompanied the opening of the Canadian West. Here gross capital formation and gross investment are compared with the gross national product. The aggregates are shown in millions of dollars for each quinquennium from 1900 to 1930. In the final two columns of the table gross domestic capital formation and gross investment are expressed as percentages of gross national product. Gross domestic capital formation exceeded 25 per cent of the gross national product from 1901 to 1915. An average of almost 27 per cent was maintained from 1906 to 1915. The 26.9 per cent average for the years from 1911 to 1915, which include two years of reces-sion, suggests the unusual levels attained in the peak years, 1911-13. The average dropped off to 19.3 per cent from 1916 to 1920, reached a low for the thirty-year period of 16.1 per cent from 1921 to 1925, and recovered to 20.3 per cent after 1926. The remarkably high levels of domestic capital formation before 1915 were made possible by large inflows of British and foreign capital funds. The inflows of British and foreign funds are shown in column 3. Adding these algebraically to gross domestic capital formation yields the gross investment shown in column 4. The importance of foreign savings varied considerably over the period. They were relatively more important before 1915 than after and also absolutely more

TABLE V

Domestic Investment, Foreign Investment, and Gross National Product, 1901-30(a)
(millions of dollars)

	1 Gross national product	2 Gross domestic capital formation	3 Foreign invest- ment	4 Gross invest- ment (2 + 3)	5 Percentage 2 is of 1	6 Percentage 4 is of 1	3 as percentage of 2
1901-5	5,650	1,283	-301	982	22.7	17.4	23.5
1906-10	8,482	2,287	-784	1,503	27.0	17.7	34.3
1911-15	12,178	3,279	-1,515	1,764	26.9	14.5	46.2
1916-20	20,923	4,033	-262	3,771	19.3	18.0	6.5
1921-25	22,589	3,641	72	3,713	16.1	16.4	—
1926-30	28,758	5,831	-563	5,268	20.3	18.3	9.7

(a) *Sources*: Appendix tables H and I.

important from 1905 to 1915 than from 1926 to 1930. Only in the depressed period from 1921 to 1925 were they not a factor at all. An approximation of the relative importance of gross domestic savings appears in column 6, where gross investment is expressed as a percentage of gross national product. Direct government investment would have to be deducted from gross investment and the residual adjusted for the net surplus or deficit of governments to obtain a conceptually accurate measure of domestic savings offsets. This adjustment is made in the preliminary section of Chapter VI, which deals with the role of internal savings and external funds in the finance of capital formation in Canada in the period from 1900 to 1930.

IV. The Statistics of Investment

The last six chapters are an account of the statistical investigations upon which the commentary in Chapters II to VI was based. The primary results were quinquennial estimates of the major components of domestic capital formation and gross investment and some direct estimates of investment in different sectors of the economy. In addition, annual series of the production, imports, and exports of construction materials and machinery and equipment, by types were obtained. Supplementary estimates include several reliable series based on records of building permits, real estate transfers, mortgages, discharges of mortgages, and subdivisions registered in metropolitan areas, and less reliable but, for restricted purposes, useful measures such as the rough estimates of gross national income.

The estimates of the total volume of construction are explained in Chapter VII, the flow of machinery and equipment in Chapter VIII, investment in inventories in Chapter IX, and net foreign investment in Chapter X. In all but certain components of the inventories, the estimates were prepared on an annual basis and then combined in five-year totals. The estimates of the annual flows of construction materials and machinery and equipment at producers' prices are firm enough to serve as indexes of annual investment. The records used to establish the two series were reasonably good from 1900 on. However, production records from 1896 to 1899 and the records available to support the procedures involved in passing from producers' prices to cost to final users were much less satisfactory. The seriousness of the possible errors introduced by these procedures would be greatly reduced in the quinquennial totals of new construction and outlays on machinery and equipment. The estimates of inventory investment are the weakest of the major components of gross investment; while the margin of error is reasonably small for some types of inventories, the possible error in the totals is fairly large even on a quinquennial basis.

Chapter XI deals with the various direct estimates mentioned above. The quality of most of these is demonstrably good. The least reliable are the estimates of municipal investment, investment in housing, and gross national production, which contain arbitrary elements.

A basis for judging the quality of the estimates is provided in Chapters VII to XI. These chapters are arranged to allow an examination of the statistical investigations at two depths. The first two sections of each deal with definitions and concepts and provide a summary of the statistical procedures. The third section of each chapter contains detailed descriptions of the sources and procedures.

All the basic estimates are presented together, for convenient reference, in the tables of the Appendix. With one exception the figures are given in that detail which in my own opinion their quality supports. The exception is section 2 of Table A, which shows the estimates of total construction, and the percentage of construction materials in the total, annually from 1896 to 1930.[21] This information is relevant to any judgment of the reliability of the quinquennial estimates of new construction – the largest component of gross investment – and it also provides a point of departure for any revisions which might seem warranted to another user.

2.
Investment in the Wheat Economy

I. Rise of the Wheat Economy

1. Western Land

Following the transfer of Rupert's Land and The Northwest Territories from Hudson's Bay Co. to the Dominion of Canada in 1870,
the federal government established a free land system to attract
settlers. The first Dominion Lands Act, 1872, provided for homestead entry on a quarter-section of land with a fee of ten dollars and
a residence requirement of three years. In 1874, to promote development from the 160-acre homestead to a 320-acre farm, the homesteader was given a "pre-emption right" which allowed him to buy
at a low price 160 acres of Dominion land adjoining his homestead
as soon as the patent had been issued on his original homestead.
The privileges of "pre-emption and purchased homesteads" were
repealed in 1890 and restored for the period 1908 to 1918.[1]

A railway land-grant system was set up to provide transcontinental railways at a minimum cost to the public treasury. Grants
were made until 1894 and all lands earned by railways were located
by 1908. Besides the grants of land to railways, a large grant was
made to the Hudson's Bay Co. as part of the terms of the transfer.
In addition, two square miles in each township were reserved from
homestead entry as school lands.[2] These were to be sold as the
progress of settlement valorized the land and the proceeds applied
to the cost of providing educational facilities for the children of
settlers.

Incoming settlers could enter for free land and acquire additional land by pre-emption or homestead purchase (when these
privileges were in effect) or by direct purchase from the railway land
companies, from the Hudson's Bay Co. and certain other land companies established under federal auspices, or at the auctions of
school lands. The gross total of acres of original homestead entries
in the prairie provinces from 1870 to 1927 has been estimated at 99
million acres but the total patented and under homestead in 1930
was 58.2 million.[3] Settlers bought more land than they acquired

free: 11 million acres were alienated directly by federal pre-emptions, purchased homesteads, and direct sales policies, and, in addition, approximately 50 million acres were sold by railways and other companies (railway lands: 31.8 million acres; H. B. Co. lands: 7 million; school lands: 9.3 million; other: 2 million).[4] These land sales from 1893 to 1930 and homestead entries from 1880 to 1930 are shown annually, on a ratio scale, in Figure 2.

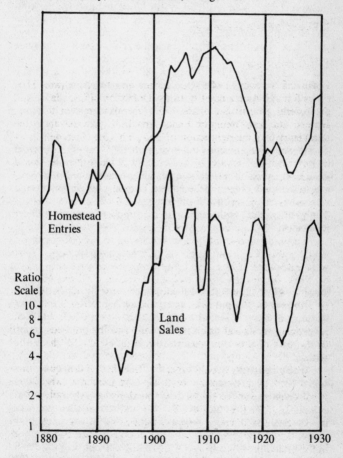

FIG. 2.   Homestead entries and land sales in western Canada. (Source: *Canada Year Book*.)

In this type of chart, which is used frequently in this study, the degree of slope in the curve indicates the rate of change from one year to the next. The steeper the slope the more rapid the rate of development. The approximate percentage change in the level of the data from year to year can also be determined by applying the scale given in the left hand corner of the chart. The level of homestead entries, for example, more than doubled from 1881 to 1882. The spectacular Winnipeg real estate boom induced by the construction of the Canadian Pacific Railway in the early eighties also reached its peak in 1882, the year the railway link with the East was completed.[5] The price of wheat reached a relative peak in the same year. It was not until after 1896 that homestead entries again doubled in a single year. That the year 1896 marked a major turning point in the rate of prairie settlement is evident in the chart. The level of homestead entries quadrupled from 1896 to 1901; and quadrupled again from 1901 to 1903. The average level of homestead entries from 1903 to the major peak in 1911 was about ten times the level of the eighties.

The rate of increase in land sales from 1896 to 1903 – shown in the lower curve of Figure 2 – was even more rapid than the rise in homestead entries. The recessive tendencies in 1904 and 1907, evident in the curve of homestead entries, appear more sharply in land sales. The difference in the patterns of the curves after 1915 is mainly the product of the decline in the supply of accessible homestead lands.

2. Some Physical and Economic Factors in the Turning Point of 1896

The short growing season and light rainfall were the major physical problems facing the pioneer prairie farmer.[6] Frost was the chief hazard in southern Manitoba and an effective substitute for Red Fife wheat, which had rapidly achieved a leading position among wheat varieties following its introduction in the West in the eighties, was not found until 1910.[7] More important was the problem of drought west and northwest of southern Manitoba. This problem was met by the summer-fallowing technique which had been developed for dry-farming in the United States and spread through the northwestern wheat states to western Canada. Its "capabilities were known in western Canada at practically the time (1886) of the establishment of the experimental farm system."[8] American immigrants who knew its merits applied it in the West and others, encouraged by the educational propaganda of the Experimental Farms, quickly followed.[9]

The cost of transporting wheat from North America to the

United Kingdom improved steadily after the mid-seventies, but there was no significant change during the years when the major turning point occurred: the average cost (from Regina to Liverpool) was 27.9 cents a bushel from 1893 to 1895 and 26.7 cents from 1896 to 1900.[10] The price of "good red foreign" wheat in Liverpool, which reached the lowest point of the century in 1894, rose steadily from $0.67 in that year to a relative peak of $1.05 in 1898. (This peak price, 50 per cent above the price prevailing four years earlier, coincided with a record crop in western Canada.) The rising price in these years supplied a major stimulus to the expansion. The total consignment of wheat, wheat meal, and wheat flour to the United Kingdom from all countries increased from 1894 to 1895, declined in 1896, again in 1897, then increased in 1898 and 1899; but in each of these years the volume consigned from Canada increased and its relative share in the total improved. Canada's share in the trade increased by over 100 per cent from 1894 to 1899 in both relative and absolute terms.[11] Neither the Liverpool nor the Winnipeg price was so high as in 1898 until ten years later, but the prairie opportunity had been demonstrated in the few years after 1895 and the expansion got well under way.

The price factor is only one aspect of economic opportunity. There had been similar periods of rising prices in the previous twenty years accompanied by more favourable drops in transportation costs, but these did not initiate secular expansion. The Winnipeg price rose by an approximately equal amount from 1878 to 1882 and from 1886 to 1889: these represented smaller relative changes than the rise from 1896 to 1898 only because the level of prices prevailing in the earlier periods was considerably higher.[12] These peak prices coincided with relative peaks in immigrant arrivals and homestead entries. There were large movements of population into the West during the eighties, but the bulk of the migrants passed on after the railway construction boom to superior attractions on the American frontier. The Canadian Pacific had been completed to the west coast in 1885 and feeder lines to the north had been constructed by the end of the decade. "The Regina and Long Lake line was built from Regina to Prince Albert in 1889 and 1890 . . . About the same time the Calgary and Edmonton was built . . . Saskatoon, at the crossing of the South Saskatchewan river, was in the midst of what was often called 'The Desert.' Its main business came from being the station for Battleford, eighty miles away. Ten years after the line was laid there was only one homesteader between Saskatoon and the Qu'Appelle. The land grant was considered worthless."[13]

The timing and shape of the tidal waves of migrants entering Canada before 1915 were roughly the same as those reflected in

American statistics.[14] There was one large wave extending from the mid-seventies to the mid-nineties. The existence of good free land in the United States at this time explains why the major turning point in Canada had to await the next mass movement of population. Vast areas of the open continent were settled by these successive waves of population and accompanying each wave were the violent booms and collapse characteristic of economic growth based on land speculation.[15] The fortunes of American commerce, industry, and finance rose and fell with movements on the frontier. The last open land and railway boom of major proportions in the United States culminated in the late eighties. Chicago, whose development reflects more clearly than any other city the opening of the interior, achieved peak rates in its spectacular growth in this last land boom of the nineteenth century.[16] The remaining regions of unsettled country adjacent to the developed wheat lands lay beyond American territory, and when the next wave of migration began the Canadian West held the balance in alternative opportunities. The same dynamic combination of land and speculative pioneers which had operated over the previous century continued. The pattern was roughly the same, but now Canadian cities and Canadian commerce, industry, and finance experienced the expansive impact of the process of occupation of the continental plain.

3. Production and the Growth of the Prairie Farm Market

The prairie provinces became the major export region of Canada after 1900. Eastern farm producers became more dependent upon domestic markets in the rapidly growing metropolitan centres and, accompanying this shift, the cultivation of available land in the east grew more intensive. There was very little increase, and in some cases even a decline, in the amount of land and labour employed in agriculture in the eastern provinces during this period of transition. The rapid expansion of agriculture in the West is reflected in Table VI. The first section of the table shows the total number of farms and the occupied and improved acreage for Canada as a whole and the percentage of these in the prairie provinces. The percentages indicate the extent and the rapidity of the frontier development over this period and also the larger land units characteristic of the western farms. The second section of the table shows the total farm labour force distributed between the prairies and other provinces. Again the expansion in the West is evident, but the form of presentation brings out clearly an additional tendency implicit in the other data. After 1891 there was a definite stability in the number of workers employed in agriculture in the other provinces. Examination of the first section of the table indicates a similar tendency in

TABLE VI

Relative Expansion of Land and Labour in Prairie Agriculture(a)

A. Land

Year	No. of farms All Canada (No.)	Prairies (percentage of total)	Occupied acreage All Canada (thousands of acres)	Prairies (percentage of total)	Improved acreage All Canada (thousands of acres)	Prairies (percentage of total)
1881	464,025	2.2	45,358	5.9	21,866	1.3
1891(b)	-	-	-	-	-	-
1901	511,073	10.8	63,422	24.3	30,166	18.5
1911	682,389	29.2	108,969	52.9	48,734	47.1
1921	711,090	36.0	140,888	62.4	70,770	63.4
1931	728,623	39.5	163,114	67.3	85,732	69.8

B. Labour

Persons occupied in agriculture (thousands)

Year	Prairie provinces	Other provinces	Total
1881	15	647	662
1891	48	687	735
1901	79	638	717
1911	283	651	934
1921	376	666	1,042
1931	444	688	1,132

(a) Source: *Decennial Census.*
(b) Data for this year are omitted because they are not comparable

the use of the land. The number of farms in the other provinces actually declined from 454 thousand units in 1881 to 441 thousand in 1931.

Wheat became the major western crop but there were variations in the production pattern in different parts of the region during the period of expansion. As settlement proceeded, dairy farming emerged on lands adjacent to Winnipeg and other cities and mixed farming developed throughout the Park Belt especially in Manitoba but also in the other provinces (in northeastern Saskatchewan and, away from the Park Belt, in northwestern Alberta and on irrigated land). Ranching, which had developed in the dry areas in southwestern Saskatchewan and southeastern Alberta before the turn of the century, reached a peak in 1900, then declined as homesteaders poured in, but remained of considerable importance in the southern and foothill regions of Alberta. At the end of the period, about 75 per cent of the crop land was devoted to cash crops, and the remaining 25 per cent to growing feed for livestock. Wheat accounted for 80 to 85 per cent of the crops grown for sale.[17] The changing pattern of acreage sown to the principal cereal crops is summarized in Table VII.

TABLE VII
Percentages of Prairie Field Crops in Wheat, Oats, and Barley(a)

	1900	1906	1911	1916	1921	1926	1930
Manitoba							
Wheat	71.3	64.5	60.0	53.3	48.1	33.3	36.3
Oats	20.8	22.1	25.3	28.2	30.6	26.4	22.6
Barley	5.1	8.0	8.7	13.4	14.1	28.1	30.1
Saskatchewan							
Wheat	74.3	64.7	57.5	64.6	65.6	69.3	65.4
Oats	21.6	27.6	25.5	27.1	27.3	20.0	16.9
Barley	1.8	2.4	3.0	2.6	2.4	4.5	8.2
Alberta							
Wheat	22.8	24.4	48.5	47.3	57.3	67.2	66.7
Oats	62.5	51.9	36.1	38.6	29.9	20.9	18.2
Barley	5.9	11.8	4.9	6.1	4.6	4.5	5.9

(a) *Sources: Statistical Atlas* and *Decennial Census*, 1931.

The shift from wheat to coarse grains accompanying the trend to diversified farming in Manitoba is evident in the table. The shift from oats to wheat in Alberta reflects the relative decline of ranching in that province. The relative decline in oats in Saskatchewan after 1921 was largely the result of the substitution of mechanized equipment for horsepower. The prairies also produced the bulk of the national output of flax and rye (86 per cent of total flax acreage and 99 per cent of the rye acreage from 1924 to 1928 were in the West), but these crops were unimportant in comparison with the other cereal crops. Flax was a very popular first cash crop from 1900 to 1924 owing to an unusually favourable price relation.[18]

There was a decline in the acreage sown to wheat in eastern Canada from 2.4 million in 1880 to just under 1 million acres in 1930. Wheat acreage in the West exceeded the eastern acreage for the first time in the early nineties. The period of rapid expansion extended from 1896 to 1921. The total wheat acreage was 4.2 million in 1900, 8.9 million in 1911, 15.4 million in 1916, and 23.3 million in 1921. (A rise of approximately 5 million acres occurred in the single year from 1920 to 1921 following the peak price of 1920.) The acreage dropped to 20.8 million after four years of agricultural depression, and then rose in the subsequent expansion to 25.2 million at the end of the twenties.[19]

Meanwhile Canadian wheat assumed an important position in

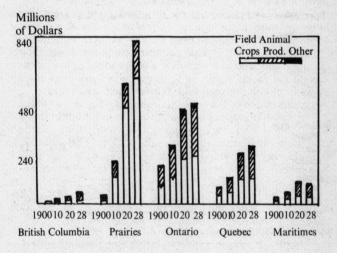

FIG. 3.   Gross value of farm production by regions, selected years, 1900-28. (Sources: *Decennial Census* and *Canada Year Book*.)

the international market. Canada ranked third among the major exporters by 1912, rose to second place by 1918, and to first place after 1922. Canadian exports accounted for approximately 40 per cent of the total world exports of wheat from 1922 to 1930. Wheat and wheat flour accounted for 32.0 per cent, 33.7 per cent, and 25.4 per cent of Canada's commodity exports in 1913, 1926, and 1929, respectively. There are no accurate figures on the relation of exports to national income over this period; but at the end of the period, in 1926 and 1929, exports of goods and services were the direct source of 40.8 and 35.1 per cent of the national income.

The expansion of wheat production for export in the prairie provinces implied an expanding domestic market and, to the extent that the other, formerly isolated regions were able to integrate their respective economies with the expanding export region, they shared in the expansion. Figure 3 provides an approximate index both of the expansion of the prairie farm market and of some of its effects. It shows the gross value of farm production by regions and by types of products in selected years from 1900 to the peak year in 1928. The change in the prairie region was closely associated with the expansion of wheat exports, whereas the expansion in the other regions, especially in Ontario and Quebec, was related to domestic urban markets as cities expanded under the impact of the frontier. Cash cereal crops "were replaced on eastern farms by crops grown to be consumed on the farm for the production of milk and animal products and by specialized crops such as potatoes, roots, tobacco, vegetables, fruit, etc."[21] This secondary expansion in agricultural income in the dependent regions was added to the primary expansion in the export region to broaden the national farm market exploited by industry, commerce, finance, and transportation.

Interpretation of the value totals shown in Figure 3 to indicate the expansion of regional farm markets must be qualified in several ways. Three concepts are commonly used to describe agricultural production and farm income: gross value of agricultural production, farm cash income, and net farm income. The first concept is used here because it is the only one available over the whole period. It overstates the final output because it includes the values of grains grown for seed and feed. This double counting is relatively smaller in the prairies totals: the bulk of prairie field crops was exported; elsewhere a large portion of field crops was fed to animals.

The second concept, farm cash income, is gross receipts from the marketing of farm products. The third concept, net farm income, is gross cash income adjusted for changes in inventory minus operating expenses plus government transfer payments (which were negligible before 1930) and income in kind. This last measure, with slight adjustments, appears in the national income accounts, but it is the second aggregate which is relevant in any consideration of the spending power of the farm community. Gross value of production is a better approximation to it than net income.

Farm cash income in the West, expanding with exports, was – indeed still is – an autonomous factor in the national economy. But in the period of expansion the annual expenditures of western farmers exceeded farm income by a considerable margin. Total expenditures included net proceeds from borrowing as well as expenditures from current cash income and past savings. The growth in farm debt also depended upon the expansion of exports.

There were other incomes that varied with wheat exports. Among these were the incomes of domestic investors in transportation equipment, of workers employed in transporting the product, and of a host of agents providing marketing facilities including grain merchants, elevator companies, banking and insurance institutions, and so on. The costs of their services were paid by the foreign buyer of wheat and were included either in the export price of the commodity or in the service components of current transactions in the balance of payments. In an ideal measure of the impact of the development of the wheat economy, one would have to add to changes in gross expenditures of the exporting farm groups an allowance for changes in income and expenditures of these complementary producers and relate the total to induced changes in national investment and consumption.

II The Expansion of Western Farm Plant, Equipment, and Inventories

The last section outlined the growth of the wheat economy in western Canada and indicated the shift in the character of agricultural production in other regions of the country induced by this development. Directly and indirectly wheat supplied a dynamic vitality to the whole agricultural industry, and the innumerable small-scale opportunities that opened for thousands of commercial farming units contributed to a vast aggregate investment outlay. The larger part of these expenditures was made on the prairies. Prairie farms accounted for 72 per cent of the total farm investment from 1900 to 1930. Two aspects of farm investment can be distinguished in the development. The first was related to the spread of new farm units over the frontier and can be called, in Hansen's terminology, the extensive aspect; the intensive aspect was related to the substitution of the gasoline motor for animal energy as a source of power and the adoption of improved machinery.[22]

As a result of an emphasis on mechanization after 1915, farm

investment outlay was well maintained in absolute dollar terms until
1930. But the slowing down in the extensive aspect of the investment process after 1915-20 implied a sharp decline in the relative
importance of the western farm region as a field for investment.
The region accounted for 14.6 per cent of domestic capital formation from 1901 to 1915 and for only 7.9 per cent from 1916 to
1930.[23] Furthermore, this apparent decline in the West would be
increased if the investment figures were expressed in "net" instead
of in "gross" form, since the relative importance of replacement
expenditures would grow with the stock of durable physical assets.
However, even as they stand, the figures demonstrate that, despite
the high levels of expenditure in the later years when prairie farm
methods were undergoing rapid transformation, relatively more
abundant investment opportunities accompanied the extensive
phase of the development. Even if all passenger automobiles bought
by prairie farmers were treated as producers' goods, in addition to
trucks, this observation would still hold. The addition would raise
prairie farm investment from 7.9 per cent to 9.5 per cent of gross
domestic capital formation from 1926 to 1930. If gross investment
were used as the comparison base the drop in the percentages after
1915 would be even more pronounced owing to the larger negative
net foreign balances in the earlier period.

The economic aspects of farming in western Canada were
closely bound up with home and family life. But the speculative
character of the original settlers,[24] combined with the specific
nature of the land resources and a consequent reliance upon a single
cash crop sold in world markets under competitive conditions, contributed to a highly commercial outlook. Prices and climatic forces
were the immediate determinants of the farmer's real income, but
variations in the rate of expansion appear to have turned almost
entirely on the price of wheat. The annual expansion of wheat
acreage provides an accurate index of the rate of expansion. Figure
4 has been prepared to illustrate the importance of the price of
wheat in the expansion of farm plants.[25] The annual physical product, the top curve in the chart, is shown to illustrate that, however
fundamental variations in real output may have been to the success
of the region in the long run, they had very little significance for
short-run decisions. Taking his luck with the weather, which
affected yields through rainfall, temperature, and hours of sunlight
and through its effects on weeds, insects, and plant disease, the
farmer varied his investment outlays almost directly with the price
of wheat. The impact of the upward trend in the price curve is
reflected in the sharper trend in wheat acreage. One effect of the
demand for more land in the extension of productive capacity
appears in the lowest curve on the chart, which shows annual selling

prices in dollars per acre of all lands sold by the registered land companies and the Hudson's Bay Co. Financial investment in land became an important element in farm enterprise at an early stage in the development despite the federal free land policy. It has already been pointed out that a greater acreage was sold through the various companies that received federal grants than was alienated under the homestead policy and that a great deal of the free land was "proved" for early resale.

Referring again to the product, price, and acreage curves in Figure 4, it will be observed that prices and output almost always moved in opposite directions. Conspicuous exceptions are the years 1896 to 1898 when prices and yields moved sharply upward, with implications which have been discussed above. Significantly the record crop in 1901 following a mediocre crop in 1900 (yields per acre increased from 13 to 21 bushels) was not in itself enough to reverse a decline in acreage which continued from 1900 to 1902. A bumper yield (24 bushels) in 1902 and the improvement in price evident in 1903 led to a further expansion of acreage in 1903 and 1904. Expansion was continuous from 1904 to 1911 with the single exception of 1907. The hesitation in that year, despite good yields the year before, is a clear reflection of the sharp drop in price in 1906.

The period from 1910 to 1914 was an important one. The price of wheat reached its pre-war peak in 1909 and was lower in each of the four following years. As a result acreage declined in 1912, 1913, and 1914. In this period, the forces underlying the secular expansion which had begun in 1896 appeared finally to have spent themselves and for the first time the expansion process showed definite signs of coming to a halt. The price movement reversed its direction with the outbreak of war in 1914, rose to inflated levels, and reached a peak in 1920. The response of the acreage is apparent in the chart. The expansion of productive capacity was renewed at an accelerated rate in 1915 and the upward trend was continued until 1921. Acreage contracted from 1921 to 1925 when the wartime price inflation was reversed, but expansion was once more resumed, although at a slower rate, in 1926. This last period of expansion was preceded by a sharp rise in price as well as in yields in 1925.

Examination of the movements of price and acreage has revealed that, with one exception, every movement in the price was followed by a similar movement in acreage. An examination of land sales and homestead entries[26] would show an even more sensitive response to wheat prices in these quantities. It should be added that whereas the wheat acreage reacted sensitively to upward movements in price, it tended merely to level off when the price fell and to contract only when the adverse price movement continued over a period of several years. The net result was that the upward trend in

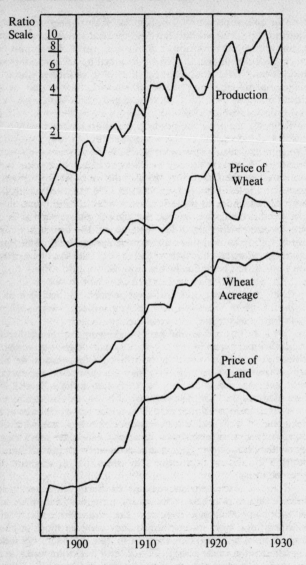

Ratio
Scale
10
8
6
4

2

Production

Price of
Wheat

Wheat
Acreage

Price of
Land

1900   1910   1920   1930

FIG. 4.   Indexes of prairie expansion. (Source: see note 25.)

price was accompanied by a similar but sharper trend in acreage, while a falling price was accompanied by a flat acreage trend. Other factors influenced the shape of the acreage curve. In the post-war years, for example, coarse grains were substituted for wheat in production on a fairly large scale, particularly in Manitoba where the urban market expansion was most marked. Also a part of the expansion from 1915 to 1930 was related to the development of power farming which increased the land scale of the optimum farm unit. Finally, the production costs of the wheat farmer as well as the price of wheat determined the net profitability of wheat production. The price of consumption goods purchased by farmers also affected incentives. However, a strong emphasis on these other prices is not warranted by the facts.[27] An index of the ratios of farm prices to domestic wholesale prices from 1895 to 1930 does not correlate as well with the index of expansion as an index of farm prices alone. The general trends are similar, but there is little sympathy in the year-to-year movements in the two indexes. The correlation is not significantly improved when a more appropriate index of the farmer's terms of trade, i.e., ratios of farm prices to prices of commodities farmers buy, is used in the comparison.[28]

The discussion of expansion so far has been based on an index of land. Total investment in buildings, equipment, and inventories on prairie farms reflects the same general pattern. Table VIII presents the quinquennial figures in some detail. If an allowance is made for the changes in the cost of building materials and labour, the construction component shows a pattern of growth similar to that for land.[29] Farm residential buildings did not move in step with urban residential building. Urban housing construction increased in each quinquennium from 1901 to 1915, fell in 1915-20, and then rose again in the two following quinquennia, exhibiting the long cycles characteristic of that field of building activity.[30] In contrast, the value of farm building construction shown in the table rises from the first quinquennium to the second, falls in the third, rises in the fourth, falls in the fifth, and rises again in the sixth. Again a measure of western farm expansion varies in sympathy with the price of wheat.

The two remaining components, machinery and inventories, taken together follow the same general movement, but taken individually show conflicting tendencies. The equipment totals in Table VIII display a more consistent buoyancy than the totals of either land or building. They increase steadily from 1901 to 1930 with a single exception in the period 1921-25. Two trends are fused in this series: the general expansion of productive capacity and the increasing mechanization of farm production.[31] The trend to more machinery was evident before the war and was greatly accelerated by the

TABLE VIII

Prairie Farm Investment
(millions of dollars)

	1 Housing	2 Other buildings	3 Farm machinery	4 Trucks	5 Grain inventories	6 Livestock inventories	7 Subtotal 1 to 6	8 Passenger cars
1901-5	41.7	37.6	76.1	—	13.1	52.7	221.2	.3
1906-10	64.4	57.9	104.4	.3	32.0	60.2	319.2	2.5
1911-15	26.5	23.8	129.3	1.2	168.4	113.3	462.5	13.0
1916-20	66.9	60.2	188.7	5.5	-33.6	82.1	369.8	50.7
1921-25	16.9	15.2	157.4	5.8	38.2	11.6	245.1	59.1
1926-30	72.0	64.8	265.0	15.9	37.6	-1.4	453.9	106.9

relative scarcity of labour and the successful application of the gasoline engine after 1915.[32] The substitution of machine power for
horse and man power was continued under pressure of competition
in the post-war years to reduce production costs.

Approximately 100,000 tractors were sold in the three prairie
provinces from 1918 to 1930, half of them in Saskatchewan.[33] The
growing importance of the new source of power affected both livestock and grain inventories. The demand for horses was affected
directly and, as an indirect result, the relative costs of maintaining
other stock increased. Feed grains were affected directly and, with
faster haulage by trucks, year-end wheat inventories on the farms
also became relatively smaller. The sharp reduction in the rate of
growth of grain inventories is evident in Table VIII.

Table IX shows the changes in livestock inventories from 1901
to 1930. The investment in horses rose to a peak in 1911-15 and
then declined, becoming negative from 1926 to 1930. Horses
accounted for the greater part of the large investments in livestock
up to 1920. The decline in the value of this component after 1915
offset to a considerable extent the increased expenditures on machinery and equipment. These latter expenditures were offset further
by the movement in grain inventories. Investment in cattle and milk
cows also declined in the twenties. The earlier drop in cattle investment from 1906 to 1910 reflects the federal government's release of
land from grazing leases to meet the demand for homesteads. A
great deal of this land, which was too dry for wheat, was thrown
open to settlement in 1911.[34] The recovery in swine stocks after the
period of high wartime wheat prices reflects the greater settlement
activity during the twenties in the province of Alberta where a
greater land area was well adapted to coarse grains.

The fact that end-of-year wheat inventories on farms did not
keep pace with the increase in the size of crops is attributable to the
automobile, and to a lesser extent, the combine.[35] In 1921 approximately 34 per cent of all registered trucks and passenger cars were
on farms (157,000 out of 456,000). In 1931 approximately 30 per
cent of all trucks (48,400 of 165,800) and 32 per cent of all passenger cars (321,300 of 1,024,200) were on farms. At both dates about
45 per cent of these farm vehicles were on prairie farms.[36]

Another approach to the expansion of farm capital is available
in the records of the census of agriculture. These cover the reported
value of land, buildings, machinery, and livestock. The census
materials for the prairie provinces are assembled in Table X. The
value data, biased by price movements, all show peaks in 1921; but
when the values per farm of the various components are distributed
as percentages of the total value per farm at each census date, the
trend from livestock to machinery is evident. The sharp drop in

TABLE IX

Prairie Farm Livestock Inventory Investment

A. Value of the Physical Change in Livestock
(millions of dollars)

	Horses	Milk cows	Other cattle	Swine	Sheep	Total
1901-5	31.0	4.9	15.0	1.2	.6	52.6
1906-10	60.0	.2	-1.4	1.1	.3	60.3
1911-15	79.3	13.8	19.2	-.1	1.0	113.3
1916-20	52.2	6.5	26.1	-6.0	3.3	82.1
1921-25	2.5	9.3	-9.0	8.9	-.1	11.7
1926-30	-9.6	-.2	.2	3.6	4.6	-1.4

B. Physical Change in Numbers of Livestock
(thousands)

	Horses	Milk cows	Other cattle	Swine	Sheep	Total
1901-5	349	150	815	215	127	1,656
1906-10	518	90	-12	287	12	895
1911-15	610	286	526	516	189	2,127
1916-20	430	80	442	-287	230	895
1921-25	35	188	-317	724	-8	622
1926-30	-140	-1	-163	265	486	447

TABLE X

Values and Percentage Distribution of Prairie Farm Capital and Land, 1901-31(a)

A. Values

| | Total all farms ($000,000) | Value per farm (dollars) | | | | |
		Land	Buildings	Machinery	Livestock	Total
1901	231	2,343	522	330	982	4,177
1911	1,789	6,215	901	550	1,314	8,979
1916	2,174	6,324	1,000	759	1,864	9,947
1921	3,256	8,026	1,765	1,343	1,602	12,735
1926	2,609	6,348	1,725	1,271	1,171	10,515
1931	2,705	5,955	1,566	1,192	676	9,389

B. Percentage Distribution

	Land	Buildings	Machinery	Livestock	Total
1901	56.1	12.5	7.9	23.5	100.0
1911	69.2	10.0	6.1	14.6	100.0
1916	63.6	10.1	7.6	18.7	100.0
1921	63.0	13.9	10.5	12.6	100.0
1926	60.4	16.4	12.1	11.1	100.0
1931	63.5	16.7	12.7	7.2	100.0

(a) Source: *Census of Agriculture*.

livestock from 1901 to 1911 is the result of the relative decline in cattle ranching as settlement proceeded. The decline thereafter, however, is clearly related to the increased importance of machinery and equipment.

Another point of interest in the table is the very large share of land in the total financial investment reported by farmers. Also, an examination of the changes in the values will show that these reflect a lull in the rates of expansion of both land and buildings from 1911 to 1916 as compared with both the preceding and succeeding quiquennia. The rate of expansion of the capital value of equipment in this same interval was not nearly so damped. The inferences are once again that the extensive aspect of prairie farm investment was correlated closely with the price of wheat and that the intensive aspect accompanying the trend toward greater mechanization operated continuously throughout the period.

TABLE XI
Land and Equipment Per Farm Worker in the Prairie Provinces

	Improved land per worker (acres)	Machinery and equipment per worker (1926 dollars)
1901	67	342
1911	81	350
1916	101	524
1921	119	822
1926	119	763
1931	145	842

The price aberrations of the war period make meaningful comparisons of these census values over the whole period impossible. However, the values of machinery may be deflated with an index of farm implement prices from Chapter VIII of this volume. Ratios of real machinery and equipment per worker and of acres of improved land per worker on prairie farms at each census date are shown in Table XI. The figures provide a rough indication of the trend in economic organization on western farms. There was a marked increase in the use of machinery and land per farm worker. A measure of the gains in product per worker may also be devised. The ratio of product in current prices to numbers of farm workers increased fourfold from 1900 to 1925.[37] Meanwhile farm prices approximately doubled.[38] This implies that the product per worker doubled while, since the ratios of improved land per worker and of equipment per worker shown in Table XI approximately doubled over the same period, the ratios of real product to improved land and to equipment remained almost constant.[39] Even though these calculations are rough, the indicated trends would be nearer the truth than the broad trends reflected in unadjusted data.[40] Since output doubled with a doubling of land and equipment while the relative labour input remained unchanged, the improvement in production methods over the twenty-five years involved a displacement of one out of every two workers. This implies a total displacement of about 400,000 men. Meanwhile direct employment in the agricultural implements industry did not increase by more than 6,000 men. An allowance for the indirect labour engaged in research of various types, in extension and other educational services, and in producing component materials and marketing implements might double but would hardly triple this number.

In summary, two distinct aspects may be recognized in the process of prairie farm capital formation during the period under review: an extensive aspect accounting for most of the investment as farm units spread over new geographical regions, and an intensive aspect associated with mechanization and the consequent increase in the size of the average productive unit. The extensive phase began on a large scale with favourable market conditions prevailing after 1895 and the closing of the American frontier in the decade of the nineties, rapidly gained momentum, reached an apparent peak from 1909 to 1911, and then started to subside. In the decade from 1901 to 1911 the occupied acreage increased from about 15 to 58 million acres, with gains of 24 million in Saskatchewan, 15 million in Alberta, and 3 million in Manitoba; the acreage under wheat increased from 2.5 to 10 million or 400 per cent. This was the period of most rapid growth.

The outbreak of war in 1914 provided a powerful new external stimulus and the extensive phase was revived. Disruption in Europe and the distance of Australian and Argentine competitors from the major markets favoured North American producers. Wheat acreage in Canada increased from 10 to 20 million acres despite military demands for labour, the cessation of immigration, and persistently bad climatic conditions. The only good crop during the war years was that of 1915, but high farm prices more than offset reduced yields.

The full impact of price deflation following 1920 was relieved to some extent by improved yields and the continued disorganization of wheat production in the Danube countries and in Russia. This last factor and improvement in international economic conditions after 1924 contributed to a rise in the price of wheat and the extensive phase was resumed at a comparatively modest rate until 1928.

The intensive aspect of the investment process operated throughout the whole period with only a mild break in its continuity induced by the severe post-war deflation.

3.
Investment in Transportation

I. The Development of Transportation in Canada[1]

RAILWAYS were the fundamental industrial innovation enabling the shift from a maritime economy, based on timber and fish, to a transcontinental economy, based on wheat. Their construction completed the shift from short-term to long-term credit which had started with canals. Timber replaced fur as the major export from British North America in the early nineteenth century. Since water routes determined the accessibility of forest resources, the timber trade involved no fundamental change in domestic transportation, adding only minor trails as cutting moved back from water. But the new trade encouraged immigration, and population grew rapidly on the narrow base of native French and Loyalist immigrants in the Maritimes and the Canadas. The implications of frontier wheat as settlement spread revolutionized prevailing conceptions of adequate transportation. The demand for canals to overcome the barriers of falls and rapids in the St. Lawrence system and capture the trade with the western states was strengthened by the prospect of a domestic surplus of wheat as immigration increased and settlement spread. Investment in canals was carried forward with great vigour on an enlarged credit base following the political union of Upper and Lower Canada in 1841; but in 1850, twenty-five years after the completion of the Erie Canal had diverted the western trade to New York, the Canadian achievement had proven too meagre and too late to offset the advantages of the American seaboard. Meanwhile the progress of railroads in Great Britain and the United States provided a new instrument to attract private promotion of government support.

The first railroads in Canada were short portage lines. Their total mileage in 1850 was 66 miles. The first large-scale undertakings were completed in the decade from 1850 to 1860. Of chief importance were the Grand Trunk and the Great Western (a competitive road eventually acquired by the Grand Trunk). These provided lines running east and west across southern Ontario and Quebec. By 1860, over 2,000 miles of road had been built.

From 1860 to 1867, the year of Confederation, only 213 miles were added. In Nova Scotia, by 1867, lines had been completed from Halifax to the Bay of Fundy and to the Gulf of St. Lawrence. In New Brunswick there was a road from Saint John to the Gulf. In the Canadas, in addition to the two major roads built in the fifties, a series of short roads running north and south had been built to the limits of the agricultural frontier.

The Intercolonial and the Canadian Pacific, both products of Confederation, were the major developments in the period from 1867 to 1896. The Intercolonial was begun by the federal government in 1868 and completed in 1876 from Rivière du Loup, eastern terminal of the Grand Trunk, to Truro, Nova Scotia. The provincial roads which linked it to Halifax and Saint John were taken over along with the provincial debts by the new federal government. In 1873 a road under construction in Prince Edward Island was also taken over by the federal government when the island province joined the union under pressure of debt. Meanwhile numerous small, private ventures, encouraged by federal subsidies and local government support, raised the total railway mileage of the dominion to over 5,000 miles. Nine hundred and fifty miles of this total were operated directly by the federal government.

A Pacific railway was essential to the development of the prairie region, but the immediate pressure for construction of the railway arose with British Columbia's entry into Confederation in 1871. After initial arrangements for its construction by a private syndicate had failed, the road was started as a public enterprise in 1873. Construction proceeded very slowly until 1880 when a contract was negotiated with the syndicate that established the present Canadian Pacific Railway Co. By virtue of an aggressive personnel and generous government assistance, the road was completed by 1885 from Lake Nippissing, north of Toronto, across the southern prairies, through the Kicking Horse and Rogers' passes to the Thompson River, and down the Fraser Canyon to the coast. Acquisitions and new construction in the East extended the main line from Lake Nippissing through Ottawa to Montreal.

The Canadian Pacific competed with the Grand Trunk at this time for acquisition of many of the independent lines which had been built in the years immediately following Confederation and which now served as feeders to these two dominant roads.

The total railway mileage in operation in 1895 was 15,977. The three major roads were the Canadian Pacific, the Grand Trunk, and the Intercolonial. The bursts of construction activity from 1867 to 1873 and 1880 to 1885 had contributed to short, violent booms, but the economic growth of the new dominion was not impressive.

In addition to its railway programme during these years the federal government expended one hundred millions improving the Great Lakes-St. Lawrence waterways without affecting appreciably the flow of trade from the interior.

The high rate of investment in transportation promoted by government activity from 1867 to 1895 was exceeded in the period after 1895. In the former period the investment was undertaken without any major inducements immediately apparent in the way of resources and markets. Expert opinions on the possibilities of the prairie region as an agricultural frontier were pessimistic.[2] Support of government railway policy in the face of rather bleak economic facts revealed an excessive optimism and indifference to the implications of government debt. In a community of this outlook, which would support the construction of railways across thousands of miles of unsettled and apparently unproductive territory, it is not surprising that the beginning of the wheat boom should induce a scale of investment in transportation far in excess of requirements. Two additional transcontinental railways and several smaller roads were built from 1895 to 1915-20.

The first of the new transcontinentals had its beginning in Manitoba. The partnership of MacKenzie and Mann, two contractors who had taken part in the construction of the C.P.R., acquired the Lake Manitoba Railway and Canal Co. in 1895. The partners obtained liberal support first from provincial governments in the West anxious to promote a competitor of the C.P.R. and later from the federal government. A complete list of the numerous companies of this new system, the Canadian Northern, is given in Chapter XI. Nine thousand miles were developed by new construction and through acquisitions. The excessive ambition of MacKenzie and Mann and the recession beginning in 1913 led to financial difficulties which were further complicated by the outbreak of war. Government intervention saved the company from bankruptcy.

The Grand Trunk's ambition to share in the western wheat boom led to the construction of a third transcontinental system. Failure to secure co-operation between the Grand Trunk, with lines in the East, and the Canadian Northern, with lines in the West, was followed by an agreement between the Grand Trunk and the federal government. Under this agreement the Grand Trunk Pacific was built from Winnipeg northwest to Saskatoon and Edmonton and on through Yellowhead Pass to the northerly Pacific port of Prince Rupert. This section of the line, which followed closely the route of the Canadian Northern as far as the Yellowhead, was constructed by the company with government guarantees of its bonds. An eastern section was built by the government east from Winnipeg to Quebec City and across the St. Lawrence to Moncton,

New Brunswick. Its completion in 1915 raised the mileage of government railways to 4,393 miles. The Grand Trunk had agreed to lease this section, called the National Transcontinental, at a rent based on its cost of construction, but was neither willing nor able to fulfill the agreement. The company had been under serious financial pressure before 1914 and the war greatly increased its difficulties. Like the Canadian Northern, the Grand Trunk became dependent upon the public treasury. A Royal Commission was appointed in 1916 to investigate the whole railway problem.

The majority report of the commissioners recommended public ownership of the Canadian Northern and Grand Trunk group. The recommendation, duly enacted, raised government railway mileage to over 22,000. After a period of transition, all the federal lines were consolidated into a single system, the Canadian National Railways. Mileage operated by the Canadian Pacific at that time was approximately 13,000 miles. Together the two systems accounted for just over 90 per cent of the national railroad mileage. Their chief investment activities in the twenties were competitive branch-line construction, mainly in western Canada, and intensive improvement of existing road and equipment.

The federal government continued its traditional waterways development throughout this period of expansion. The largest project was the construction of the Welland Ship Canal. This canal, the fourth built between Lakes Ontario and Erie to circumvent Niagara Falls, was under construction from 1913 to 1931, with one major interruption during the war years. The federal government was also active in harbour construction, and its expenditures in this, and in the related field of river dredging, are included in the analysis below. A major development in external transportation during the period was the opening of the Panama Canal immediately after the war. The Panama reduced the relative importance of the St. Lawrence with important implications for the city of Vancouver whose trade hinterland was now extended as far inland as western Saskatchewan.

Meanwhile the rapid development of the motor car converted roads from a position of minor to major importance among government transportation expenditures. The responsibility for roads had been assigned to provincial and local governments by the B.N.A. Act. Departments of Highways were established in the various provinces during the period of expansion. "The days of turnpikes and statute labour virtually came to an end towards the end of the nineteenth century."[3] The provinces enacted legislation reorganizing the financing and construction of roads. The total mileage of roads in 1930 was 400,000 of which 80,000 miles were either gravel or hard-surfaced.[4]

Local transportation facilities, especially the substitution of electricity for horse power in the operation of street railways and the provision of streets and sidewalks in cities, towns, and villages, were major fields of investment. Complete estimates of the investment in street railways have not been prepared, but sufficient data to indicate their relative importance are incorporated in the discussion below. Streets and sidewalks, subjects of direct municipal investment, are dealt with along with other direct government investments in Chapter V.

II. Investment in Transportation, 1896-1930

Transportation facilities are not different in kind from the other durable producers' assets covered by the definitions of this study. But railways, canals, and roads in Canada differed in degree from most other types of capital equipment in two important ways:

(1) They were the essential prerequisite to so many other types of economic development that their initial appearance generated large repercussions in investment in other fields and, also, great speculation in land.[5]

(2) The size of an effective unit of transportation equipment was very large. The point here is not the degree of capital intensity but merely the absolute size of the initial outlays relative to private capital resources.[6]

The mass and complexity of steam engines and large numbers of heavy rolling stock involved large outlays on equipment. But the initial expense of a main road greatly exceeded the cost of equipment. An elaborate roadbed was required even on the prairie where the track had to be raised several feet above the surrounding countryside to avoid drifts of snow in winter. Building through mountains and over muskeg involved the additional costs of blasting, fills, tressels, bridges, and tunnels. Muskeg in the Canadian Shield often appeared bottomless. After 50 years of dumping thousands of tons of fill, parts of main-line roads are not yet firmly founded. Thus climate and geography accentuated the implications of the size of the railway unit. Reliance on an agricultural staple added the difficulty of an unusual seasonal peak.[7]

Many structures and much equipment are specific with respect to locality and use, but none more so than railway. Excessive and misplaced expenditures cannot be recovered. In Canada these are borne as a national overhead of dead debt, a product of the character of the equipment and of government direction of its accumulationg during the period of extensive expansion.

Once the initial roads were established, fields for large investment outlays were not exhausted. Again, as with prairie farm investment, the extensive phase (spreading mileage over new territories) gave way to a costly process of intensive investment. This is an additional reason why records of railway mileage and the numbers of locomotives and cars, often used as criteria of the volume of railway investment, are very imperfect indicators of actual outlays. With some growth in traffic, and facing competition from other railroads and alternative modes of transportation, the individual lines continued investment in the improvement of existing facilities to reduce operating expenses and increase or maintain revenues. Heavier trainloads reduced operating expenses by spreading fixed costs over a greater freight revenue. More powerful locomotives were necessary to pull the larger trains. With passenger cars there was an ever-widening array of attractive improvements. The heavier locomotives and longer trains required heavier rails and better ballasting. Whether these were charged as renewals or not they represented net investment in road. Another important phase of intensive investment was found in the possibility of a continual reduction of gradients and improvement of alignments. Substitutions of treated for untreated ties like the earlier replacement of steel for iron rails (completed in 1916) constituted net additions to railway property. Terminals, switching and yard facilities, shops, and road crossings offered other avenues for investment.

The extensive phase of railway building in Canada ended about 1915. Large expenditures were later undertaken by the Canadian National group to replace temporary structures. Thirty-five per cent of all C.N.R. mileage was taken over from contractors from 1915 to 1918. Wooden tressels with an average life of seven to ten years had to be replaced.[8] Fresh fills were still settling. Many roundhouses, section buildings, water facilities, stations, and terminal plants remained to be built or improved. Some of the expenditures in this transition period might be classified as extensive, but the bulk of the expenditures were of the intensive variety. In Table XII the estimated railway investment expenditures are compared with changes in mileage and numbers of rolling stock. The table illustrates the unreliability of changes in physical units as indexes of railway investment. The mileage series alone would greatly exaggerate the implications of the shift from extensive activity after 1915 for the level of the net expenditures on road. The drop in net investment was nevertheless very large, and the higher prices prevailing after 1915 do not mask it. Even the rise in replacement expenditures plus higher costs of construction were insufficient to offset a drop in gross railway construction at current prices in the years following 1915. Net investment in equipment was much better maintained and, when replacements are added, the gross equipment series shows a fairly steady rise from 1896 to 1930.[9] The intensive phase of railway development involved net additions to both road and equipment. But railway rolling stock is more flexible than road property and, from the outset, equipment outlays were more closely adjusted to prevailing traffic demands than the initial outlays on road. The ratio of road to equipment expenditures therefore fell in the period of intensive expansion.

The lower section of the table shows the investment in equipment and the net additions to rolling stock. Here the inadequacy of the changes in physical units as a guide to railway investment is even more marked than with road. The numbers of locomotives and cars added reached a peak in 1911-15. After 1920 the retirals of locomotives and freight cars exceeded the gross additions with the result that the net additions were negative. Nevertheless, the net expenditures on rolling stock at current prices reached their peak from 1926 to 1930.

Reasons for these high equipment expenditures after the period of extensive expansion may be cited.[10] The character of the demand for freight services grew more complex. Whereas the number of all freight cars increased 107 per cent from 1907 to 1930, the numbers of refrigerator cars and of oil tank cars increased 341 per cent and 228 per cent, respectively. This specialized equipment was more expensive than other kinds of rolling stock. A more important factor contributing to larger outlays was the change in the capacity of the cars. In 1908 there were more cars in the 30-ton class than in any other, with the 20-ton class ranking second in this respect. Twelve years later cars in the 30-ton class were still the most numerous, but the 40-ton class had risen to second place. By 1930 cars of the 40-ton class were most numerous. The increase in the average capacity from 1907 to 1929 was 35 per cent for box and flat cars, 63 per cent for coal cars, and 77 per cent for tank cars. The larger cars were more expensive for reasons of size and because steel was substituted for wood in their construction. A steel underframe and frame were necessary for strength in the larger cars, and all-steel construction was favoured on the grounds that lower maintenance and longer life offset the greater initial outlay.

Another factor contributing to the high equipment expenditures of the twenties was the large re-equipment programme of the C.N.R. The standard of its inherited equipment was below the national average owing to the financial stringency that had plagued the component companies. In the five years from 1924 to 1929 the C.N.R. retired 17,722 cars while the C.P.R. in the ten years from 1920 to 1929 retired only 12,736. The average capacity of C.P.R. freight cars rose from 36.3 tons in 1920 to 41.1 tons in 1930. Aver-

TABLE XII

Measures of Steam Railway Expansion, 1896-1930 [a]

	Road construction (millions of dollars)			Net additions to railway mileage
	Net	Replacement	Gross	
1896-1900	42	13	55	1,680
1901-5	102	22	124	2,830
1906-10	348	33	381	4,244
1911-15	490	47	537	10,151
1916-20	158	94	253	3,923
1921-25	138	115	253	1,545
1926-30	258	132	389	1,697

	Equipment expenditures (millions of dollars)			Net additions of rolling stock		
	Net	Replacement	Gross	Locomotives	Freight cars	Passenger cars
1896-1900	12	4	16	250	12,557	-514
1901-5	34	7	41	633	21,577	496
1906-10	82	10	92	1,173	28,616	1,190
1911-15	132	13	145	1,407	82,077	2,006
1916-20	141	30	170	544	22,699	231
1921-25	96	37	133	-278	-262	282
1926-30	146	48	194	-301	-9,200	507

(a) *Source*: Appendix table J and Chapter XI.

age capacity of C.N.R. freight cars increased from 34.8 tons in 1920 to 37.8 tons in 1930.[11]

There was a parallel change in locomotive capacity. While numbers declined in the twenties, the average tractive power of locomotives increased from 33,519 pounds in 1924 to 36,228 in 1930. The average tractive power of all C.N.R. freight locomotives was 42,901 pounds in 1930. The C.N.R. spent much more in this field than the C.P.R., with the result that the average for all its locomotives was 38,814 in 1930 whereas the average for all C.P.R. locomotives in the same year was 35,550 pounds.[12]

The progressive substitution of heavier and more specialized equipment accounted for the continuing high levels of net investment in rolling stock after 1915.[13] At the same time, rising replacements echoed large net additions of earlier periods. As a result the total demand for equipment was well sustained up to 1930. Road improvements, which necessarily accompanied the use of longer, heavier trains, also involved considerable net expenditures. But the ratio of net investment in road to net investment in equipment was not maintained at anything like the pre-1915 level for the reason given above. And road renewals tended to grow more slowly and more evenly than equipment renewals.[14] Total gross investment in railway road and equipment therefore fell after the period of extensive development. This absolute decline implied a very sharp drop in the relative importance of railways as a field for investment. This may be demonstrated by comparing the gross investment in railways with the national gross investment in durable physical assets in different periods from 1896 to 1930. Railways accounted for 23.4 per cent of the national expenditure on all structures and machinery and equipment over the ten years from 1906 to 1915. Their relative importance in this respect was cut in half after 1915, since railways accounted for 12.3, 11.1, and 11.2 per cent of all expenditures on durable physical producers' assets in the three quinquennia 1916-20, 1921-25, and 1926-30, respectively.[15]

It is sometimes assumed that the development of the automobile opened new fields of investment in the twenties sufficient to offset the relative decline in railway investment. This is not true. It was shown in Table III that a group of transport facilities including highways, bridges, and producers' automobiles as well as railway road and rolling stock accounted for approximately 25 per cent of gross domestic capital formation in 1906-10 and 1911-15 and just under 21 per cent in 1920-25 and 1926-30.[16] At the end of the period the railways were still the most important component of this group despite the absolute and relative decline of gross investment in railway road and equipment. The changing relative importance of the three major types of producers' transport facilities in this group is shown by their percentage distribution in Table XIII. Harbours and canals were a fairly stable part of the total over the whole period. Railways declined from over 80 per cent of the total before 1915 to about 50 per cent after the war. They accounted for 47.6 per cent from 1926 to 1930 whereas highways, bridges, and producers' automobiles accounted for 41.1 per cent.

A striking contrast between the two major types of transport facilities is in the far greater implications which railways had for construction. The highways and bridges (used by both consumer and producer vehicles) fell very far short of the railway roadbed as a field of investment expenditure. Highways were undergoing an extensive expansion throughout the twenties yet absorbed less expenditure than railways in this period. The construction expenditures in these transport fields and their percentage distribution are shown in Table XIV. Growing highway expenditures brought the total expenditure, expressed in current prices, slightly above the pre-war peak at the end of the period, but these expenditures on roads and bridges were only 20 per cent greater than the sums going into harbours, canals, and river work and less than half as great as those going into the intensive expansion of railway road property. It was this difference in railroads and automobiles with respect to construction demands that determined the change in the relative position of transportation as a field for investment in Canada after 1915. It has been pointed out that, on the equipment side, the absolute level of railroad demands was well maintained. The demands did not keep pace with the rising total flow of machinery and equipment that accompanied the growth of the economy. However, growing demands for automobile transport among transport equipment demands in general more than offset this tendency.

TABLE XIII
Gross Investment in Major Transport Facilities, 1901-30[a]
(percentage distribution)

	Railway group	Automobile group	Canal group	Total
1901-5	82.1	1.9	15.9	100.0
1906-10	87.3	3.4	8.9	100.0
1911-15	80.5	8.4	11.1	100.0
1916-20	64.0	27.0	9.0	100.0
1921-25	51.2	34.1	14.6	100.0
1926-30	47.6	41.1	11.3	100.0

(a) *Source*: Appendix Tables J and K

TABLE XIV

Gross Construction Outlays in Major Transport Fields, 1901-30(a)

A. Values (millions of dollars)

	Railways	Highways	Canals and harbours	Total
1901-5	124.3	3.3	32.1	159.7
1906-10	380.7	11.7	48.0	440.4
1911-15	537.4	38.5	93.7	669.6
1916-20	252.5	39.4	59.7	351.6
1921-25	253.2	100.4	109.8	463.4
1926-30	389.4	172.4	138.2	700.0

B. Percentage Distribution

	Railways	Highways	Canals and harbours	Total
1901-5	77.8	2.1	20.1	100.0
1906-10	86.4	2.7	10.1	100.0
1911-15	80.3	5.7	14.0	100.0
1916-20	71.8	11.2	16.9	100.0
1921-25	54.6	21.7	23.7	100.0
1926-30	55.5	24.6	19.7	100.0

(a) *Source:* Appendix Tables J and K and Chapter XI.

Expenditures on producers' automobiles exceeded expenditures on railway rolling stock for the first time in the years from 1921 to 1925 and were approximately 65 per cent greater in the five years that followed. This positive net change in the transport equipment pattern was not great enough to offset the opposite drift in the construction pattern.

If the definition of investment were broadened to include consumers' automobiles and these were added to the group of transport facilities mentioned above, then the gross investment for the group would be slightly more important in 1926-30 than in 1911-15 (about 30 per cent as compared with 29 per cent of gross capital formation). But if the vehicles replaced by the automobile and the investment in non-farm and farm horses were taken into account, the result of the comparison would be shifted quite definitely the other way. These comparisons leave out the secondary repercussions. For example, the automobile involved large investment outlays on manufacturing plant and equipment, garages, filling stations, and so on. However, it is probably safe to say that these repercussions were of less relative importance than those which accompanied the extension of railroads at an earlier period. It is also clear that, within the present definition of investment and considering only the direct expenditures, the automobile, in its extensive phase, did not offset the relative decline in investment outlays on railroads that occurred after 1915. The expenditures on automobiles and railway rolling stock are shown in Table XV.

The addition of investment outlays on street railways and municipal expenditures on streets, highways, and bridges – purely local forms of transportation – to the major facilities considered above would not alter the general pattern. Publicly and privately owned street railway companies expended $44 million on road and equipment from 1926 to 1930.[17] If an index based on changes in their total capital liabilities can be relied upon to indicate their capital expenditures, the chief period of expansion of electric railways occurred from 1905 to 1915. Large additions to capital liabilities after the war suggest another burst of activity: the completion of the earlier extensive phase with a lag imposed by the war. There was only a small change in capital liabilities after 1925. Exact figures on municipal outlays for streets, highways, and bridges are not available. From 1926 to 1930 these outlays were in the neighbourhood of $100 million.[18] These are not large compared with railway expenditures in this period. Total municipal expenditures from 1911 to 1915 were only 20 per cent below the level of 1926 to 1930.[19] Taken together both forms of local transport expenditures are much smaller than the total expenditures on transport facilities

TABLE XV

Gross Expenditures on Railway Rolling Stock and Automobiles, 1901-30[a]

	1	2	3	4	5	6
	Value (millions of dollars)			Percentage distribution		
	Rolling stock	Producers' autos	Consumers' autos	Percentage 1 is of total	Percentage 2 is of total	Percentage 3 is of total
1901-5	41	1	2	93.2	2.3	4.5
1906-10	92	7	18	78.6	6.0	15.4
1911-15	145	34	92	53.5	12.5	33.9
1916-20	170	139	360	25.4	20.7	53.9
1921-25	133	157	420	18.7	22.1	59.2
1926-30	194	331	760	15.1	25.8	59.1

(a) *Source*: Appendix Tables J and K.

and, since they also reflect the impact of the wheat economy to a large degree, their pattern is not dissimilar.

III. Appraisal

This examination of transportation development from 1896 to 1930 has indicated the importance of this field of investment in the Canadian economy. The construction of railways was the most impressive aspect of the development. Initial activity in the wheat economy before 1905 provided the ignition. Induced investment in railroads rose very rapidly, continued at high levels until 1913, and then tended to decline. This declining tendency was largely, although not fully, offset by the innovation of the automobile as a means of transportation. Automobiles were first concentrated in local transportation, but at an early stage in their development they began to exert a depressive influence on the railways, taking a growing share of the remunerative short haul freights as highways improved. The automobile also reduced greatly the public demand for railway passenger service.[20]

Railways absorbed more foreign investment during the period of extensive expansion than any other single industry in Canada.[21] Farm expansion, the basic development, and housing, the largest single investment field, were financed largely by domestic savings. Government intervention rather than the profitability of railroading in Canada was responsible for the large flows of foreign capital attracted to the railway field. (The financial aspect of railway investment and the allocation of foreign capital among industries is dealt with in Chapter VI.) The relative size of the investment opportunity in railways has been emphasized, but the labour opportunities were also very great. In the period before 1915, a job with the railway builders provided many a farmer with the cash to carry him over the first years of settlement. The unusual demands for unskilled construction workers carried many other immigrants through the first difficult years in the new country. When the pre-war construction boom collapsed thousands of the immigrant construction workers were absorbed as permanent urban residents by the wartime expansion of manufacturing production which followed. The large railway industry itself absorbed many workers on a permanent basis. At the end of the period, from 1926 to 1930, railway revenues averaged 11 per cent of the national income. The railway labour force accounted for approximately 7 per cent of the national labour force.[22]

To classify the railroads among the developments that depended upon the emergence of the wheat economy is not to imply that the railway development was attributable solely to wheat or that the wheat economy was not dependent on transportation. But wheat was the prime mover, and the expansion of prairie farm production did valorize a great deal of the investment in railways either directly or as the essential catalytic agent in innumerable new and apparently independent exchange relations across the country.

Some part of the extension of railroads was a necessary complement of the wheat economy and some part of the intensive investment after the extensive period can be rationalized in terms of growing traffic density; but both forms of expansion were greatly overdone. One traffic bridge over the Canadian Shield may have been justified on non-economic grounds, but hardly two, and certainly not three. Since there was obvious over-building one might have expected a lag in investment after 1915-20 while traffic caught up with the initial indivisible road units. However, intensive investment was apparently continuous (at least, after 1907) and appeared to accelerate as extensive investment dropped.

The growth in traffic density after 1920 was too small to warrant high levels of investment during the twenties. Traffic density in 1928 was 26 per cent higher than in 1920, but 1928 was a unique year. Traffic density was slightly higher in 1920 than in 1913, but it was lower in 1924 than in 1913 and lower still in 1931.[23] The average carload did not increase as rapidly as the size of the cars after 1920, and shippers were admonished by railway officials for not taking advantage of the larger cars.[24] Since there was an absolute decrease in the numbers of cars loaded with heavy staples like grain, forest products, and coal,[25] the admonitions were better directed to the railways for not adapting their equipment to the demands of the shippers. The railways appear to have expanded capacity for capacity's sake.

In the passenger field there was an absolute decline in density after 1920. Expenditures to improve passenger service reflected an effort on the part of the railways to recover losses to the automobile in this field.

Some part of the intensive investment may have been an economically justifiable substitution of capital for labour. The well organized railway unions did succeed in retaining the larger part of wartime wage gains. The prospect of the growing power of the unions would have further strengthened the inclination of railway executives to expand capital equipment. Since the relative changes in labour and capital costs per unit of output over this period cannot be determined from the available data, it is not possible to test for this factor.

Probably the most important determinant of the high levels of railway investment after 1920 was the competition between the two major systems. Capital expenditures of the C.N.R. were subject to government approval and, since faith in indefinite progress and expansion continued to prevail among the legislators, these expenditures were large. The C.P.R. was compelled to expand in order to maintain its relative position.[26] Consequently, the level of investment in railways was largely determined by public policy in the intensive as well as in the extensive period of development. Since railway rates were administered by a government agency, there was a concomitant tendency to determine the price of railway service by the stock of railway capital instead of the other way around. This economic waste of politically determined over-investment was induced by prairie expansion; and, since the prairies were the only region within the economy where competition of water and road did not limit the level of railway rates, the cost of the economic waste was also largely borne there.

4.
Urban Building

THE RELATION of the extensive railway boom to the wheat economy was simple and direct. At the same time developments on the prairie generated construction activity on a large scale elsewhere in the economy, particularly through its relation to the growth of towns and cities. Although western expansion was clearly the basic development before 1915 and continued to be a major factor until 1930, other developments complicate the interpretation of investment activity from 1915 to 1930. After 1915, the first world war, the opening of the Panama Canal, the development of hydroelectric power, and the new export staples of mine and forest contributed along with the western frontier to the formation of the economic structure within which the urban construction cycles operated.[1] Government railway and tariff policies affected the growth of cities over the whole period. The concern here is with the link between these primary factors and the process of urbanization with its cycles of construction. Before dealing with the nature of urban building fluctuations in Canada, it will be useful to consider construction in general to indicate some of its major characteristics.

I. Construction in General

Detailed analysis of censuses of the construction industry and the flows of construction materials (see Chapter VII) indicates that a very large share of the expenditures on construction from 1896 to 1930 went directly to domestic skilled and unskilled labour in the form of wages and salaries. In addition to these payments to on-site construction labour, some part of overhead and profit was wages and salaries of office personnel. Furthermore, capital intensity in the industry was low and much of the capital was owned by small-scale domestic enterprisers whose whole income, comprised of wages, rent, and interest, would not put them in the upper income brackets. Thus it may be inferred that about 50 per cent of the expenditure on structures emerged as direct income widely dispersed among domestic factors. Raw materials and supplies accounted for the balance. The bulk of these raw materials was domestically produced. (For example, about 90 per cent of the domestic disappearance at producers' prices was domestically produced in the five years from 1926 to 1930. See Appendix table A.) Since most of these construction materials were forest products and simple mining products, like clay bricks, cement, and building stone, the import content was small. About 75 per cent of the material costs of construction emerged as indirect labour income.[2] Adding the indirect to the direct income makes it apparent that from 85 to 90 per cent of a dollar spent on structures from 1926 to 1930 became domestic factor income. (The percentage was lower before 1915. Imports (plus duties) were only 11.7 per cent of the domestic disappearance of construction materials from 1926 to 1930, 20.9 per cent from 1911 to 1915, and 26.5 per cent from 1901 to 1905.) This implies an unusually low leakage to imports at a time when imports ranged between 37 and 41 per cent of national income at factor cost. The leakage to savings would not be high owing to the large domestic labour content. Also the types of forest and mining industries affected were not typically large-scale, nor was the capital invested in them foreign-owned to any great extent. One would expect a large leverage effect on all counts. This is an important consideration. The large incremental variations characteristic of construction, whether induced or not, must have contributed powerfully to fluctuations in the level of economic activity.[3]

The impact of variations in expenditures on machinery and equipment, taking them as a whole and over the whole period from 1900 to 1930, was much less dynamic. The direct leakage to imports was high. Approximately 40 per cent of the domestic disappearance of machinery and equipment from 1926 to 1930 was imported. This reliance on foreign supply did not change significantly over the thirty-year period.[4] Then, with the proportion of the supply that was finished in domestic plants, leakages were high for several reasons: (1) the share of direct domestic labour was small; (2) the import content of the materials, which accounted for about 45 per cent of the producers' price, was large relative to construction materials, reflecting dependence on the iron and steel industry of the United States; (3) capital intensity in machinery industries was and still is relatively high, with ownership concentrated very often in foreign hands; and finally (4) administered prices were the rule in the protected equipment industries and this monopolistic element would contribute to a relative distortion of the income structure. Leakages through imports and savings were consequently much higher for marginal gross revenues of the machinery and equipment industries than for those of construction.

Another characteristic of investment in structures relevant to an understanding of its role in the dynamics of the economy was its heterogeneity. The pattern of decisions involved was more complicated than that respecting machinery and equipment, if only because the demand for structures arose in all fields where machinery and equipment were in demand and also in two others where machinery and equipment were not significant factors, namely, residential housing and government investment. Government construction and housing have been two of the largest components of gross construction. Some of the factors governing decisions to invest in these two fields were peculiar to these fields. Differences in structures and equipment with respect to durability and flexibility have contributed to a divergence in the trends in the expenditures on them in the railway field. Peculiar trends also developed in other major fields.

The broad movements of three major types of construction may be discerned from quinquennial estimates. Housing, government, and railway construction from 1900 to 1940 are shown in value terms and as percentages of gross construction in each quinquennium in Table XVI. The data in the table reflect several things worthy of remark, only two of which are relevant here: the great size of these three components relative to the total and the variation in their relative importance over the years. Together, these three components accounted for about two-thirds of all construction activity in Canada from 1900 to 1940.[5] This is an important consideration in view of the probability that decisions to invest in these types of construction have been less subject than most other forms of investment to the rational restraints assumed in economic theory. The movement of the railway component from 1900 to 1930 has already been examined in a previous chapter. It will be noted that the drop in its relative importance after 1915 was followed by a further drop after 1930 and complete failure to recover after 1935. Contrasting with the trend in the railway component is the opposite trend in government construction; and contrasting with both is the relative stability in the ratio of housing to gross construction over the whole period. Each appears to have followed a peculiar pattern. The levels of railway construction were determined to a very large extent by government policies and financed by government credit. Government construction was wholly so governed and financed. Public decisions were not governed by the motives of profit and loss and success and failure dominating behaviour in trade and industry. Housing was also in a different category. The evidence we have supports the view that the demand for housing did not respond so sensitively to short-run changes in the level of general economic

TABLE XVI

Gross Construction, by Major Types, Quinquennially, 1901-40(a)

A. Value (millions of dollars)

	1 Steam Railways	2 Housing	3 Government	4 Other (5-1+2+3)	5 Gross Construction
1901-5	124	222	79	256	681
1906-10	381	468	149	441	1,439
1911-15	537	568	342	560	2,007
1916-20	253	641	256	972	2,122
1921-25	253	742	436	840	2,271
1926-30	389	1,060	578	1,082	3,109
1931-35	122	483	515	480	1,600
1936-40	106	765	772	456	2,099

B. Percentage Distribution

	1 Steam Railways	2 Housing	3 Government	4 Other (5-1+2+3)	5 Gross Construction
1901-5	18.2	32.6	11.6	37.6	100.0
1906-10	26.5	32.5	10.4	30.6	100.0
1911-15	26.8	28.3	17.0	27.9	100.0
1916-20	11.9	30.2	12.1	45.8	100.0
1921-25	11.1	32.7	19.2	37.0	100.0
1926-30	12.5	34.1	18.6	34.8	100.0
1931-35	7.6	30.2	32.2	30.0	100.0
1936-40	5.1	36.4	36.8	21.7	100.0

(a) *Sources:* Estimates for the period 1901-30 are from Chapters VII and XI; estimates for the period 1931-40 are from *Public Investment and Capital Formation,* with the exception of the housing figures which are from Firestone, *Residential Real Estate in Canada,* 279. (Direct investment in steam railways by the federal government is included in column 1. See Appendix table L for the amounts involved.)

activity as the demand for structures in industry and trade. Consequently any one of these major components may have played at times a major independent role in the economic system.

The contention that the pattern of different types of construc-

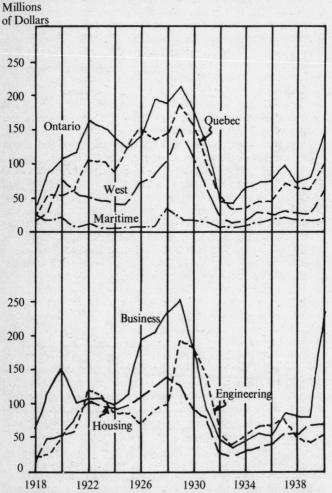

FIG. 5. Construction by regions and types. (Source: Hugh C. MacLean Publications Ltd., Toronto.)

tion may vary through time and, further, that the level of construction activity may vary regionally, is supported by evidence given in Figure 5. The indexes in this chart are based on the values of construction contracts awarded from 1918 to 1940.[6] Contracts awarded are the best records available on regional construction in Canada and the only records on types of construction over so many years. Coverage probably increased gradually over the period but this trend would not mask the cyclical changes. It is apparent in the upper section of the chart, which displays the regional pattern, that the Maritimes failed to share in the construction boom of the twenties. Also, the construction industry of the prairie provinces experienced depression through the first half of that decade. The construction industry in the Maritimes experienced stagnation from 1920 to 1940. After the collapse of the wartime boom, and in the absence of both basic and dependent opportunities, the region lost most of the natural increase in its population. Nova Scotia and Prince Edward Island experienced an absolute decline in population from 1921 to 1931. Secondary industries in the Maritimes were unable to compete with those in the central provinces after the first period of extensive frontier expansion closed. The severe deflation of agricultural prices following the war explains the sluggishness of construction activity on the prairies from 1920 to 1925. Since the hinterland was depressed, it is perhaps surprising that construction activity was so buoyant in both Ontario and Quebec at this time. Despite price deflation and the sharp national recession that began in 1920 and cumulated to a depression trough in 1922, the value of contract awards in central Canada was rising through 1920, 1921, and 1922, out of phase with the national business cycle. Examination of the lower section of the chart indicates that commercial and industrial investors, whom one would expect to respond most sensitively to current levels of aggregate demand, did in fact respond to the post-war recession. The buoyancy of construction activity in Ontario and Quebec through the recession and depression of 1920-22 was the result of a rise in residential and engineering construction. The latter reflected actions of governments and public utilities which were finally cut back after 1922. Residential construction displayed the most remarkable pattern, moving against the level of aggregate demand, rising when aggregate demand fell from 1920 to 1922, and levelling out when it rose from 1922 to 1925. Following the rapid rise in new residential construction from its wartime trough, the rate of increase in house building fell in 1920 when commercial and industrial construction was most active, perhaps reflecting the competitive weakness of housing in a period of peak costs, and then accelerated in 1921 as costs fell. Urban growth in Ontario and Quebec during the war laid the basis for this post-war surge of house building. The high level of residential construction reached in 1922 was fairly well maintained until 1925. After 1925, as economic recovery became more general, housing construction rose to still higher levels, finally reaching a peak towards the end of the decade. Resumption of western expansion was a major factor in this latter period.

A significant contrast between house building and the other types of urban building construction is evident in Figure 5. The movement of the housing index, particularly in the up-swing, is relatively persistent. In contrast, the index of commercial and industrial building reacts sensitively from year to year – probably to changes in the general level of economic activity. When the level of commercial and industrial building is compared with exports of goods and services, one finds that annual changes in the two indexes are almost always in the same direction. When they are not, the commercial and industrial building index follows the trade index with a lag. The index of housing construction does not display this close dependence upon the level of trade.

Building permit data do not provide as much information on types of construction as the records of contract awards, but permit records cover a much longer period of time. These records are used in the following section to establish the long-run pattern of urban residential building construction.

II Urban Building and Real Estate Fluctuations

The top section of Figure 6 is an index of urban building activity in Canada from 1866 to 1946. This index reflects four-and-a-half major cycles in the eighty years since the Dominion was established. The cycles are similar in many respects to those found by American students.[7] This Canadian index, like those used to illustrate the long cycles in American building, is based on building permits issued in major cities, and has been adjusted to eliminate the influence of changes in the cost of construction.[8] Table XVII compares upper and lower turning points in the index with those reflected in Riggleman's index of deflated values of urban building permits per capita in the United States. It is evident that the length of the cycles was roughly the same in both countries. The most remarkable differences are the four-year lead in the Canadian turning point of 1896, and the three – and four-year lags in the Canadian peaks of 1912 and 1929.

There are numerous limitations to the usefulness of permit data as measures of construction activity.[9] Since the chief concern here is whether there have been long wave-like movements in urban residential building, most of the limitations of permit data are not serious. However, the inclusion in the building index shown in Figure 6 of commercial, industrial, and some public buildings, many of which have a very high unit cost, involves the possibility that they and not housing may have determined the shape of the cycles. To test further the suggestion that urban residential building has followed a long cycle, several indexes of building and real estate activity in greater Toronto were prepared in which the influence of non-residential activity was reduced. These are shown in Figure 7. The basic data were compiled as far as possible for the metropolitan region.[10] Two indexes of building were developed: an index of the number of new building permits issued annually per capita from 1886 to 1946, and an index of the number of dwelling permits per capita from 1920 to 1945.

TABLE XVII
Urban Building

Upper turning points		Lower turning points	
Canada	United States	Canada	United States
1871	1871	1880	1878
1889	1890	1896	1900
1912	1909	1918	1918
1929	1925	1933	1934

Numbers rather than values of permits were used in the former index to avoid the distortion introduced by the high unit values of commercial and industrial permits. The number of new building permits is heavily weighted by housing permits in the years before 1915-20 when the automobile was not common; later, large numbers of permits were issued for small garages. This difficulty was met by compiling a second index of dwelling permits per capita covering the years when garage permits became numerous. The two building indexes appear in the centre of Figure 7. The first index suffers greatly, in the years from 1885 to 1895 or thereabouts, from limitation of the area of the city to which the permit law applied and failure to comply with the law within this area.[11] Although the index is too low in these years, it is good enough for the present purpose.

At the top of Figure 7, appear annual indexes of real estate activity in greater Toronto from 1880, when Toronto was a town of 95,000, to 1948, when the population had reached a million. For the period from 1880 to 1894, an index of all instruments registered is shown. Its movements are dominated by the total numbers of deeds (property transfers), mortgages, and discharges of mortgages registered.[12] Two indexes are shown for the years 1894 to 1948: the number of transfers and the number of property mortgages registered each year.[13] The series based on numbers were used for the chart because they are more likely to be dominated by residential property.[14] The annual index of the number of subdivision plans registered from 1880 to 1948, which is shown at the bottom of the chart, reflects another form of activity that is clearly related to the promotion of housing.

The Toronto building indexes follow a long wave-like pattern similar to that displayed in the more comprehensive index of Figure 6. The indexes of real estate activity appear to corroborate the suggestion of a long cycle in urban residential construction. The long cycle is particularly evident in the index of subdivisions. The major turning points in all the series occur within a year of one another, with the single exception of transfers which reached a peak in 1920, two years before mortgages, permits, and dwellings, and three years before subdivisions. A comparison of numbers of building permits per capita with numbers of new dwelling permits per capita from 1920 to 1945 confirms the view that the weight of housing dominates the former series even in these years when the proportion of housing to total permits is at its lowest. The value series for permits, transfers, and mortgages all show a peak in the late twenties. This later peak in the value series is the result of the higher levels of commercial and industrial building and real estate activity which prevailed in the second half of the decade. Thus an index of the value of permits issued in Toronto, adjusted for changes in the cost of construction, would show a peak in the late twenties as does the index of Figure 6.

Further evidence respecting the nature of urban real estate fluctuations in Canada is given in tables in the Appendix. Registrations of deeds, transfers, mortgages, and discharges of mortgages for Winnipeg over a period of seventy years, and the numbers of permits for new buildings in Montreal over the same period also confirm the existence of long fluctuations.

Numerous factors have a bearing on the demand for urban dwellings. Data on vacancy rates, the levels of gross and net rents, costs of construction, amortization and other terms of mortgage loans, the degree of mortgage solvency, the structure of interest rates, the level of income, net family formation, and population

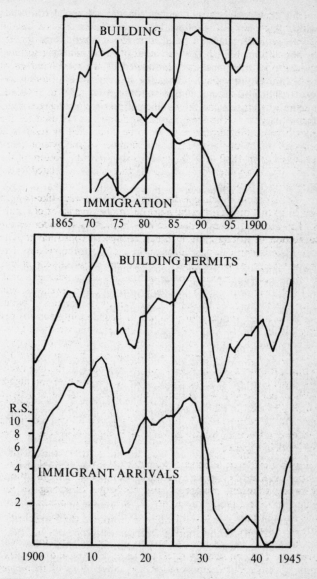

FIG. 6.   Urban building activity and immigration in Canada. (Source: Chapter XI and Appendix.)

growth and movement would be required for a reasonably complete analysis. Also, in view of the marked divergence in regional building activity evident in the past, it is probable that national aggregates would be too crude for the purpose. In the following section only the population factor is considered. The growth and geographic movements of the population in some of the periods of active building are examined and an attempt is made to compare population movements with the fluctuations in building and real estate activity.

III. Relation of Urban Building to Population

There is no direct relation between cycles in the rate of growth of the population and the building cycles reflected in the charts. The long population cycles described by M. C. MacLean extend over periods several times longer than the fifteen to twenty years of the urban cycles.[15] In any event, it is increments in the population and in numbers of family and non-family households, not rates of growth, which should be considered in connection with the demand for dwellings. These increments may continue to rise long after the rates of growth have passed their peak. For example, in Canada the peak rate of growth in the nineteenth century occurred from 1831 to 1841, but decade increments continued to rise until 1851-61. The decline in the following four decades is shown in Table XVIII.

Accompanying this decline in population growth there were two long cycles in urban building and real estate activity from the mid-sixties to the mid-nineties. The first cycle reflected in Figure 6 reached a peak in 1871. Activity remained fairly high until 1875, then fell sharply to a trough in 1880. The evidence shown is based on Montreal, but, since Montreal was the only city exceeding 100,000 in population before 1881, its experience should reflect adequately whatever developments may be termed "urban" in that period of Canada's history. In 1871 less than 20 per cent of the population lived in incorporated villages, towns, and cities. It was not yet clearly established that Toronto and not some other of the several large towns on the north shore of Lake Ontario would become the metropolitan centre of Ontario. Hamilton did not enter its period of rapid growth until after the protective tariff was introduced in 1879. The population of Quebec, the second city in 1871, was relatively stable for the thirty years following Confederation.

From a trough in 1880, building and real estate activity rose continously through the decade of the eighties, with one or two hesitations, to a peak in 1889, and then dropped again to a trough

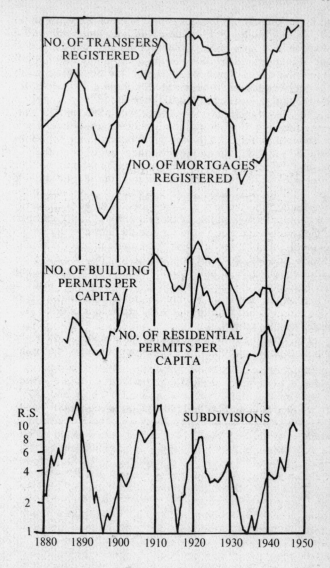

NO. OF TRANSFERS
REGISTERED

NO. OF MORTGAGES
REGISTERED ∨

NO. OF BUILDING
PERMITS PER
CAPITA

NO. OF RESIDENTIAL
PERMITS PER
CAPITA

R.S.
10
8
6
4

2

1

SUBDIVISIONS

1880   1890   1900   1910   1920   1930   1940   1950

FIG. 7   Building and real estate activity, Greater Toronto. (Source: Chapter XI and Appendix.)

in 1896. The city of Toronto, which achieved a population of 100,000 shortly after 1881, and the city of Hamilton, which reached 49,000 in 1891, were added to the index of Figure 6 in this period. The Winnipeg data indicate that this small city (8,000 in 1881) experienced a level of real estate activity in the early eighties which was not surpassed until well into the next boom which culminated in 1912 (population reached 140,000 in 1912).

The second cycle may be examined with profit since its nine-year expansion phase falls within two decennial census dates. It will be observed in Table XVIII that the increment in the population from 1881 to 1891, the decade when the major cities experienced building and real estate booms, was smaller than the increments on either side of it; that is, than the increments from 1871 to 1881 and from 1891 to 1901. Although total population grew more in the seventies and nineties than in the eighties, urban building activity was buoyant throughout the eighties and declining over a large part of the seventies and nineties. Increases in the number of households followed a similar pattern over these three decades: 152,000, 108,000, and 149,000 in the decades 1871-81, 1881-91, and 1891-1901, respectively.[16] In this illustration, drawn from the relatively simple economy of Canada before 1900, it is easy to see that it is the geographic movement and not the growth in total numbers of population which is fundamental to the explanation of urban residential building activity.

The changing pattern of regional differentials in economic opportunities will determine to a large extent when and where and

TABLE XVIII

Decade Increments in Population, Canada, 1851-1941[a]

Decade	Increments (thousands)
1851-61	793
1861-71	460
1871-81	636
1881-91	508
1891-1901	538
1901-11	1,835
1911-21	1,581
1921-31	1,589
1931-41	1,130

(a) *Source*: Dominion Bureau of Statistics, *Eighth Census of Canada*, 1941, I, 7.

for how long people will move; and vacancy rates, rents, cost of building sites, along with other secondary factors, will be more or less determined by the movements of people. It is conceivable that total population might be stable, as it was tending to become in Canada from 1860 to 1896, while movements from one set of towns and cities with declining opportunities to another set with expanding opportunities induce an urban investment boom. If the waves of population movement are long, the building cycles will be equally long.

The size and duration of the movement will be determined by the character of the factors creating the differential opportunities in the first place. If the differentials necessary to overcome non-economic costs of movement are very large, it is reasonable to expect that particular movements once started on a large scale will persist over a fairly long period before the initial opportunities and the dependent opportunities cumulatively induced by the process of movement itself are finally exhausted. Superimposed on the major waves will be the ripples of minor cycles of varying severity reflecting sensitive marginal responses to immediate economic conditions.[17] The major turn occurs when the opportunities have been fully exploited.

An elaboration of this simple thesis cannot be fully tested even in a small economy like the Canadian because of lack of information on the scale and direction of annual internal migrations. It can always be contended that a rise in building activity may induce and, through cumulative interactions, sustain population movements.[18] The more reasonable view suggested by Silberling that social, political, religious, and economic conditions operated in the past to cause intermittent movements out of one region or country into another[19] does not conflict with the one emphasized here. The direction of movements would be influenced by the pattern of economic opportunities. Within Canada this pattern has been largely determined by the status of primary resources relative to world markets, by government policies, and by wars.

The major factors creating the opportunities underlying the long building fluctuations in Canadian cities may be enumerated: (1) Confederation; (2) tariffs and the c.p.r.; (3) western expansion; (4) the first world war, new staples, and, again, wheat; (5) the second world war with its aftermath, and new resource developments. The bases of the first two were established by political action. The stimulus of the wars was also, in a sense, artificial. Economic disruption accompanying the wars afforded special protection to many domestic industries. Inflated demands with restricted competition led to urban expansion similar to that induced by tariffs. The growth of urban centres, which accompanied the expansion of the wheat economy, took the form of a building boom which ran from 1896 to a peak in 1912-13. The frontier forces underlying this expansion appeared to have exhausted themselves soon after 1909. After a short lag the opportunities in secondary and tertiary industries induced by the settlement of the frontier were also exploited, and recession set in. The more intricate pattern of repercussions from the first world war, new staples, and hydro-electric power, from the final short burst of extensive activity on the prairie frontier, and, although less important, from the growth of the automobile industry and the opening of the Panama Canal will not be examined here; but the impact on urban building and real estate activity from 1918 to 1930 is apparent in the several charts of this paper.[20]

Favourable conditions in world markets, the stimulation of inter-regional trade following Confederation in 1867, the extension of railroads, and especially the construction of the Intercolonial Railway from Canada to the Maritimes by the federal government were among the factors that contributed to the growth of Montreal from the mid-sixties to the mid-seventies. The building boom in Montreal collapsed in 1875, the year before the Intercolonial was completed. Timing of this initial cycle cannot be related to data on population movements taken from census records, because the building cycle straddled the first Dominion census and had run its course before the second census was taken.

From 1881 to 1891 the population of Canada increased by a meagre 11.8 per cent, 6 per cent less than the increase of the previous decade. The net addition to the population was 508,429 compared wity 635,553 the decade before. Estimated immigrant arrivals numbered 903,264 from 1881 to 1891, but the immigrant population grew by only 41,000. In the same decade the Canadian-born in the United States increased by 264,000. Emigration during the eighties apparently exceeded 1,100,000 so that the balance of migrations was negative.[21] In spite of this poor showing with respect to growth in the country as a whole, the various indexes indicate urban building booms of considerable proportions in this decade. Internal migrations were a major factor in urban growth. Census records on farm labour indicate that over-all employment of agricultural workers in central and eastern Canada was relatively stable from 1881 to 1931. This implies that after 1881 eastern farms were unable to absorb the natural increase in farm population. It is known that excess farm population will remain on the farms if there are no alternative opportunities, and that when cities experience deep depression as in the 1930's there may even be a reverse movement from cities to farms.[22] However, in the eighties alternatives were open on frontiers and in cities, chiefly in the United States. M. C. MacLean's analysis of net changes in population by counties provides a basis for appraising the scale and direction of the internal movements of population.[23]

There was an absolute decline of 2,916 people from 1881 to 1891 in 120 of the 154 counties in eastern Canada (Ontario, Quebec, and the Maritimes). These counties, which held 75 per cent of the total population in 1881, could not hold their native increase let alone absorb immigrant workers.[24] The remaining 34 counties made an absolute gain of 329,869 people. Most of this growth occurred in cities. Urban centres in the 34 counties gained 300,416, with over 200,000 of the gain concentrated in Montreal, Toronto, Hamilton, and Ottawa and their suburbs.[25] Western population, which had been 168,165 in 1881, more than doubled with an increment of 181,481. Some of this increase occurred in Winnipeg and other small incorporated centres but most of it represented growth in farm population.

If an average native increase of 14 per cent is assumed, it appears that about one half of the net movement away from declining agricultural counties in eastern Canada went to other parts of Canada, either to eastern cities or to the West; and the other half went to the United States, as did virtually all the immigrants who came into the country after 1881. The movement into eastern cities accounts for the building and real estate booms in Toronto, Montreal, and Hamilton during the decade. With alternatives in American cities (which experienced building booms in the same decade) and on the western frontier, the movement into the Canadian cities must have been a response to opportunities available there. The introduction in 1879 of a protective tariff designed to industrialize the country was a major factor creating urban opportunities in Canada during the eighties. The domestic market was not large, nor was it growing very rapidly; but the tariff established a portion of this market as an exclusive, profitable opportunity for domestic producers. Government railway policy also contributed to the boom. Construction of the c.p.r. induced a land boom in Winnipeg that rose to quite sepectacular heights only to collapse in 1882 after the railway reached the city. It has been said that the price per foot of business frontage on the main street at one point in this ill-founded, speculative boom exceeded the price of the best property in the city of Chicago. "The excitement (in Winnipeg) during the fall of 1881 amongst real estate owners was intense. Nothing to equal it had ever before occurred on Canadian or British soil. Thousands of dollars were made in a few minutes. Vast fortunes were secured in a day . . . Real estate agents became as numerous as the sands on the sea-shore . . . In the evening after the stores and other places of business are closed, the hotels and real-estate auction rooms are the centres around which the great mass of the people congregate. The excitement then is even more intense than during the day – and many of the largest transactions take place."[26]

Speculative building and real estate development were also greatly overdone in Montreal and Toronto at the peak of the tariff and railway boom. The subsequent reaction was severe. According to an editorial in the Toronto *Globe* of November 2, 1891, "The city . . . is reaping the results of seed sown in several years past. The speculation which caused an abnormal rise in values, which made real estate dealers wealthy by the score, which extended streets into the country and illuminated cow pastures with electric lights, was bound to bring reaction." And in the same paper for October 31, 1891: "There are certain facts in connection with real estate matters in this city with regard to which there is no difference of opinion. That there has been over-speculation can be easily ascertained by reference to the Court of Revision, and the related experience of too sanguine speculators." In a later editorial appears evidence not only of excessive subdividing and land speculation but of excessive building as well: "(The number) of unoccupied houses proves that the building trade has been overdone and that, in order to facilitate a too rapid increase in the value of their land, owners and speculators have been putting up houses on it to an extent which now threatens many people with disaster."

Montreal, directly linked with the West by rail, was the only eastern city to experience much growth in the nineties. "The six cities, Toronto, Hamilton, Quebec, London, Halifax, and Saint John gained only 46,181 or 11.5 per cent, that is, almost certainly did not hold all their native increase, while in 1881-91, the same cities gained 34.7 per cent."[27] For the first time the West gained more population (295,871) than the East (242,205). According to MacLean, the growth came largely after 1896. "The rate of increase of the population of Canada must have reached almost a vanishing point sometime between 1891 and 1896."[28]

The next urban building boom was much less a product of political action than the boom that collapsed at the end of the eighties; the more general and resilient urban developments from 1896 to 1912 were induced by the expansion of the wheat economy. However, government policies did play an important part in the creation of opportunities, since tariff and transport policies assured the integration of industrial plants and commercial and financial organizations in eastern Canada with the expanding export region in the West.

Population increased by 1,935,380 from 1901 to 1911, the largest decade increment in the history of the country. The expansion of the West during the decade was evident in the fact that 1,090,560 of the increase occurred in the western territories. More than half of this increase, about 579,000, came in western urban centres. In Manitoba and British Columbia the urban increase exceeded the rural increase, while in Saskatchewan and Alberta it was about half as great as the growth in rural population. In the rest of the country the net gain in population was entirely urban; a slight increase in the rural population of Quebec was more than offset by absolute declines in rural population in the other provinces. Thus the opening of the West was accompanied by a total gain of 1,256,645 in urban population and 574,578 in rural population. The ten largest cities alone, not including their suburbs, gained 650,000 from 1901 to 1911.[29] Population in sixty-six rural counties in eastern Canada declined absolutely and another fifty-five gained less than their expected native increase. Besides the growth of cities in the East, one other development worthy of remark was evident in this decade; new frontier settlements in the Canadian Shield accounted for eighty thousand of the growth outside the West. Thus migrations moved along three distinct channels: the basic movement into the western farm frontier; the larger, dependent movements into cities in both the West and the East; and the smaller movements into the forest and mining frontiers in the Canadian Shield and in British Columbia. The migrants were drawn chiefly from abroad and from the declining counties in eastern Canada.[30]

The increments in the population became successively smaller in the following three decades (see Table XVIII); but the trend to urban centres continued. Farm population in the West continued to grow; and, although less spectacularly, so did the forest and mining settlements. However, the bulk of the growth was concentrated in cities. Comment on the building expansion that accompanied this growth would carry us beyond the scope of this chapter. The rest of this section deals with the question of the timing of the population movements.

MacLean distinguishes three major trends in the internal movements of the population in his study of net changes in census and county regions over the period from 1850 to 1930. From the 1850's to 1881 there was a movement from well-settled (eastern urban) to settled (eastern rural) counties.[31] From 1881 to the 1920's there were two movements: first, a movement from the settled (eastern

rural) to the well-settled (eastern urban) counties; second, a movement from the settled to the unsettled or very thinly settled regions
(the frontiers). The former is the familiar rural-to-urban movement
accompanying the process of industrialization. Since the 1920's
there has been a fourth tendency: a movement from what had been
frontier regions to the well-settled. This movement reflects the end
of settlement of the agricultural frontier and the beginning of actual
displacement of farm population with technological improvements
in agriculture. This movement is another manifestation of the
rural-to-urban trend which had been more than offset previously by
the expansion of settlement on the frontier.

The first trend from well-settled counties would probably have
continued until the mid-nineties had political factors not inter-
vened. There was the slight check from 1867 to 1875 incidental to
commercial revival following Confederation and the Confederation
railway programme. A definite check came when the government
encouraged the process of industrialization through its tariff and
railway policies. Both contributed to the movement back to the
cities and the railway contributed to the movement to the frontier.

Railway construction and urban building in the eighties provided immigrants with temporary employment, but as construction
contracts ran out the recent arrivals were forced to move on to the
United States. Internal migrants would have an advantage in the
competition for more permanent employment in the few growing
cities, and at the same time they might be more reluctant to leave
the country. Immigrants were employed on a much larger scale in
the construction boom from 1896 to 1912. Alternative opportunities were also abundant on the frontier and in the cities. After the
war began, the carrying capacity essential for the permanent
absorption of immigrants was further increased. Had it not been for
the war, the depression which had barely started after 1913 would
probably have persisted. Many of the recent immigrants would
have moved on. As it was, the wartime boom provided employment
opportunities; expansion continued in the post-war period on the
basis of new staple exports, and, after a lag, renewed agricultural
prosperity. Net foreign migration which had been negative for the
forty years from 1860 to 1900 was positive from 1900 to 1930.

It is necessary to break down these broad trends in foreign and
domestic migrations to annual movements to establish that the fif-
teen- to twenty-year fluctuations reflected in the indexes of urban
building and real estate activity were products of the movements of
population. Residents of Canadian cities came both from within
and from without the country. There were probably many differences in the circumstances of migrants originating abroad and those

originating at home, but both must have been governed to some extent by the pull of employment opportunities. Census records show that most of the first migrants to western Canada were natives of North America. They were followed by British immigrants, who were followed in turn by continental Europeans. This is the sequence that one would expect, and it was probably the sequence of the response not only to the opportunities in the West, but to the tertiary and secondary opportunities that emerged in railway construction and in the cities and towns across the country as well. All types of migrants would communicate with friends, perhaps provide some financial aid, and, in any event, encourage others to follow so long as attractive employment was available. The process would be encouraged by the press and by government and private agencies. As a result each movement would be cumulative so long as good opportunities continued to prevail. At the start, natives would lead in the movement if only through better knowledge and geographical proximity. They would hardly lag behind the immigrants, particularly if they resided, as so many of them did, in the economically unattractive agricultural counties in eastern Canada. When both had started, the movements from abroad and from within the country would be roughly synchronized, keeping in step as the degree of attraction varied.

If this view of the nature of the movement of population is accurate, an index of gross immigration will provide an approximate index of the total movements of population toward economic opportunities in periods when immigration was a large part of the total. A comprehensive index, combining both the foreign and the domestic components of annual population movements in Canada, would probably lead the gross immigration index. Furthermore, with respect to the present use of this index, some of the immigrants went to farms and railways on the frontier as well as to the cities; and, although all those covered by the index expressly declared their intention to settle in Canada, many of them stayed only a short while. In view of the intimate relation between basic opportunities, tariff and railway policies, and the induced expansion of secondary and tertiary occupations in cities and towns, the intervals between the responses of immigrants to the emergence of the various types of new opportunities were probably short. In any event, the immigrants who went to farms and railways and those who went almost directly to the United States all passed through urban centres and contributed temporarily to the growing pressure of demand for living space in these centres.

Two indexes are shown together in Figure 6, the index of building activity in Canadian cities from 1870 to 1946, and an index of annual gross immigration to Canada over the same period.[32] There is a clear relation between the two curves.[33] The index of population movements follows a long fifteen- to twenty-year cycle rather like the index of building. At no time do the lower turning points in the urban building index precede the recoveries in the population index. There is nothing here to support the view that the urban building booms caused the initial rise in the immigration. In fact, gross immigration led urban building in every major up-turn except that of 1933 (by which time immigration was a minor part of the total movement of population). Immigration began to increase in 1876, four years before building. It rose from a second major trough in 1895, a year before building, and from a third in 1916, two years before building began to recover. The high peak of immigration in the early eighties probably reflects the land boom in the West and the availability of jobs in railway construction. However, the interest here is not to analyse immigration but merely to consider what support can be found for the view that general population movements followed long cycles similar to urban building cycles and probably initiated the building cycles, and that the population movements in turn were induced directly and indirectly by frontiers, by wars, and by government policies.

If the movement of population from one region to another generates a cycle of residential building, it follows that real estate booms in the two regions will not occur together. The region losing people should experience a slump while the region attracting people has a boom. Most of the immigration to Canada was from the United Kingdom. Large British migrations to the United States followed almost precisely the same time pattern as migrations to Canada. In Table XVII it was shown that the timing of the long urban building cycles in Canada was roughly the same as the timing of those in the United States. One would expect therefore that cycles in residential building in the United Kingdom could not follow the same pattern as cycles in United States and Canada during those years when international migrations were not restricted. And indeed the cycles in London house building were almost perfectly out of phase with urban building cycles in North-America over the fifty-odd years from 1871 to 1913. This is demonstrated in Figure 8 which shows the number of houses built annually in London from 1871 to 1913, and, as a convenient reference to the North American building cycles, the number of new buildings erected annually in Montreal, which conforms to the general pattern of Riggleman's index.[34] When the one index is rising, the other is falling; when the one is falling, the other is rising; troughs correspond with peaks, and peaks with troughs.[35]

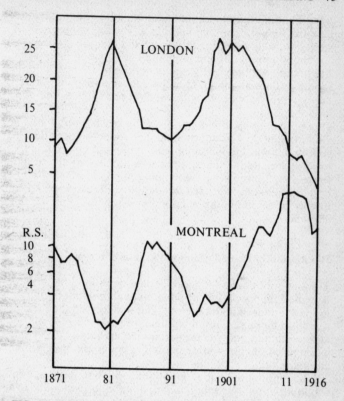

FIG. 8. Houses built annually in London, England, compared with permits for buildings in Montreal. (Source: Chapter XI and the Appendix for Montreal data. For London data see note 34.)

Over these years a large part of British foreign lending went to North America. It is not surprising that the volume of lending tended to move, in its longer cycle, in phase with emigrations overseas.[36] British emigrants began to respond to expanding opportunities in Canada earlier than British capital funds in both the major up-turns of the seventies and the nineties. With one exception, the major troughs in urban building coincided with deep depressions in Canada.[37] Major revivals, based on new opportunities which began immediately to attract migratory individuals, would have to continue for some time before levels of investment began to approach the limits of the capacity of the domestic economy to save; only when this stage was reached would the net inflow of overseas funds necessarily begin; and then only if the investment opportunities were sufficiently attractive to warrant the flow, or governments guaranteed investors against loss. Although slower to start, capital flows varied more sensitively over short periods and contributed to short-run fluctuations in domestic capital formation. Capital inflows apparently were not independent factors in the development.

One may conclude with confidence that building permit data in Canada, as in the United States, do show long cycles, and that the cycles were related to similar movements of population. The industrial and commercial building covered by permits may also be subject to long fluctuations, but one would expect the minor cycles to be much more clearly marked than in the residential permit series. Further refinement of the building data is required to answer this question.

IV. Relation of House Building to the Level of Income

The long urban building and real estate cycles in Canada reflect movements of population into urban centres in response to employment opportunities in those centres. One would expect these critical changes in the rate of growth of cities to coincide with some but not all lower turning points in the national income because the income would reflect the rise in urban purchasing power as employment in cities increased.

A change in the rate of growth of a city where employment opportunities were beginning to expand would not usually lead to a high rate of building activity unless vacancy rates were low. Vacancy rates would be fairly high in the typical case as a result of over-building in some previous period and because of the over-crowding of occupied dwellings characteristic of periods of depression. At the same time construction costs would be relatively low. As the vacancy rate fell rents would begin to rise in response to the changing circumstances. A rise in rents stimulates new construction in two ways. Since construction costs lag behind the rising rents, owner-occupation of a new house grows increasingly attractive. Net rents rise more rapidly than gross rents with the result that investment in rental projects grows more attractive.[38] The new construction activity adds to the employment opportunities open in the city. Meanwhile every aspect of the real estate market assumes new life and the speculative interest in land and building grows. Absorption of vacant building lots in and immediately adjacent to the city gives speculative value to more remote vacant land. The momentum of subdivision activity and speculative building accelerates. Rising land costs are added to rising building costs, but so long as the population pressure continues to inflate rents the level of activity climbs. As the peak is approached the inflation of land values and the high costs incidental to pressure on the limited physical capacity of the construction industry operate to restrict the current demands. However, owing to the ease of entry to the real estate market, a large speculative element provides momentum sufficient to carry the supply of lots and dwellings beyond effective physical needs. All the elements of cost that, with a tendency to lag, contributed to the upswing as gross rents rose, now continue to lag and accelerate the downswing as gross rents fall. Meanwhile, difficulties with mortgage loans secured on both new and old properties begin to increase. These difficulties have been inevitable in the past because the terms were usually too short and most of the loans were made on the basis of the inflated values of land and structures at or near the peak. The number of foreclosures would increase not only because the absolute volume of outstanding mortgage loans rises with the cycle, but also because recession in income is now accentuated by the decline in building activity itself.

This impressionistic sketch of an urban building cycle does not conflict with the annual data on volume of real estate mortgages, numbers of foreclosures, vacancy rates, rents, building costs, and so on, available for recent years. The data fit into the pattern of the cyclical movements of permits issued and deeds and mortgages registered since 1920. The role of income is not so clear. While it is true that, apart from periods of war, the major valleys of the building and real estate cycles have coincided with recessions and troughs in national income, recessions in national income have been more frequent than recessions in residential construction. Also the peaks in the building and real estate indexes have not always coincided with peaks in national income and expenditure. The relation between national income and housing construction appears at times to be unlike the relation between national income and other types of construction. The explanation may be found in the class structure of income. A very large proportion of the new dwellings built in the past decade have been bought or rented by middle and higher income groups, and more often bought than rented. The needs of other income groups are largely met by a process of "filtering down". Lower income groups, who comprise the bulk of the population, typically rent old dwelling units.

In a period of sharp income recession, like that which occurred in Canada from 1920 to 1922, the people losing their incomes are, for the most part, not the people who buy or rent new dwellings. For this reason, when the pressure for accommodation is high or rising, an income recession does not affect adversely all potential demanders of new housing. The recession may even strengthen the demand, because a slackening in other types of construction sensitive to national expenditure lowers the costs of construction and consequently raises the real command over new dwellings held by a large section of the principal buying group. In a period of recession, therefore, housing construction can continue to rise with a favourable effect on the course of the recession and depression of income itself. Something like this appears to have happened in eastern Canada and the United States after the first great war.

In Toronto, Montreal, and other eastern cities that grew rapidly during the war, many new residents in the higher income brackets and older residents who had reached these brackets during the prosperous war years were unable to build the dwellings they could afford because of wartime restrictions. Many of them built immediately after the war. The shrewder ones among them, and some of the investors in expensive apartment buildings, waited until costs of construction eased down from the inflated peak in 1920. These people could and did build in 1920, 1921, and 1922 despite the depression. The wartime growth of Toronto also increased the pressure on the margins of the better districts, lowering property values, and contributing to one of those periodic migrations of the "better families" characteristic of North American cities. Rapid growth has reduced the social status of successive districts in the typical city. Once the retreat from a district begins, the process cumulates. These class movements also appear to follow a long cycle. It is significant that the highest peak in the residential building cycle in Forest Hill Village, a suburban municipality of the Toronto region occupied by middle and upper income groups after the twenties, came in 1933 when national income and the city's income were at their lowest.

Thus while income is a factor in the demand for new housing, it is the income of the people who buy or rent new dwelling units, not the national income, that matters. For this reason cycles in residential construction did not follow the pattern of the shorter cycles in national income. Mass movements of people into the cities created the congestion and pressure underlying the real estate cycles. In addition to the residential building which supported income in certain periods of recession, the movements of population also contributed to municipal engineering and building construction: streets, sidewalks, sewerage, water works, schools, hospitals, and other essential complements to urban growth.[39] Commercial and industrial construction in urban centres was not unaffected by population growth. But housing was related to multitudes of people in a direct fundamental way. The decisions to invest in housing were distributed among many people and were dependent upon the incomes of certain classes and not the level of national expenditure. The demand for structures by mercantile, industrial, and financial establishments was more flexible, was easily increased or postponed, was concentrated among fewer people, and reflected profit expectations that were greatly influenced by current levels of national expenditure.

5.
Public Investment

I. Introductory

THE MAJOR ROLE of government in the field of investment has been developmental: opening up and encouraging the settlement of new regions, promoting the production of staples for export, providing the connecting facilities with world markets, and creating channels of interregional trade as staple export regions have provided potential domestic markets upon which secondary and tertiary production could grow. From 1867 to 1930 federal policies with respect to land, transportation, trade and tariffs, immigration, and agriculture were conceived and executed to establish a national economy. The design was essentially mercantilistic. Whereas the New England colonies had revolted against the restrictions of a mercantile empire, the Canadian colonies threatened to revolt when the restrictions were removed. Confederation in 1867 was part of the reaction to free trade. It reflected an evolution of political institutions within the British North American colonies as means to support economic development in the interests of commercial capitalism on the St. Lawrence.[1] The scale of government intervention necessary in this process of development provided powerful stimuli in the short run and contributed to the short-run cycles in economic activity in the Dominion. But the short-run effects were subordinate to the long-run benefits that were created by government investment policies. Federal government policies found their immediate motives in the interests of the dominant commercial, industrial, and financial groups, and their justification in the resources of the country and the capacity of these to support a growing population actively engaged in trade in international markets.

So thoroughly did the function of providing investment opportunities permeate federal and, although to a lesser extent, provincial policies, that a full examination of the role of governments in the field of investment would go far beyond the limits of this study. Land policy in the West and the enormous volume of aid extended to railways in cash and land subsidies and through guarantees of railway bonds are dealt with in other chapters.[2] The relation of agricultural and immigration policies to the provision of investment opportunities has received detailed analysis in another study.[3] The chief interest here is in the development and pattern of public investment from 1900 to 1930. A distinction is drawn between two forms of public investment: direct government outlays and outlays by publicly owned public utilities. The largest of the utilities, the Canadian National Railway system, has been dealt with. Other utilities are treated briefly in this chapter, but the major emphasis is upon direct government investment. The order of discussion is first, the growth of public investment and the changes in its pattern; second, provincial investment; and third, federal investment.

II. Growth and the Changing Pattern of Public Investment

Public investment was chiefly in the form of construction outlays.[4] The quinquennial outlays by each level of government and the relation of the totals to gross construction are shown in Table XIX. Government construction increased most rapidly from the first quinquennium to the second, when it rose from just under $100 million to $248 million. This gain of 164 per cent reflects the effect of earlier developments in the West upon government investment policy. It was followed by a further gain of 77 per cent in the third quinquennium, when government construction achieved its peak value relative to gross construction for the thirty-year period. Since these outlays occurred during the initial extensive phase of western farm expansion, public investment in the years before 1915 may be considered as a unit.

In the period of expansion from 1900 to 1915, the federal government accounted for approximately 60 per cent of public investment. The federal railway programme was the major item. Direct expenditures on railway construction, which had averaged about $3 million annually before the construction of the National Transcontinental, jumped to an average of $20 million a year for the ten years ending in 1915. The total outlay on railway construction equalled total municipal construction during the same period, and exceeded other federal and total provincial construction outlays which were $190 million and $102 million, respectively. Federal outlays on canals, harbour and river works, and on public buildings also contributed to the expansion. These outlays tripled and railway construction increased six fold from 1901-5 to 1911-15. The following expenditures were made:

Although the Dominion's activities dominated the pattern of public investment in this period, there was an equal relative expan-

TABLE XIX

Direct Investment by Governments, 1901-30(a)

	Federal	Provincial	Municipal	Total	Percentage of gross construction
			(millions of dollars)		
1901-5	57.5	4.5	32.0	94.0	13.8
1906-10	162.3	24.2	61.4	247.9	17.2
1911-15	224.6	78.1	137.0	439.7	21.9
1916-20	126.3	65.7	100.1	292.1	13.7
1921-25	130.3	148.7	159.8	438.8	19.3
1926-30	214.8	216.1	171.1	602.0	19.4

(a) *Source*: Chapter XI and the Appendix.

	Railways ($000,000)	Other transportation ($000,000)	Buildings ($000,000)
1901-5	15	32	10
1906-10	99	48	15
1911-15	98	94	33

sion in municipal outlays and a very much greater expansion in provincial construction, which rose from 5 per cent of direct public investment in 1901-5 to 18 per cent in 1911-15. There was a great diversity among the various provincial investment programmes, but two items accounted for most of the expansion. Provincial highway expenditures were growing. In the first five years after 1900, when the responsibility for roads still rested largely on local authorities, the provinces spent only $5 million on highways. In the five years from 1911 to 1915, they spent $38 million. The other important item of direct provincial investment in this period was building construction. Farm settlement and urban growth throughout the West created demands for a wide range of facilities within the sphere of provincial responsibility, including legislative and administrative buildings, universities, court houses and jails, hospitals and sanitaria. Manitoba's investment outlays from 1901 to 1905 were negligible. Over the following ten years, from 1906 to 1915, the three prairies governments invested $42 million. These expenditures accounted for 40 per cent of all provincial investment and more than half of all provincial outlays on new buildings.

Large provincial outlays were also made in the utility field during the decade from 1906 to 1915. An approximate estimate of the expenditures on provincially owned public utilities indicates a level at least 60 per cent as high as that for direct investment. Prairie telephones, the T.N.O., and Ontario Power developments cost $24, $20, and $6 million, respectively, to the end of 1913. Total provincial direct investment outlays were $75 million from 1900 to 1913.

The pattern of public investment changed considerably in the second half of the period from 1900 to 1930. During the war years the value of government construction fell while the value of total construction in current prices continued to rise. The relative position of government construction was consequently lower than at any other time from 1900 to 1930. It dropped from 21.9 per cent of total construction in 1911-15 to 13.7 per cent in 1916-20. There was a marked revival after the war. In the first five years after 1920, direct public investment approximated the pre-war level in absolute, current dollar terms. In the next five-year period it increased by more than a third to a new current dollar peak of $602 million. Accounting for about 19 per cent of gross construction in both quinquennia, it did not achieve its former relative importance.

The curtailment of the federal railway programme during the war years and the transfer of its lines to the Canadian National Railway system marked the end of the Dominion's dominance in the direct public investment field. While outlays declined at all levels of government in the period 1916-20, federal outlay was cut by 44 per cent as compared with 27 and 15 per cent for municipal and provincial outlays. The federal government was still the largest spender, but for the first time the combined provincial and municipal outlays exceeded the federal government's investment. In the post-war quinquennium, federal investment was lower than either provincial or municipal investment. Railways had cost $98 million from 1911 to 1915, $36 million from 1916 to 1920, and only $2 million from 1921 to 1925. Not until construction of the Hudson Bay Railway was resumed after 1925 did direct railway investment reach a significant level.

Municipal construction rose by 60 per cent in the first quinquennium of the twenties; provincial outlays more than doubled. The automobile and the new federal policy in the railway field radically altered the pattern of public investment. Not only were larger outlays required for highways and bridges, but an increasing share of the cost had to be borne by the provinces.[5] Highways had accounted for just under 50 per cent of total provincial investment from 1911 to 1915; they accounted for two-thirds after 1920. In absolute terms, provincial highway construction almost tripled, whereas outlays on new buildings declined slightly. This expansion of highway construction continued throughout the twenties while other types of provincial investment remained relatively constant. From 1926 to 1930 provincial investment surpassed municipal and was the largest component of public investment for the first time. Meanwhile federal investment recovered and was almost as large. The federal expansion in the late twenties reflected among other things two major projects: the Welland Ship Canal and the Hudson Bay Railway.

At the end of the period 1926-30 direct public investment in structures was approximately 20 per cent of gross construction. Federal and provincial outlays were about equal and both were slightly greater than municipal. Federal construction comprised a slightly smaller percentage of all new construction than it had at the beginning of the period (about 7 per cent, 1926-30; about 8 per cent, 1901-5). Municipal construction was slightly higher (rising from about 5 per cent to 6 per cent). Federal construction reached its relative peak in the pre-war period when it was 11.2 per cent of gross construction (1906-15). Municipal construction also achieved its relative peak before the war: 7 per cent from 1911 to 1915. Provincial construction expanded from 1 per cent of gross construction in 1901-5 to 7 per cent in 1926-30. It reached its relative peak in this last quinquennium.

Provincial investment is the sum of the outlays made by nine different governments, and there were marked differences in the policies pursued. The magnitude of provincial investment outlays was not determined by the size and wealth of the various provinces. Quebec, for example, was the second largest in population and revenues, but it made relatively minor contributions to the total of provincial investment. Quebec was the only province to adopt a strict laissez-faire position. Other provinces, notably Nova Scotia and New Brunswick, undertook large-scale public works and their share in the total is consequently greater than their populations would lead one to expect. Maritime policies reflected the economic depression which became general in that region after 1920. The share of the wealthiest and largest province, Ontario, was very high, particularly in the twenties. Its wealth and active developmental programmes were responsible for high levels of expenditure; but in the pre-war decade, Ontario, with a population double that of the prairies, spent less than the three prairie governments. Owing to the state of their economic development, the four western provinces spent more, both in absolute and in relative terms, in the immediate pre-war years than in the twenties.

There were also important differences in the types of projects undertaken in the various provinces. Before the war Ontario's direct investments were about evenly divided between highways and buildings. British Columbia and the Maritimes spent more on highways whereas the prairie provinces spent twice as much on buildings as on roads. Prairie governments had to acquire public structures already in existence elsewhere. They left a larger share of the responsibility for road construction with municipalities. Municipal organizations were less highly developed in British Columbia and in the Maritimes, and as a result the burden of providing roads rested more heavily on the provincial governments. In the post-war years, very nearly 70 per cent of all provincial investment was on highways, but the proportion ranged from about 90 per cent of the provincial totals for Ontario and the Maritimes to less than 50 per cent for the prairie provinces.

The relative importance of publicly owned public utility investment at the end of the period may be judged from Table XX, which shows total direct government investment and government-owned utility investment in selected years from 1926 to 1930. Railways were by far the most important of the government utility fields; their development was examined in Chapter III. Other major utility developments are noted in the following section on provincial investment.

TABLE XX

Gross Investment in Durable Physical Assets by All Public Authorities, Selected Years, 1926-30[a]

(millions of dollars)

	1926	1929	1930
Direct gross investment by all governments	97	168	208
Gross investment by government utilities			
Railways	42	106	88
Electric power	11	33	35
Telephones	3	5	4
Other	4	8	8
Total: All public authorities	157	320	343

(a) *Source:* P.I.C.F., 54.

III. Investment by the Provinces

1. Ontario

Throughout the period under review the government of Ontario assumed an active role in the development of the province. In the early years of the century the desire to open up the northern portions of the province and to connect Toronto with both this northern area and the prairie hinterland induced the provincial government to undertake the construction of the Temiskaming and Northern Ontario Railroad. A second major developmental programme was also initiated in this decade with the establishment of the Ontario Hydro-Electric Power Commission.[6] The Commission did not at first generate power, but during the pre-war period it built up a comprehensive system for the distribution of power.

Ontario accounted for approximately 30 per cent of the small total of direct investment by the provinces from 1901 to 1905. The proportion declined to 14 per cent in the next two quinquennia as a result of the expansion of prairie governments, but Ontario's investment increased from $1.4 million in 1901-5 to $11.1 million in 1911-15. The major utility ventures absorbed greater sums than direct investments: while direct investment outlays totalled $16 million from 1900 to 1915, the construction of the T.N.O. alone absorbed some $19 million, and $12 million was advanced to the Hydro-Electric Commission in the same period.

Highway construction in Ontario accounted for slightly smaller outlays than building construction before 1915. Investment in neither was very large. Annual gross investment on the provincial highways did not reach $.5 million until after 1910. Municipal investment expenditures on rural roads were more than ten times as large as those for provincial road construction in 1900, and were still four times as large in 1910. Most of the provincial projects in this period were colonization roads in northern Ontario. A department of Highways was organized in 1903, but it did little beyond supervise provincial assistance to the municipalities.[7] When the provincial highway system was introduced in 1917, the province carried out the construction work, met 70 per cent of the costs, and charged the balance to the municipalities. Under this system, provincial highway construction expenditures exceeded municipal by 1920 and, with the extension of the provincial system in the twenties, were approximately double municipal by the end of the period.

The economic development of the province continued to be an important aspect of provincial policy after the war. During the twenties the T.N.O. was extended to James Bay and short branches were built into mining areas at a cost of some $10 million. In the pre-war period the T.N.O. was the most costly venture; in the twenties highways and power were the principal commitments. The Hydro-Electric Power Commission, which entered the field of power generation at the end of the war, maintained a large construction programme throughout the twenties. Provincial advances to the Commission totalled $80 million from 1921 to 1925 and $41 million from 1926 to 1930. The cost of highways, at $55 million from 1921 to 1925, was ten times the level of the five years ending in 1915. The level of building construction, at $6 million, was unchanged. Owing chiefly to the scale of its highway programme, the province of Ontario contributed 40 per cent of the total direct investment by provinces from 1921 to 1925. The percentage declined to 30 per cent in 1929 with the expansion of public works in other provinces after 1925.

2. Quebec

Quebec occupied a unique position. In comparison with every other provincial government, the government of Quebec was relatively inactive in the investment field over the whole period under review. Developmental policies had little place in the provincial budget. The public works undertaken were for the most part those that could not be avoided. At the time when the Dominion was engaged in the construction of the National Transcontinental, and the other provinces were rapidly expanding their public works programmes and supporting developments in the railway and other utility fields, Quebec was expanding its public works programme slowly and leaving utilities to others. Quebec had been active in the railway field during the seventies and eighties. The modest growth in debt resulting from railway subsidies and the construction of the Quebec, Montreal and Ottawa (later sold) was followed by reaction. Despite buoyant revenues after 1900 a conservative policy prevailed and budget surpluses were applied to the cost of necessary capital works. The provincial debt was small relative to the debts of the other provinces.

Quebec contributed less than 10 per cent of total provincial investment during the first decade covered by the estimates. If utilities were included in the total, the percentage would be considerably reduced. Highway policy was virtually confined to grants to municipalities. Construction outlays increased after the passing of the Good Roads Act in 1912 which authorized provincial road construction for the first time. By 1915 the province incorporated

1,600 miles of road into a provincial highway system and spent $7 million (excluding grants). The highway system was gradually extended in the twenties, the province taking over more of the responsibility from the municipalities. There were 7,500 miles of provincial highways by 1926. Highway construction for the five years ending in 1925 cost $8.5 million. The addition of highway grants would raise the amount to approximately $20 million, which is much less than the $55 million, exclusive of grants, spent by Ontario in this period. Total investment in Quebec was 11 per cent of the total for all provinces in these five years and was only slightly higher at the end of the period (13 per cent in 1930).

3. The Maritimes

Nova Scotia and New Brunswick were particularly active in the investment field during the period from 1900 to 1930. Public works beyond the provision of essential community facilities were undertaken as part of a conscious policy aimed at stimulating economic development of the region. Investment policy in some other provinces, notably Ontario and British Columbia, was also developmental, but circumstances giving rise to the policy differed. In Ontario, for example, large investment outlays were made under prosperous economic conditions to hasten northern development which, left to private enterprise, might have lagged. But the problem in the Maritimes was that of economic stagnation. Even in the pre-war period the Maritimes shared in the national boom to a lesser extent than other regions, and Maritime agriculture and forest industries felt acutely the competition of the West. Governments in both New Brunswick and Nova Scotia undertook substantial investments in transport facilities to stimulate depressed areas in their respective economies.

In the five years from 1901 to 1905, the Maritimes accounted for 20 per cent of all provincial direct investment. Approximately $6.5 million was spent on highways from 1901 to 1915 as compared with $7.6 million in Ontario which had almost three times the population. Both New Brunswick and Nova Scotia were also active in the railway field, giving aid in the form of subsidies and guarantees of bonds. Large increases in debts were incurred as a result of these developmental activities.

The stagnation which had affected only certain industries in the pre-war period spread over the whole Maritime economy in the twenties. Temporary wartime demands had disrupted much of the limited integration achieved with central Canada before the war. The provincial governments intensified their efforts after the war.

Both New Brunswick and Nova Scotia entered the hydro-electric power field and greatly expanded their highway programmes. Highway construction expenditures increased from $3.9 million in 1911-15 to $8.5 million in 1916-20 and $15.7 million in 1921-25. In the last two periods the outlays exceeded those in all other provinces except Ontario. The Maritimes contributed about 13 per cent of all provincial investment from 1921 to 1925 and approximately 15 per cent of the total in 1930. The levels of expenditure were slightly higher than in Quebec, with a greater emphasis on highways than on buildings. New Brunswick also expanded in the railway field, taking over the Saint John-Quebec Railway in 1917.

The scale of public investment in the Maritimes improved the depressed situation but fell far short of solving the problem of economic stagnation.

4. The Prairie Provinces.

Like Ontario and the Maritimes, the three prairie provinces – Manitoba, Saskatchewan, and Alberta – were very active in the investment field in the pre-war period. Expenditures were maintained at a high level until 1920 and then were very sharply curtailed during the agricultural depression of the early twenties. Even during the prosperous period of rapid extension of the prairie frontier the revenues of prairie governments were more restricted and inflexible than those of other provinces, because the Dominion had retained control of the public domain. In Saskatchewan, for example, 70 per cent of provincial revenue in 1908 came from Dominion subsidy and grants; the proportion was 35 per cent in 1913. While expenditure requirements increased rapidly, the subsidy increased gradually. The public investment programmes consequently led to very large increases in provincial debts. The large-scale movement of people into regions not previously settled gave rise to a host of demands for facilities that had to be met by either the provincial or the local government. The provinces of Alberta and Saskatchewan were established in 1905, and while the new provinces acquired some of the equipment of government from the retiring federal administration, they had to make large outlays to provide for most of the ordinary provincial functions. In addition, there was great pressure upon all three governments to enter new fields.

The most insistent demands were for improved means of communications. With population spread thinly over wide areas, the private telephone companies were unable, or unwilling, to satisfy these demands. The three provincial governments assumed this responsibility at an early date. They also extended substantial aid to railway companies, and Alberta undertook some direct construction in this field. At a later date Manitoba entered the hydro-electric power field.

Most of the developmental programmes were completed by 1920, and the prairie governments, confronted with the post-war depression that persisted in the West until 1925, turned to policies of economy with respect to both current and capital expenditures. Public works programmes expanded again after the depression.

The prairies accounted for 40 per cent of all provincial investment in the 10 years ending in 1915.[8] The construction of new buildings comprised an unusually high proportion of their total investment outlays – about one-half in 1906-10 and two-thirds in 1911-15. Prairie expenditures of $27.5 million on buildings in this ten-year period made up slightly more than half of all provincial building construction. Highways were relatively less important, absorbing approximately $15 million in this period. Grants to municipalities on highway account were small and the provincial governments left the greater part of the burden with the municipalities. Later the provinces were compelled to assume much more of the burden, but highway expenditures did not dominate the investment programme as they did in other provinces. Nevertheless the highway expenditures were large relative to the size and financial resources of the prairie provinces.

Capital expenditures on the telephone systems reach $24 million by 1913. This investment doubled in the following eight years: $20 million in Alberta, $17 million in Manitoba, and $11 million in Saskatchewan by 1921. Capital advances of $10 million to railways were made by Alberta prior to 1921. The other provinces limited their railway policy to the guarantee of bonds. Together the three government guaranteed $100 million of railway bonds in the period ending in 1920.

Provincial outlays were curtailed somewhat during the war, but unlike the governments of the eastern provinces, the prairie governments greatly reduced their outlays after a brief upsurge at the end of the war. In the five years from 1921 to 1925, direct construction outlays in Ontario were five times higher than the level reached in 1911-15, in the Maritimes they were four times higher, and in Quebec 50 per cent higher; but the prairie governments spent less than they did in the earlier period. Road construction increased slightly, from $10.5 million to $11.6 million, while outlays on building construction fell from $21 million to $13.7 million. Whereas the prairies spent 40 per cent of the provincial total from 1911 to 1915, they spent less than 20 per cent from 1921 to 1925. The proportion increased with the revival of public works in the later twenties, reaching 29 per cent by 1930.

5. British Columbia

The pattern of provincial investment in British Columbia was like that in the other western provinces, with comparatively high outlays before the war followed by a decline to below the pre-war level in the early twenties. As a result, the four western provinces dominated provincial public investment from 1906 to 1915, contributing 68 per cent of the provincial total. British Columbia outlays were disproportionately high from 1900 to 1915. Part of the explanation for the high level of investment was the rapid growth of population. The geography of the province and the relative weakness of municipal organization were important contributing factors. Settlement was either scattered thinly over the province, with small communities isolated by the mountainous terrain, or concentrated in the few large urban centres. The heavy costs of providing schools, hospitals, buildings, and other facilities in the unorganized territories, as well as the maintenance of communications between settled regions, fell to the provincial government. A special factor contributing to the high level of investment was a tremendous increase after 1900 in provincial revenues from public domain, that is, from timber and mining royalties and land sales. So large were the increases in revenue during the boom that, although public works were financed largely on current account, the province had a budget surplus in every year from 1905 to 1912. Optimism engendered by this budget experience contributed to the adoption of an ambitious railway policy to open up the hinterland.

When the construction boom ended in 1912-13, provincial revenues fell drastically – by 50 per cent between 1912 to 1915 – but expenditures on public works continued at approximately the same level until the war. Public debt began to rise rapidly. During the war the works programme was curtailed but this curtailment was more than offset by railway commitments. The Pacific Great Eastern was taken over from its private promoters in 1917. Other large-scale public works were not undertaken until the end of the twenties.

Direct public investment in British Columbia increased from just under $2 million in 1901-5 to over $20 million in 1911-15. Highway construction, accounting for approximately 60 per cent of provincial investment in the ten years ending in 1915, was much more important than on the prairies. It involved outlays equal to those of the three prairie governments combined. Expenditures on new buildings in this period were comparable to amounts spent by the prairie provinces individually, and exceeded building outlays in the other provinces. In the pre-war period British Columbia made larger direct investment outlays than any other province.[9]

The increase in provincial investment in the eastern provinces in the post-war period has been contrasted with the decline on the prairies. British Columbia investment declined from $21 million in 1911-15 to $15 million in 1921-25. Thus, in both absolute and relative terms, direct investment outlays of the four western governments declined in importance. British Columbia's outlays tripled from 1926 to 1929, with a further increase in 1930.

When the province took over the P.G.E. in 1917 only a small part of this remarkable railway had been constructed. The province assumed responsibility for $20 million of guaranteed bonds that were in default, and continued the construction work until 1921 by which time $23 million had been advanced. A provincial audit in 1926 placed the governments's investment in the road at $51 million. The capital liability at the end of the twenties was $60 million.

IV. The Federal Government

Annual increases in investment outlay after 1900 marked the beginning of a very extensive developmental programme. Federal revenue – roughly two-thirds of which came from customs duties in the pre-war era – was a factor of some importance in the formation of investment policy at the beginning of the expansion. The improvement in revenues after 1896 was accompanied by a gradual expansion in outlays. In 1900 the federal programme cost $7.5 million. By 1906 it had nearly doubled ($14 million). A large part of this increase in investment expenditures was financed on current account. There was a much greater resort to borrowing when the major railway construction programme got under way.

Expenditure increased by $20 million in 1907 and was maintained at this higher level until the war. The National Transcontinental was the chief project. A further expansion at the end of the pre-war boom – to a total of $50 million in both 1913 and 1914 – was associated with harbour and river work and building construction, but railways remained the major item. In the ten years ending with 1915, transportation projects accounted for 87.6 per cent of direct federal investment. In addition to the aid given to private railroads, the Dominion spent almost $200 million on its own railways and approximately $150 million on canals and other water transport facilities from 1906 to 1915.

In the period 1901-5, 57 per cent of federal investment was financed by borrowing (the balance by current revenues); in the next quinquennium the proportion was 77 per cent and in the five years ending with 1915 it was 72 per cent. Gross debt of the Dominion increased by $350 million from 1900 to 1915 – the direct cost of the transport programme from 1905 to 1915.

Federal policy entered a new phase with the completion of the railway construction programme. From the peak level of $54 million in 1914, investment outlays declined to $21 million by 1918, and remained at this lower level through the early twenties. During this period expenditure on canals and harbour and river work was greatly expanded but not enough to offset the virtual cessation of direct railway investment and the low level of building construction. There was a revival in federal investment in the late twenties, although it was not until 1930 that the 1913 and 1914 levels were surpassed. This revival was associated with two large projects, the Welland Ship Canal and the Hudson Bay Railway; but the increased outlays on other forms of transportation and on buildings were also notable. Federal investment increased from $29 million in 1926 to $46 million in 1929, and to $63 million in 1930.

When investment outlays are compared with levels of revenue and the change in the federal debt, the shift in federal investment policy in the post-war decade appears even more marked. Revenue sources were more diversified and budgets larger after the war than before. The pre-war peak of $436 million in fiscal 1921 was surpassed in fiscal 1929 with total revenues of $460 million. Gross debt was reduced from a peak of $3 billion in 1920 to $2.5 billion in 1930. Although the gross federal debt in 1930 was five times as large as the debt of 1914, public works were no longer a contributing factor.

6.
Savings and Capital Flows

I. Domestic and Foreign Savings in the Supply of Investment Funds

CAPITAL FORMATION implies saving: some part of current income must be withheld from consumption expenditure if economic resources are to be available to produce investment goods. Within a closed economy – and ignoring the effects of the fiscal programme of governments – investment outlays of privately and publicly owned enterprises are financed by the savings of business units and households. The annual flow of investment is precisely matched by the flow of savings. This equality is slightly complicated by international economic relations and government budgets. Domestic investment can exceed domestic savings to the extent that foreign capital funds are drawn upon; or domestic savings may exceed domestic investment, with the surplus savings flowing abroad to finance capital acquisitions in other countries; but total investment – as opposed to domestic investment – is equal to domestic savings in either case. The other complication arises because the direct investment expenditures of federal, provincial, and municipal governments may be financed, wholly or in part, from current revenues, and the net proceeds of their borrowings from domestic and foreign capital markets may be used for purposes other than investment. In general, governments absorb a part of the national income to finance their expenditures on goods and services. When this net transfer from the community to governments – which roughly speaking, equals taxes of all kinds less transfer payments and subsidies – is less than government expenditures on goods and services, the governments borrow from private savings to the extent of the excess expenditure or deficit. Thus, while investment by business enterprises provides offsets to the savings of the community and, if they occur, to capital imports, it is the deficits of governments that provide comparable offsets. When the revenues of governments exceed their expenditures, the surplus is available to supplement the savings of the community in the finance of investment. Accordingly, domestic savings can be measured by

TABLE XXI
Gross Savings Offsets in Canada, 1901-30

	1 Gross private domestic investment	2 Government deficits	3 Capital inflows	4 Gross private domestic savings $(1 + 2 - 3)$	5 Gross savings as percentages of G.N.P.
	(millions of dollars)				
1901-5	1,189	40	301	928	16.4
1906-10	2,039	255	784	1,510	17.8
1911-15	2,839	770	1,515	2,094	17.2
1916-20	3,741	2,195	262	5,674	27.1
1921-25	3,202	525	-72	3,799	16.8
1926-30	5,229	400	563	5,066	17.2

deducting direct government investment from total investment and adding back the deficit, or subtracting the surplus, of government. The foregoing applies when investment and saving are taken in either the gross or the net sense, because the shift from a gross to a net basis involves the deduction of an estimate of replacement investment from gross investment which is offset by the portion of gross savings required to finance the replacements and which must be deducted from gross savings to obtain net savings.

High rates of private capital formation and recurring government deficits exceeded the savings of the Canadian community in most of the years from 1900 to 1930, and the domestic supply of capital funds was augmented by British and foreign funds.[1] The importance of these funds relative to domestic savings is apparent in Table XXI. Private gross domestic investment is shown in column 1; government deficits in column 2. Taken together, these are offset by capital inflows, shown in column 3, and private gross domestic savings, shown in column 4. Private gross domestic savings (hereafter, gross savings) are obtained by deducting column 3 from the sum of columns 1 and 2. The table also indicates the relation of domestic gross savings to gross national income in this period.

There is apparent in the table – ignoring, for the time being, the inflated years from 1916 to 1920 – a remarkably stable relationship between gross savings and gross national product.[2] If one could assume no change in the disposition to save over the period, the estimates would appear to be mutually corroborative, since, on that assumption, the minor changes in the proportion of the national product saved may be plausibly explained in terms of known variations in the level of domestic income. In the quinquennium 1926 to 1930 an average of 17.2 per cent of G.N.P. was saved. Since the G.N.P. for these years is the official estimate, this average provides a reliable basis for comparison. With the exception of 1930, a depression year, these were prosperous years. Assuming no change in the disposition to save, one would expect to find the average running at about the same level in the period 1901-10, as it appears to have done. There were minor recessions in 1901 and 1904 not quite as severe as the recession of 1907-8. The first major break in the pre-war expansion came after the peak of 1912-13. The recessive tendency continued into 1915. The post-war depression would account for lower relative gross savings in 1921-25. Although the period of severe unemployment during 1921-22 was brief, it is perhaps surprising to find the rate of gross savings so high. However, the worst of the depressions from 1900 to 1930 was mild compared with that experienced after 1930.

The whole period from 1900 to 1930 was characterized by a general prosperity and expansion without parallel in the country's development. However, while the levels of capital formation from 1900 to 1930 imply that investment outlets were sufficiently-abundant to absorb high average levels of domestic savings, there was a considerable decline in the availability of investment outlets for imported capital after 1912-13. Capital imports were more than half as large (57.4 per cent) as domestic savings from 1901-1915 and less than one-tenth (9.7 per cent) from 1921 to 1930. This change came not gradually but abruptly, and was attributable largely to the close of the extensive phase of the frontier development described in Chapter II. It should be added that the scale of capital import before 1915 was not altogether justified by opportunities associated with the frontier. Much of the capital would not have come without government guarantees. Favourable expectations induced by the frontier were unduly strengthened by government actions. The full impact of error was fortuitously avoided as a result of the war.

The figures on capital imports and gross domestic savings given in Table XXI greatly understate the magnitude of the change in circumstances after 1911-15, because the capital imports were offset by net additions to productive capacity (or public debt) while gross savings were offset by net additions and replacements. The ratio of estimated depreciation and similar business costs to gross national product in the current national accounts for Canada runs slightly higher than 10 per cent even in years of high average employment and income like the late twenties.[3] Dr. Kuznets' estimates of average replacements bear a very stable relationship to his overlapping decade estimates of gross national product for the United States, running fairly consistently between 10 and 11 per cent over the fifty years from 1889 to 1939. One may therefore take 10 per cent of the average gross national product of Canada in each quinquennium from 1900 to 1930 as a reasonable approximation of average replacements. Despite the crudity of this estimate it will improve the illustration of the relative importance of external funds in the growth of Canada's real capital.

Results of making an allowance for replacement investment are shown in Table XXII. Column 1 is net private domestic capital formation broken down into investment in structures and machinery and equipment, and investment in inventories. The inventory component is shown separately because, as will be seen later, it was largely financed by domestic savings. Column 2 shows government deficits. Column 3 is capital imports and column 4 net private domestic savings. The sum of columns 1 and 2 is the total capital formation financed by capital imports and net domestic savings and

TABLE XXII

Rough Estimates of Net Private Investment and Net Savings, 1901-30

(millions of dollars)

	1		2	3	4	5	6
	Net private domestic investment ~~Structures Inventories and equipment~~	*STRUCTURES INVENTORIES + EQUIPMENT*	Government deficits	Capital inflows	Net private domestic savings	Capital inflows as percentages of G.N.P.	Net savings as percentages of G.N.P.
1901-5	402	222	40	301	363	5.3	6.4
1906-10	929	262	255	784	662	9.2	7.8
1911-15	1,261	360	770	1,515	876	12.4	7.2
1916-20	1,060	589	2,195	262	3,582	1.3	17.1
1921-25	784	159	525	-72	1,540	-0.3	6.8
1926-30	1,728	625	400	563	2,190	2.0	7.6

is, of course, equal to the sum of columns 3 and 4. In the last two columns the percentage relationships of capital imports and net savings to the gross national product are shown.

The unusually high rate of savings from 1916 to 1920 requires comment. The net addition to durable physicl assets was lower during this period than from 1911 to 1915 even when the values are expressed in current dollars. In view of the inflation accompanying the war the drop in volume must have been considerable. (Average construction costs were over 50 per cent greater from 1916 to 1920 than from 1911 to 1915.) Additions to farm and business inventories at 2.8 per cent of G.N.P. do not appear unreasonable considering the great expansion of manufacturing and agricultural output during this period. Thus the proportion of the national product saved and channelled into private capital information was only slightly lower than in other prosperous periods. Superimposed on this level of savings was an additional 10 per cent induced by deficit spending and absorbed by the federal government to finance the deficits incurred as a result of the war. The federal government, without access to foreign capital markets and unwilling to alter radically the prevailing system of taxation, relied upon domestic bond sales on an unprecedented scale to war-enriched corporations and individuals. The primitive methods of financing the war greatly distorted the distribution of money income. Deutsch has estimated that 75 per cent of all war-bond subscriptions were from large corporations and wealthy people who reaped the profits of inflation.[4] The process of wartime finance added to the breadth and liquidity of the domestic bond market and indeed may be said to have created this market. In five years, federal fiscal policy placed in the hands of domestic bond holders assets which matched in volume the sum of British investments in Canada from 1900 to 1914. Gross savings amounting to 26 per cent of G.N.P. were achieved during the war of 1939-45. In view of the contrast in the methods of war finance, it is not surprising that a higher rate prevailed in the earlier period.

The marked decline in the relative and absolute importance of capital imports is evident in Table XXII. Capital imports were $0.3 billion in 1901-5, equivalent to 5.3 per cent of G.N.P. At $0.8 and $1.5 billion in the following two quinquennia, they were much greater relative to G.N.P. than were net domestic savings. The small inflow during the years 1916-20 was replaced by a small outflow in 1921-25. Capital imports rose again to a significant level in absolute terms from 1926 to 1930, but they were equivalent to only 2.0 per cent of G.N.P. Net savings in this period were 7.6 per cent of G.N.P. In fact, apart from 1916-20, net savings were not far from 7 per cent of G.N.P. over the thirty-year period.

The pattern displayed in Table XXII tends to confirm the view, stated earlier, that the level of capital imports from 1900 to 1915 was probably excessive. Comparison of capital inflows with the net additions to structures and machinery and equipment indicates that, until after 1915, external claims to Canadian assets were growing at a rate which was hardly warranted by the rate of expansion of the nation's physical plant and equipment. An examination of Canada's international indebtedness requires other data to supplement those shown in Table XXII.

It would appear from Table XXII that Canada's international indebtedness grew very rapidly from 1900 to 1915, much less rapidly from 1916 to 1930. Total net capital imports were $2,600 million from 1900 to 1915 and only $753 million from 1916 to 1930. But meanwhile, according to the various estimates of Viner and Knox and the Dominion Bureau of Statistics, the value of net external liabilities increased by approximately $2,500 million in both the earlier and the later period. Gross liabilities were $1,200 million in 1900, $3,840 million in 1914, and $6,171 million at the end of 1930. Gross assets abroad at the same dates were $100, $237, and $1,443 million. There was a large reinvestment of earnings of non-resident capital in the later period which would not show in capital imports, but some part of the discrepancy noted above may be explained by errors in the 1914 estimates.[5] Net interest and dividend payments abroad relative to gross national product reached a peak for the six quinquennia in 1910-15; the successive quinquennial percentages were 3.27, 3.85, 5.38, 4.04, 4.45, and 4.19.

The year 1915 also marks the close of the period of major reliance upon the United Kingdom as a source of external capital and the beginning of the period during which American capital predominated. According to Viner's estimates, approximately $1,050 million of the $1,200 million of claims outstanding in 1900 were held in Great Britain, chiefly in government and railway securities. Most of the small balance was held in the United States. By 1914 British claims had increased to $2,780 million and United States claims to $880 million. The first section of Table XXIII shows the distribution of capital imports from 1900 to 1914 by country of origin and by field of investment.[6] The second section of the table shows the value of British and foreign capital in Canada at December 31, 1930.[7]

The major changes in the pattern of Canada's international indebtedness from 1900 to 1930 may be outlined with the aid of Table XXIII. Imports of capital from Great Britain of $1,750 million from 1900 to 1914 raised the outstanding debt to Great Britain

TABLE XXIII

A. Distribution of Total Flow of Capital to Canada, 1900-14
(millions of dollars)

	All countries	Great Britain	United States	Other countries
Dominion and provincial governments	179	175	4	—
Municipal governments	260	200	60	—
Railroads	767	670	50	47
Industrial	630	420	180	30
Land and timber	305	80	145	80
Mining	125	65	60	-
Insurance	82	32	50	-
Other	198	111	81	6
Totals	2,546	1,753	630	163

B. External Investments in Canada at December 31, 1930
(millions of dollars)

	All countries	Great Britain	United States	Other countries
Dominion	682	235	441	7
Provincial	592	69	517	6
Municipal	432	182	247	2
Railways	2,244	1,352	833	60
Other utilities	634	100	522	12
Manufacturing	1,573	275	1,286	12
Mining and smelting	334	74	255	5
Merchandising	203	62	137	4
Financial	543	243	251	49
Other	377	176	170	31
Totals	7,614	2,766	4,660	188

to approximately $2,800 million. This was apparently the all-time peak. The value of British investments in Canada declined to $2,636 in 1926 and, after an increase in the late twenties, stood at $2,766 in 1930. Before 1900 virtually the whole British investment had been in government and railway securities and mortgage debentures. Government and railway securities continued to occupy an important position after 1900. Governments and railways accounted for $1,045 million of the total of capital imports from 1900 to 1914, but industrial investment also became prominent, accounting for $420 million of the imports in this period. There was no marked change in the distribution of British claims among the various fields in the period from 1915 to 1930. Of the total of $2,766 million outstanding in 1930, $1,938 million were in government and railway securities. Investment in manufacturing had become slightly less important, and insurance investments slightly more. British investments in Canada had been, and remained over the whole period from 1900 to 1930, typically portfolio investments, with a greater part in bonds than in equities.

The change after 1914 was not a simple shift from London to New York as it is sometimes regarded. American capital of a different character from British had already assumed prominence before 1914 in the form of direct investments in Canadian branches and subsidiaries of American firms, chiefly in manufacturing, mining, and the forest industries. Management accompanied the capital, and ownership and control remained in the United States. Various political, sociological, economic, and geographic factors underlying this extension of American industry into Canada have been treated in other studies.[8] This development accounted for well over half of the $880 million of American investment up to 1914.[9] By 1930 the value of this direct investment had grown to $2,000 million.[10] This growth, which to a large extent was financed by reinvestment of earnings, was independent of the shift from London to New York. After 1914 the value of the portfolio investments held in the United States grew very rapidly as a result of the shift. By 1930 they exceeded the value of the direct investments. Government securities held by American institutional and individual investors in 1930 were about equal to United States investments in Canadian manufacturing. Holdings of utilities were of approximately the same size and very nearly as large as the total British investment in Canadian public utilities, although not so highly concentrated in railways. These changes are apparent in Table XXIII.

As a result of the direct movement of American enterprise into Canada and its subsequent growth with the expansion of the economy, American interests owned and controlled approximately 40 per cent of all capital invested in Canadian manufacturing, mining, and smelting at the end of the period covered by the present study. The percentage was well above this average in non-ferrous metals, chemicals, automobiles, rubber goods, electrical appliances, and refining of oil. It was 50 per cent in the important staple export industry, pulp and paper.[11]

Utilities and governments were the major fields for all non-resident portfolio investors. British and American claims at the end of the twenties represented at least 45 per cent of all capital claims against Canadian utilities. External ownership of railway capital alone approached 60 per cent. The large external holdings of government securities were a smaller percentage of the total outstanding as a result of the enormous domestic sales of federal bonds during the war period and greater reliance upon the domestic market thereafter.

On the basis of this brief survey of the pattern of external investments it is possible to indicate the more important outlets which remained for private domestic (net) savings. In view of the weakness of the domestic capital market, in which large gaps were long to remain, one might safely guess that a very large share of the domestic net savings was channelled directly into investment without benefit of market intermediaries. Many members of the labour force were small-scale capitalists operating unincorporated business enterprises. Small private entrepreneurs were typical in agriculture, the largest industry, in other primary industries, such as fishing and trapping, in construction, and in retail and wholesale trade. In all of these industries, direct reinvestment of earnings in plant, equipment, and inventories would be the common policy. Even in manufacturing there were many small private units in 1900, and many of the large firms which were incorporated during the period grew out of family concerns that expanded with the wheat boom. Reinvestment of earnings financed much of the expansion of these domestically controlled firms. The expansion of firms controlled in the United States was also financed to a large extent directly out of earnings.

Before the war of 1914-18, virtually all federal and provincial securities, and a large part of municipal securities, were sold abroad. The relative weakness of private domestic capital was reflected in the great extent to which public utilities were publicly owned, or, when privately owned, dependent on government guarantees of their bond issues. Most of the public utility issues were also sold abroad. Thus, of the three major fields of real investment – government, railways, and housing – only housing found its chief source of funds at home. Direct investment of personal savings and of funds borrowed from private mortgage lenders were supplemented by the mortgage loans of the insurance companies and the trust and loans companies, which succeeded the earlier building societies. Some part of these institutional funds was secured abroad.

The commercial banks were the major institution in the domestic capital market. They held bonds, and, to a very minor extent, equities, but their chief activity was the financing of inventories and receivables. Indirectly they financed equipment purchases to some extent. For example, through advances to farm implement companies, the banks provided short-term credit to finance purchases of implements by farmers. The banks were forbidden by law to lend

on real estate or chattel mortgages. Thus it may be said that, until
the expansion of the bond market during the war, the domestic
mortgage market was the most important market for the financing
of durable capital formation in the country. In the post-war period
the bond market assumed a new function. Bonds became a favour-
ite instrument for the financing of new firms and the refinancing of
old firms in manufacturing and trade. The sociological basis of an
adequate market for new equity issues did not appear. Internal
financing and direct use of personal savings remained the characteristic mode of applying venture capital. Individuals with surplus
investment funds over and above the demands of their own business
and those without a business of their own typically bought bonds of
governments and corporations. The banks and insurance companies
secured the bulk of the small savings. The insurance companies
specialized in bonds but also invested a liberal proportion of their
funds in urban mortgage securities. The trend in bank assets was
only slightly away from loans and discounts toward bonds, chiefly
of governments.

In the foregoing examination of the relation between domestic
capital formation and offsets in the form of replacement reserves,
net domestic savings, and capital imports, the emphasis has been
upon the relative size of the offsets. The significance of measuring
offsets is easily exaggerated. Sources and channels of actual money
flows of capital formation have been indicated, but in a most super-
ficial way. In the remainder of the chapter the sketch of this aspect
of the development is filled in to a slight extent for two fields:
western agriculture, which relied mainly upon internal sources of
finance, and the railways, which drew largely upon external capital
markets.

II. Western Farm Finance

Prairie farmers secured funds to finance investment in plant, equipment, and inventories from several sources. Trust, loan, and insurance companies, financing land and buildings on a mortgage basis,
were the most important institutional lenders. These channelled
savings from central Canada and from abroad into the expansion.
As the prosperity of the region increased, individual lenders within
the region became a factor in the mortgage field. The large farm
implement companies supplied the credit for implement purchases
by accepting payments in two to four annual instalments.[12]

Sample studies indicate that a significant portion of the credit
requirements was supplied by the personal funds of settlers at their

arrival on the frontier.[13] The relative size of these individual funds increased with the period of settlement. If the data on initial capital is distributed quinquennially, it is found that the average initial investment of new settlers was $1,249, $1,812, $1,993, and $4,943 in the periods 1901-5, 1906-10, 1911-16, and 1916-20, and approximately $5,000 in the post-war period. A comparison of these values with the average capitalized values of farm property reported in the census at the same dates, shown in Table X, indicates the importance of personal funds.

Studies have also been made to measure the relative importance of savings from farm income. These savings were usually invested in the farm or used to pay off debt. "Seldom less than 20 per cent and frequently as much as 55 per cent of net income is devoted to reinvestment in the home farm or the payment of principal and interest of debts formerly contracted."[14]

Western expansion offered new opportunities for eastern financial institutions. The commercial banks extended their branches to the hundreds of new marketing centres that sprang up, and through these channelled eastern funds to finance grain and livestock. Financing the movement of the wheat crop rapidly became one of the most profitable aspects of their business.[15] The most important operators in the long-term field were the so-called loan companies.[16] These were rescued from stagnation by their western business. The loan companies, which had originated as building societies, became specialists in the farm mortgage field in the central provinces. Their loans on real estate increased from $3 million in 1867 to $117 million at the end of the century. There was evidence in the decade of the nineties of a plethora of domestic savings. The loan companies were finding it increasingly difficult to compete with individual lenders and began themselves to shift from British funds, upon which they had chiefly relied, to the cheaper supplies afforded by domestic sources.[17] By 1900 "company lending had definitely given way before competition of the savings of individual investors"[18] in central Canada, but expansion in the West created new demands and the companies were rescued from their plight. The trend among them to increasing reliance on Canadian sources continued until 1903 and was thereafter reversed as the pace of unfolding domestic opportunities for capital investment outstripped the supply of domestic savings. Meanwhile the insurance companies entered the farm mortgage field on a large scale and eventually replaced the loan companies in relative importance in the post-war period.

A partial compilation of the company mortgage debt in western Canada at 1914 shows a total of $275 million, with the loan companies holding about two-thirds of it and the insurance companies most of the remainder.[19] Excessive optimism in the initial boom coupled with the inevitable difficulties associated with the common practice of five-year maturities led to early provincial government investigations of the farm mortgage field, small-scale public intervention, and the beginning of a retreat of the institutional lenders. The retreat was accelerated during the post-war deflation and completed in the collapse of farm prices after 1928.[20]

The census of agriculture made a partial enumeration of farm mortgage debt in 1931.[21] The census covered owner-operated farms which accounted for only 60 per cent of all farms in the prairie provinces. Total mortgage indebtedness for this sample in 1931 was $344 million: an average of $3,100 for reporting farms. Dr. Mackintosh raised this figure to $488 million to cover the unreported farms and added $49 million as the prairie farm debt to implement companies $48 million to banks, and $65 million to stores, automobile dealers, and supply companies for a total estimate of $650 million.[22]

III. A Note on Railway Finance

Total capital liabilities of Canadian railways in 1895 were $693 million. The gross liabilities of the Canadian National Railway system at December 31, 1931, slightly exceeded $3 billion. About $1.5 billion of these were capital liabilities, chiefly long-term debt ($1.3). In addition there were $1.4 billion on Dominion government account for government-built railways, loans, and accrued interest on loans. The profit and loss deficit, including accrued unpaid interest on government loans, was $.7 billion. The assets of the system were carried on the books at $2.4 billion. The total liabilities (equal assets) of the Canadian Pacific at this time were $1.4 billion of which $.9 billion were distributed about evenly between equities and long-term debt with $.4 billion allocated to surplus, reserves, and stock premiums.[23] The magnitude of these railway liabilities relative to the size of the country may be indicated by comparison with the direct debt of the government of Canada. The gross debt in 1930 was $2.5 billion, most of which was attributable to the war (gross debt rose from $.5 to $3.0 billion from 1914 to 1920).

1. Canadian Pacific Railway

The terms of the contract, ratified by Parliament in February 1881, provided a federal cash grant of $25 million and a grant of 25 million acres of land. The roads built by the government from Selkirk to Lake Superior and from Kamloops to Port Moody at a cost of $37.8 million were given to the company. Additional lands for roadbeds and other railway purposes were granted free. Various tax exemptions were included: all C.P.R. lands were free of tax for twenty years after the actual grant; materials imported for original construction were duty free, and domestic materials required for construction and operation were to be exempt forever. In addition, the C.P.R. was allowed a monopoly of traffic in the West for twenty years. Loans totalling $34.5 million were made by the government during the period of construction.[24]

The directors of the new project displayed remarkable ingenuity in avoiding mortgage bonds. Land grant bonds, stock sales, and government aid were the chief expedients until the road was completed.[25] Thereafter fixed charges were kept down and by 1908 the value of declared dividends exceeded fixed charges and continued to do so until the depression of the thirties.

The capital stock outstanding in 1885 was $65 million and there was no change until 1903.[26] From 1903 to 1913 an additional $195 millions were sold. Sales in 1927 and 1929 of 75 millions raised the total to $335 million. Taking the par value of the stock at $25 a share, the average premium was $5.86.[27] Four per cent preference stock, authorized to the extent of 50 per cent of the common stock outstanding, was first issued in 1893 and thereafter continuously when market conditions in London were favourable. The last issue was made in 1931. Most of the common stock and virtually all of the preference stock (which always carried full voting rights) were sold in London.

Perpetual 4 per cent consolidated debenture stock, authorized in 1889, was sold in almost every year on the London market to retire mortgage bonds and land grant bonds. The sale of these debentures in New York began in 1921 when $25 million were sold there. (The last sale was made in London in 1937 when the last mortgage bonds were retired.) The company's capital liabilities and the book value of the property at the end of each quinquennium from 1890 to 1930 are shown in Table XXIV.

Throughout its history the C.P.R. pursued a liberal policy in the disposal of its vast land holdings. Gross sales to 1930 were just over 16 million acres for a sum of $154 million. According to official estimates, the total proceeds from sales of agricultural lands (after allowing for cancellations) and town sites to 1934 were $176 million.[28]

TABLE XXIV
Canadian Pacific Net Property Investment and Capital Liabilities (a)
(millions of dollars)

	Net railway property investment	Capital stock		Long-term debt	
		Preference	Common	4% consol. debenture stock	Bonds, notes, eqt. obligations
1890	221	–	65	12	66
1895	252	6	65	42	67
1900	293	31	65	60	65
1905	368	38	85	89	55
1910	510	56	150	137	41
1915	780	81	260	176	71
1920	912	81	260	184	63
1925	924	100	260	264	54
1930	1,022	129	335	291	155

(a) *Source:* Submission of the C.P.R. to the Royal Commission on Transportation, 1949, Appendix to Part 1., 27.

2. *Canadian National Railway System*

Only the Grand Trunk, of all the components of the C.N.R. system, was built without large-scale government assistance. Since the company came into existence in 1851, before the era of federal subsidies and guarantees, it relied on its own ability to raise funds in London. Shareholders received very small returns, but the company always managed to meet its fixed charges. The experience of the Grand Trunk Pacific system and of the Canadian Northern was quite different. These lines were wholly dependent upon government assistance in one form or another. They received less than the C.P.R. in the way of cash and land grants, but very nearly all their bonds carried guarantees. The outstanding stock ($25 million for the G.T.P. held by the parent Grand Trunk and $100 million for the C.N. issued to its owners) was pure water. With the exception of $4 million of Canadian Northern securities sold in France in 1911, the funds raised by public subscription for the two lines were

TABLE XXV
Dominion Assistance in Cash and Credit to Railways
(millions of dollars)

First Period (1867-1903)		
Roads now comprising Canadian National system	114.9	
Canadian Pacific Railway system	91.7	
All other roads	3.1	209.7
Second Period (1903-1917-20)		
Roads now comprising Canadian National system	508.6	
Hudson Bay Railway	18.4	
Canadian Pacific Railway system	12.0	
All other roads	5.8	544.8
Third Period (1917-20-1923)		
Roads now comprising Canadian National system	1,287.9	
Hudson Bay Railway	2.4	
Canadian Pacific Railway system		
All other roads	0.5	1,290.8
Fourth Period (1923-31)		
Roads now comprising Canadian National Railways	576.5	
Hudson Bay Railway	28.0	
Canadian Pacific Railway	0.7	
All other roads	2.0	607.2
Grand total, cash and credit		2,652.5

TABLE XXVI
Land Grants to Canadian Railways(a)
(thousands of acres)

	Total	Govt.-owned and controlled	Canadian Pacific	All other roads
By dominion	31,782	5,727	24,953	1,102
By provinces	15,509	1,806	10,612	3,091
Total acreage	47,291	7,533	35,565	4,192

(a) *Source*: *Duff Report*, 87-89.

secured in London.[29] The other components of the Canadian National system were financed directly by the government.

Following the period of difficulty which began with the war, federal government assistance was extended from development to the assumption of deficits. A large-scale investment programme of consolidation and further expansion received government support in the post-war years and throughout the following decade. Table XXV summarizes government activities in railway development up to the end of the period of expansion.

This total of $2.6 billion was about evenly divided between cash and credit support. The land grants to railways are shown in the Table XXVI. Owing to the timing of its construction, the C.P.R. received the bulk of these grants. The other major lines were built either before the main period of land granting or after settlement had begun.

Provincial and municipal governments contributed $46 million in cash subsidies and $49 million in subscriptions to railway shares.

7.
The Volume of Construction, 1896 to 1930

1. Definition and Classifications

CONSTRUCTION, in its broadest sense, includes the erection of new durable structures, such as roads and bridges, power dams, docks and harbours, buildings, and major alterations, and repair and maintenance of existing structures. Gross investment in structures is limited to the value at cost of new construction and major alterations to existing structures during the year, and excludes repair and maintenance expenditures. In some contexts, gross investment in structures is called new construction to emphasize the contrast with the repair component of total construction. Finally, gross construction is "gross" of current consumption; it includes replacement construction expenditures as well as the net additions to the existing stock of structures.

It is convenient to observe certain standard classifications of total construction in common use. The first is the three-fold classification by type of purchaser: (1) Private construction, which covers the extractive industries and residential, commercial, institutional, and industrial construction; (2) Public construction, which covers direct expenditures by municipal, provincial, and federal governments; (3) Public utility construction, which covers expenditures by a mixed group of publicly and privately owned public utility corporations.

Construction may also be classified as engineering construction or building construction, according to the nature of the specific projects involved. Building projects predominate in private construction, while engineering projects predominate in government and public utility construction.

A third classification is made according to the industrial status of the builders carrying out the work. There is contract construction, which covers work performed by general contractors, trade contractors, and sub-contractors, and force-account construction, which is the product of construction workers employed directly by governments, public utility corporations, manufacturers, and other private firms. The product of individual working proprietors, who form a considerable part of the construction labour force, falls logically into the first of these two classes because these individual builders may be regarded as one-man firms. The work of home-owners, tenants, farmers, and any others who buy construction materials and do their own building and repair work is of the nature of force-account construction.

Contract construction is performed by a few large firms, many small ones, and by individual working proprietors. It is therefore difficult to establish the number of going concerns at any one time. Furthermore, because the product of the industry is largely comprised of labour, material, and other variable cost items, the number of concerns is subject to rapid change with the violent fluctuations in construction activity. These characteristics of the contract industry, the large volume of construction work performed as a subsidiary operation in other industries, and the widespread practice among farm and urban dwellers of doing construction work on their own account explain the absence of comprehensive estimates of total construction. When the annual census of industry was established in Canada in 1917, an attempt was made to cover all establishments carrying out construction contracts. Coverage increased in 1918 and 1919 and was maintained approximately at the level attained in 1919 for four years. In 1923 general construction was dropped from the industrial census. In 1934 the census of construction was re-established and extended to include force-account work by governments and certain private firms as well as contract work. Estimates of the volume of "own-account" work carried on by urban and farm dwellers and the volume of force-account work not covered in the construction census imply that the current construction census covers less than 60 per cent of total construction.[1] The inadequacy of the earlier census would be even greater since it did not attempt to cover force-account work at all. Furthermore, it is unlikely that the earlier census managed to cover contract work as thoroughly as the current census which continues to vary in coverage despite special efforts in this respect.[2]

II. SUMMARY OF THE METHOD

The total volume of construction, measured by its cost of production, consists of four components: (1) The value of construction materials used; (2) wages and salaries paid to construction workers; (3) overhead expenses including salaries of office workers, rent, interest, taxes, depreciation and repair of plant and equipment, other sundry expenses; and (4) profits.[3] The first step in the statistical procedure was to select a bench-mark year in which the total volume of construction and the value of construction materials used could be estimated. The second step was to measure the annual flow of construction materials to construction uses from 1896 to 1930. In the third step an index of the annual flow of construction materials was applied to the value of materials used in the bench-mark year (1921) to estimate the value of the material component for each year. The fourth step was to estimate the total value of construction in each year by applying appropriate ratios to the value of construction materials used. In the final step the annual values of construction were summed for each quinquennium and the five-year totals distributed to new and repair and maintenance construction.

If the data necessary to each step of this procedure were a matter of precise record, the estimates would be completely reliable. However there were deficiencies in the records which had to be overcome by the use of more-or-less arbitrary assumptions. This section presents a summary of the procedures followed, indicates the major problems, and concludes with a test of the reliability of the general method employed. Section III deals with sources and the nature of the basic data and describes the procedures in detail to permit an evaluation of the quality of the results.

1. Bench-mark Estimate, 1921

The year 1921 was used as a bench-mark because it was the only year in the period covered when both a decennial census and a construction census were taken. The decennial census data on the total construction labour force were used to blow up the value of construction reported to the construction census.

The construction census of 1921 covered 1,501 establishments that employed 97,573 different individuals during the year with the average full-time employment at 26,583. The value of their product was $85.2 million. The distribution of the total by types of construction compared reasonably well with the more comprehensive census taken after 1933.[4]

The total number of workers engaged in construction in 1921 was determined from decennial census data.[5] A comparison of the relevant classifications of the census returns for 1921 with the more fully processed data for 1931 and 1941 indicated that the numbers of unskilled construction workers and of "other skilled workers"[6] included in these classifications for the construction industry were too low. The number of "other skilled workers" was increased by applying the ratio of "skilled" to "other skilled" from the later censuses. The ratios were virtually identical in 1931 and 1941. This adjustment raised the total of the construction labour force by 3 per cent. The number of unskilled construction workers was raised by applying the ratio of "skilled" to "unskilled" from the 1941 census (approximately 3:1). This adjustment raised the total of all construction workers by approximately 6 per cent. The total construction labour force obtained in this way was 230,618.

The "skill ratio" derived from census classifications does not reflect accurately the actual ratio of skilled to unskilled workers engaged in construction because census enumeration tends to inflate the total shown as skilled. This bias in the decennial census does not affect the reliability of the present estimate since the census ratio was used merely to determine the probable size of the adjustment required for faulty classification of "labourers" in the 1921 census. However, the relation of the actual skill ratio implicit in the estimate of the total construction labour force to the skill ratio in the portion of the labour force covered by the census of construction does matter. If the two ratios were not equal the product of the labour force covered by the census of construction would not be an appropriate basis for determining the probable product of the total labour force engaged in construction. Furthermore, if the labour force covered by the census of construction were a representative sample, as the method employed here assumes, equality of the actual skill ratios in the sample and the total would tend to substantiate the estimate of the total.

A comparison of the average annual earnings per full-time member in the two groups indicated that their composition with respect to skill was similar. The average annual wage in the census of construction, obtained by dividing total wages by the average number of full-time employees, was $1,154. The average annual earnings of skilled construction workers, census definition, in full-time employment during the year ending June 1, 1921, was $1,283, and of unskilled workers $913.[7] Weighting these by the skill ratio of 3 to 1 yielded an average wage of $1,198. When a decline in average wages of about 4 per cent from the year ending June 1, 1921, covered by the construction census was allowed for, the two averages were found to be equal. The annual index of construction wage rates declined 5.5 per cent from 1920 to 1921. The average decline from the census year ending June 1, 1921, to the calendar year 1921 would be somewhat less.

An adjustment for the average time lost by members of the construction labour force in 1921 was made on the basis of census and trade union data on employment. The percentage of unemployment (from all causes) in 1921 among members of ten classes of trade unions in the building and construction industry was 20.2 per cent. Average unemployment among skilled construction workers in the decennial census of occupations from June 1, 1920, to June 1, 1921, was 16.8 per cent. The average unemployment among all unskilled workers in this period was also 16.8 per cent. In the same period the trade unions reported average unemployment of 14.87 per cent. Average unemployment among all construction workers was apparently 12.2 per cent higher than among organized construction workers. The 20.2 per cent reported by the trade unions for 1921 was accordingly raised by 12.2 per cent. The total construction labour force in 1921, after adjustment for time lost, was the equivalent of 178,628 men working full time. The value of the product of 26,583 full-time workers in the construction census was $85.2 million. If the 26,583 workers provide a representative sample, then the value of the output of the total construction labour force in 1921 was $571 million.

An addition to the total value of construction was made for work performed by persons outside the construction labour force. These additions (for new construction by owner-builders, repairs by non-farm home-owners, and new and repair construction by farmers) were estimated by extrapolating the P.I.C.F. estimates for 1926 to 1921. These additions raised the value of total construction in 1921 to $631 million with material costs, wages and salaries, and overhead and profit at 46.2, 39.5, and 14.3 per cent, respectively.[8]

2. Flow of Construction Materials, 1896-1930

The supply method, adapted by P.I.C.F. from studies of the National Bureau of Economic Research, was used to determine the flow of construction materials. Some minor changes were made in the commodity classification set up by the authors of P.I.C.F. The extent of these changes is dealt with in the next section.

Import and export records on a detailed commodity basis were available for the whole period. Comparable production records were not maintained. A canvass of annual production data from 1896 to 1930 provided a sample of production of fairly high coverage (57 per cent of total production in 1924). In addition to these annual data, there was also the census of manufacturing, taken quinquennially from 1900 to 1915 and annually beginning in 1917.

Examination of the trends in output of the various classes of construction materials revealed marked variations. The commodity list for production was therefore broken down into two major sections with four sub-sections in section 1 and six in section 2. The four classes of production in section 1 accounted for 65.9 per cent of the total production of construction materials in 1926. Four series based on annual data from 1896 to 1930 were used to extrapolate full totals for these classes on a 1926-30 base. Taken together the sample series represented 85 per cent of the output in section 1 on the basis of average production from 1926 to 1930. The distribution of this coverage among the classes is shown in the following table:

Class of construction material	Coverage of samples. basis 1926-30 (%)
1. Wood and wood products (n. e. s.)	95.7
2. Mineral products (n. e. s.)	94.1
3. Iron and steel products (n. e. s.)	44.8
4. Railway and other force account materials	100.0
Coverage of total output in Section 1	85.8

If it is assumed that the annual series, 1896-1930, were reliable, there would be little room for error in the extrapolation of the classes in section 1, with the exception of class 3. Since this class accounted for 11.1 per cent of total output in 1926, the effect on the totals of an error in its extrapolation would be small.

Production series from the census of manufacturing were used to extrapolate full totals for each class in section 2. Possibilities of error in the extrapolations arose in two of the procedures applied: (1) Production of the commodites in section 2 for the inter-censal years before 1917 was interpolated with an annual index of the production totals in section 1, adjusted for the difference in trend in the two sections; (2) the allocation of commodities in the census of manufacturing was crude. As a general rule the whole output of each establishment was allocated according to the chief commodity produced. This difficulty was met by assembling totals for each class on both bases for the year 1926, when an alphabetical classification was also available, and applying the average adjustment required in each class in 1926 over the whole series. In view of the arbitrariness of this procedure, a test was made to determine the maximum possible error it could introduce. If it were assumed that all the errors in the re-allocations were in the same direction and of the maximum degree in any one year, the error in the total for section 2 could run to plus or minus 35 per cent. This would introduce an error in the estimate of total production of construction materials of 12 per cent in the later years, when section 2 accounted for just under 35 per cent of the total, and of less than 10 per cent in the early years of the series, when section 2 accounted for less than 30 per cent of the total.

Series on exports, imports and duties, re-exports and duty rebates were tabulated from the annual trade records. The commodity classifications in the early trade records were very detailed. No mixed classifications were encountered. An arbitrary assumption of uniform monthly distribution was used to adjust the trade totals from fiscal (June 30 until 1906 and March 31 thereafter) to calendar years. Domestic consumption of construction materials was then obtained as follows: production minus exports plus imports minus exports plus duty minus duty rebates. The values of domestic consumption were assumed to reflect producers' prices.[9]

Appropriate additions for freight margins and sales taxes were calculated and added to the series. The series was also adjusted for the flow of construction materials to non-construction uses. Owing to lack of data, it was necessary to assume that trade mark-ups were constant over the period. No adjustment for inventory changes was made in passing from producers' prices to cost to final users.

The estimates of the annual flow of construction materials from 1896 to 1930 are shown in Appendix table A.

3. Total Construction, 1896-1930

The value of construction and its major components in 1921 and the annual flow of construction materials having been established, the next step was to convert the flow into an index with 1921 equal to 100.0 and apply it to the value of the material component of total construction for 1921 to determine the magnitude of the materials component in current dollars in each year. The value of construction in each year was then estimated on the basis of ratios derived from the available data on the relationships between the material component, the labour component, and other costs included in total construction.

The overhead and profit component was relatively small – 14.3 per cent of the value of construction in 1921. An a priori expectation of relative stability in this component was supported by the results of a study of a sample of construction firms reporting to the Department of National Revenue from 1921 to 1939.[10] On the basis of this evidence, it was decided to apply the percentage for 1921 to every year in the series.

The chief difficulty arose in establishing ratios of material costs to wage costs. As a first approximation, the average ratio in the construction census data[11] was applied to the value of materials in 1913 dollars to determine annual wages in 1913 dollars. The two series were then converted to current dollars, added, a and divided by 100.0 minus 14.3 to derive estimates of total construction. A second series was computed on the assumption that the ratio of each of the two components to the sum of both, expressed in current dollars, was constant.

The two sets of estimates were compared and found similar in the period from 1900 to 1921, reflecting the general conformity in the movements of material prices and wage rates in the industry. The estimates did not differ by more than 5 per cent until 1924. From 1924 to 1930 the estimates based on constant real inputs rose as much as 20 per cent above the estimates based on constant relative value inputs, reflecting the marked divergence in the movements of prices and wage rates. Wage rates began to rise in 1922 whereas material prices continued to fall with only a slight interruption in the late twenties.

In view of the conformity in the two trends during the earlier period, there is perhaps some justification for the assumption of constant real inputs; but the divergence after 1920 made it difficult to accept the same assumption throughout the twenties.

The data covering the period between the early construction census from 1917 to 1922 and the census beginning in 1934 were scanty. The only construction activity covered by the census of industry in the intervening years was that of the so-called bridge companies. These companies engaged in a highly specialized activity that, while largely construction, was not demonstrably representative of general construction.

Comparison of averages of the ratios of material to labour costs from the earlier and later censuses of construction indicated that a considerable change took place in the intervening years. The average of the ratios of material to labour was higher from 1934 to 1940, which included deep depression years, than from 1917 to 1922 and higher still from 1936 to 1940 than from 1919 to 1922 two periods when the weights of engineering and building construction were more nearly the same. A comparison of similar averages from the bridge company data for the two periods 1919 to 1923 and 1924 to the census beginning in 1934 were scanty.

It was therefore assumed that the change evident after 1936 took place during the five years of buoyant activity from 1924 to 1929. The bridge company sample was used to extrapolate the ratios from 1921 to 1929 because it supported the assumption. A similar assumption was made implicitly in the methods employed in P.I.C.F. In that study the ratios obtained from the construction census from 1934 to 1941 were extrapolated to 1926 on the assumption that the ratios would be similar in similar phases of the cycle.

This procedure established relationships for the 1929 peak comparable to those in 1937 and 1941.

The values of materials used in each year from 1896 to 1930, obtained by applying the index of the annual flow of construction materials to the value of materials used in 1921, were deflated, and real wages paid each year were derived by applying the ratios described above. The two series, materials and wages, were then converted into current dollars, added, and their annual sum raised by dividing by the ratio of the sum of materials and wages to total construction, valued in current dollars, to secure the required estimates of total construction.

The implicit current-dollar ratios of materials used to total construction that result from the assumptions of this study are shown in Appendix table A2. The ratios for the late twenties are slightly lower than the ratios derived for the same period from the later census of construction by the assumptions of P.I.C.F. The difference may be explained by the inclusion of fuels in the materials reported in the census of construction after 1934. Fuels were reported separately in the construction census of 1921 and excluded from the present estimates of materials used.

4. Breakdown of New and Repair Construction

A breakdown of total construction into new and repair and maintenance in the years from 1926 to 1930 was made by applying the percentage distributions of new and repair construction for this period in P.I.C.F. (The distribution in P.P.I. is similar, with repair averaging 28.6 per cent for this period as compared with 29.6 per cent in P.I.C.F.)

Independent estimates of repair expenditures were developed in conjunction with the direct estimates of major components of total construction described in Chapter XI. The repair series included housing, steam railways 1896-1930, federal and provincial governments, 1900-30, and municipal governments, 1911-30. These were blown up to full coverage on the basis of their relation to the full repair totals in the period 1926-30. The relative coverage, base 1926-30, was two-thirds for the period 1911-30, just over half for the decade 1901-11, and slightly over 40 per cent from 1896 to 1900.

The quinquennial estimates of gross construction appear in Appendix table B.

5. A Test of the Method

The results of the procedures described in this section are compared with the official estimates of P.P.I. and P.I.C.F. in another study.[12]

At this point the reliability of the method may be considered by applying the same method with 1941 as the bench mark and extrapolating to 1926 with an index of the annual flow of construction materials and ratios derived from the construction census. The resulting estimates may then be compared with the estimates from the 1921 bench mark in the five years of overlap from 1926 to 1930.

Building and construction trade unions reported an average of 13.6 per cent unemployment from June 1, 1940, to May 31, 1941.[13] Average unemployment from all causes among all construction workers, census definition, during the same period was 29.42 per cent and slightly higher among unskilled workers.[14] The total construction labour force in 1941 included 213,500 skilled construction workers, 14,000 other skilled, and 71,200 unskilled workers, a total of 299,000 workers.[15] (The total of 50,000 unskilled workers reported for the construction industry proper was raised by 21,000 by applying the census skill ratio (3:1) to the skilled workers engaged in force-account construction.) This total labour force, after adjusting for time lost, was the equivalent of 224,700 members working full time. The average full-time working force reported in the census of construction in 1941 was 158,700. The total product was $639.8 million. On this basis the product of the construction labour force would be $906 million. Adding the P.I.C.F. estimate of construction by home-owners and the P.P.I. estimate of construction by farmers yielded an estimate of total construction for 1941 of $972 million.

The material component was run back to 1926 with an index of the domestic disappearance of construction materials secured from the P.I.C.F. study.[16] The ratios of materials used to total construction reported in the construction census from 1934 to 1941 were extrapolated to 1926. (Following P.I.C.F., the 1937 ratio was assigned to 1929.) The resulting estimates of total construction from 1926 to 1930 compare very closely with those derived from the 1921 bench mark:

Year	1921 bench mark ($000,000)	1941 bench mark ($000,000)
1926	703	715
1927	783	789
1928	940	919
1929	1,046	1,002
1930	928	939

III. Sources and Procudures

1. The Bench-mark Estimate, 1921

The census of occupations. Two classifications of the labour force are made in the official census of occupations: an industrial classification which shows the number of workers in each industry distributed on the basis of their occupations; and an occupational classification, which shows the number of workers in each occupational group distributed by the industries in which they pursue their occupations.

All members of the labour force employed in the construction industry itself and all persons following construction occupations in other industries or on their own account contribute to the value of total construction. Four groups of members of the construction industry may be distinguished: (1) skilled workers and apprentices who follow construction occupations; (2) other skilled workers, whose occupations are not construction by census definitions but who work on the site of construction projects and contribute to the value produced by the construction industry; (3) unskilled workers who perform "on-site" duties; and (4) office personnel: clerical, professional, managerial, and personal service workers. By census conventions, members of the first three groups are wage earners, with the minor exception of foremen and overseers included in (1), and the members of group (4) are salary earners. In 1931 and 1941 the composition of the construction industry was as follows:

	1931	1941
(1) Skilled	153,527	147,280
(2) Other skilled	15,239	14,032
(3) Unskilled	77,678	50,021
(4) Office, etc.	9,792	8,796
Unclassified	(72)	(82)
Total	256,308	220,221

(*Source: Decennial Census of Canada,* 1931, VII, 898; *Decennial Census of Canada,* 1941, VII, 670.)

Two observations are relevant to the present procedure:

(a) The relationship of "other skilled" to "skilled": the former was 9.9 per cent of the latter in 1931 and 9.5 per cent in 1941.

(b) The ratio of "skilled" to "unskilled" was approximately 2 to 1 in 1931 and 3 to 1 in 1941.

In a recent publication of D.B.S. a uniform occupational classification on the basis of the current definition of occupations shows the following figures for skilled construction workers from 1901 to 1941.[17]

> 1901- 89,165
> 1911-150,567
> 1921-162,291
> 1931-203,066
> 1941-213,493

By definition, skilled and apprentice workers whose day-by-day work is in the line of a construction skill are included in this classification. The difference between the total of 203,066 skilled and apprentice construction workers shown for this occupational class in 1931 and the 153,527 skilled and apprentice construction workers shown in the construction industry in 1931 consists of workers employed by governments, railways, manufacturers, and other firms engaged in force-account construction and also the individual proprietors or "own-account" construction workers mentioned in the introductory section of this chapter.

The construction labour force in 1921. In the original census of occupations for 1921, the classification by industries was not complete. The following data were shown for the construction industry excluding ship-building:

(1) Skilled workers	139,109
(2) Other skilled	6,312
(3) Unskilled	29,030

(Source: *Decennial Census of Canada*, 1921, IV, 24.)

The relationship of "other skilled" to "skilled" is too low. The ratio of skilled to unskilled which approximates 4 to 1 (82.7:17.3) appears to be too high. The relationship of "other skilled" to "skilled" reflected in 1931 and 1941 can be accepted, in view of its stability in these two markedly different years and the relatively small size of the "other skilled" group. The question of the ratio of skilled to unskilled in 1921 presented a more difficult problem. The 1931 ratio was immediately ruled out in view of the conditions prevailing in that year. Unemployment among trade union construction workers averaged 45.4 per cent as compared with 20.2 per cent in 1921. In 1931 governments were "making jobs" of the dirt-moving variety which undoubtedly inflated the number of unskilled construction workers reporting to the census in that year. There was evidence that governments planned their construction programmes in 1921 with some regard for the recession which began in the latter part of 1920, but the special projects were small and of a normal kind.[18] This study accepted the skill ratio of 1941. The 1921 census total of 162,291 skilled workers was accordingly raised to 217,403 to include the unskilled. The number of other skilled was taken at 13,215, i.e., 9.5 per cent of the number of skilled workers in the industry classification. The total construction labour force, by this calculation, was 230,618. The possible error in this estimate was checked by applying a 4 to 1 skill ratio as one outside limit, and the 2 to 1 ratio from the 1931 census as the other limit. The former reduced the estimate of the construction labour force by 6 per cent; the latter raised it by 11 per cent.

The skill ratio in the census of construction appeared to correspond with the one used here. Of the 97.6 thousand individual wage earners employed, 44.3 thousand were classified as labourers by the reporting establishments. This seems to indicate a lower ratio than 3 to 1. Two observations may be made. First, assuming that employers used the same definition of skill as the census enumerators, the fact that the rate of labour turn-over could be, and probably was, higher for the unskilled workers tends to refute the indication. Second, it is known that decennial census enumerations tend to inflate the size of the skilled groups[19]; but since the skill ratio was used here merely as a device to determine how many additional workers there were in the construction field, this bias in the decennial census was of no account in itself. The total classified as skilled may have included a marginal group of individuals drawing less than skilled rates of pay from employers. For our purpose, it was only necessary to establish that the average annual earnings per members of the full-time labour force – as estimated above – was the same as the average annual earnings per member of the full-time labour force covered by the census of construction. This equality has been demonstrated in Section II, part 1 of this chapter. The equality was taken as evidence that the real skill ratios implicit in the construction census and in the present estimate of the total labour force were the same, and used to justify blowing up the value of the product of the census group. The margin of error, put at minus 6 to plus 11 per cent would be reduced to the extent that the average annual value product of a complex of skilled and unskilled labour was greater than the value product of the unskilled. An inequality in average earnings of the two groups would demonstrate that, however well we had estimated the size of the labour force, its composition with respect to skill was different from the composition of the force covered by the construction census, and the latter's product would not be an appropriate basis for determining the probable product of the former.

Labour input and the value of construction in 1921. The adjustment for average time lost by members of the construction labour force on the basis of census and trade union data and the estimate of total construction for 1921 have been described in the previous section. The trade union data obtained from *Labour Gazette* (Ottawa, 1923) provided a fairly good sample. The ten skills covered corresponded to the skills included in the census classification of construction occupations. The average membership of the unions in 1921 was 27,000. The census data used to correct the trade union figures for their omission of unskilled workers and to shift from a June to a December year were from the *Decennial Census*, V, Table 16.

The data from the censuses of construction, from 1917 to 1922, were taken from the census schedules in the files of the Manufactures Branch, D.B.S. A canvass of government libraries turned up only two of the original bulletins reporting the detailed results of these early censuses. The figures published in *Canada Year Book* were scanty and inconsistent (e.g., comparative figures for 1919 and 1920 excluded subcontract work in the total for 1920 but included it in the 1919 total). The value of the product reported to the census covered a wide variety of types of construction. The distribution of the total to engineering and building construction and, within these, to public and private, on the one hand, and commericial, industrial, residential, and institutional, on the other hand, compared well with the more comprehensive census of the late thirties and the forties. The representativeness of the census need not be questioned on these grounds.

Over 40 per cent of the total construction labour force appears to have been covered by the census of construction. However, the apparent coverage would be reduced to the extent that individual wage earners worked for more than one reporting establishment during the year. Coverage was within the ratios of 26.6 thousand and 97.6 thousand to the total labour force less "own-account" workers.

The value of the wage component in the construction census of 1921 was 38.34 per cent of the value of the product. This included 2.37 per cent for the salaries of foremen and overseers who were included in the construction occupational class by census definitions. Salaries for office personnel were 2.73 per cent of the value of the product. On the basis of the census of general construction and information taken from schedules returned by bridge-building establishments, the average of the ratios of material costs to labour costs, both expressed in 1921 dollars, for the four years from 1919 to 1922, when the coverage of both records was fairly uniform, was 1.127.[20] This happened also to be the ration in 1921. It was reasonable to accept 43.21 per cent (1.127 X 38.34) as a representative percentage of materials to product in terms of 1921 prices. The value of the total product was broken down in the following way:

	Percentage	Value ($000,000)
Material costs	43.21	246.7
Wages and salaries	41.07	234.5
Overhead and profit	15.72	89.8
	100.00	571.0

This breakdown implies that part of the general overhead and profit of firms engaged in force-account construction should be allocated to the construction activity performed. In practice this allocation is probably not made.

An addition to the total value of construction was made for work performed by persons outside the construction labour force. This type of work accounted for 6.8 per cent of the value of construction in 1941, the bench mark year in the Department of Reconstruction's study. It was distributed among new construction by non-farm owner-builders, repairs by non-farm dwellers, and new and repair construction by farmers. We extrapolated to 1921 their 1926 figures for the first two items, using an index of gross investment in housing construction (cf. Chapter XI), and for the last two items, using an index of domestic disappearance of construction materials used on farms (from the supply data) combined with an index of gross farm income. The estimated value of the materials used for these projects was $45 million, and the imputed value of labour was $15 million. These additions raised the value of construction in 1921 to $631 million, with material, labour, and other costs at 46.2, 39.5, and 14.3 per cent respectively.

2. The Annual Flow of Construction Materials

Production of construction materials. The list of construction commodities produced was divided into two major sections with four sub-groups in section I and six in section II. The value and percentage of construction material production for each class in 1926 are shown in Table XXVII.

THE VOLUME OF CONSTRUCTION, 1896 TO 1930   127

TABLE XXVII
Value and Percentage Distribution of Construction Materials Produced in Canada, 1926

	Value ($000)	Percentage
Section I		
1. Wood and wood products (n.e.s.)	122,448	36.0
2. Mineral products (n.e.s.)	41,011	12.1
3. Iron and steel products (n.e.s.)	37,829	11.1
4. Railway and other force-account materials	22,877	6.7
Subtotal	224,165	65.9
Section II		
5. Paper products	9.056	2.7
6. Paints and varnishes	25,027	7.4
7. Iron and steel shapes erected	13,343	3.9
8. Planing-mill products	35,588	10.5
9. Wire and wire products	18,341	5.4
10. Miscellaneous building materials	14,426	4.2
Subtotal	115,781	34.1
Total (section I and II)	339,946	100.0

Annual series were assembled for each sub-group in section I. The sources of the data were as follows:

1. Wood and wood products – the largest group, chiefly sawn lumber, shingles, and lath. Direct records of volume and value of production from 1908 to 1930 appear in annual bulletins, *Forest Products of Canada*, Canada, Department of the Interior, and later in *Statistical Record of the Forests and Forest Industries*, Department of Mines and Resources. Indirect records, from 1895 to 1907, of lumber, shingle, and lath wood cut on crown lands were obtained from the following: *Annual Reports of Crown Land Department*, New Brunswick; *Annual Reports of Department of Lands and Forests*, Quebec; *Crown Land Reports*, Ontario; *Reports of the Department of the Interior*, Canada (the three prairie provinces and the railway belt in British Columbia were under federal administration); *Reports of the Chief Commissioner of Lands and Works*, British Columbia; R. H. Coats, *Cost of Living Report*, Vol. 2, Ottawa, 1915.

2. Minerals and mineral products data were obtained from *Mineral Production of Canada*, in annual reports of Department of the Interior, later published by Mines Branch of the Department of Mines, and more recently, Mines Branch, Dominion Bureau of Statistics.

3. Iron and Steel products (n.e.s.). *The Annual Statistical Reports* of the American Iron and Steel Association and, later, the American Iron and Steel Institute have included a section on the Canadian industry since the eighteen-nineties. Price data were obtained from R. H. Coats, *Cost of Living Report*; D.B.S. *Prices and Price Indexes*, Ottawa (annual publications).

4. Railroad force-account materials. *Canada Year Books*, 1910 to 1930; *Annual Statistical Reports* of the American Iron and Steel Association (Institute); *Crown Land Reports* listed above, and hereafter referred to by this title.

The sources of data for each sub-group in Section II were the official censuses of manufacturing taken in 1890, 1900, 1905, 1910, 1915, and annually from 1917 to 1930. The coverage was complete in each census year but there were two sources of possible error: the necessity of deriving values for inter-censal years by interpolation, and the nature of the census classifications.

The early census allocated the whole output of each establishment according to the chief commodity produced.[21] For example, the gross value of product assigned to wallpaper would include the value of any miscellaneous finished or unfinished paper products turned out by establishments whose major product was wallpaper. It would exclude the value of wallpaper produced in establishments which, while producing wallpaper to a minor extent, were chiefly engaged in some other line of production. Thus the total given for each commodity in the census required two corrections, one reducing it, the other increasing it. For 1926 the net result of the two operations was to reduce the total of the values reported under the broad commodity classifications from 10 to 40 per cent. In the earlier years the method of determining the size of the adjustment in each case was to apply the breakdown of the values reported in 1926. The possible error from this assumption is not great. It is officially held that at least 50 per cent of the value reported would represent finished output of the product named. Experience with the type of adjustment involved indicates that the possibility that 100 per cent of the value reported was of the product named is equally extreme. On the average, the final estimates lie at the mid-point between these two extremes. If, to take the strongest case, all the errors were in the same direction and of the maximum degree in any one year, then the total error in section II would run to plus or minus 35 per cent. This would introduce an error of 12.25 per cent in the total value of all construction materials in the later part of the period when section II was 35 per cent of the total, and of less than 10 per cent in the early part of the period when section II was less than 30 per cent of the total.

The interpolations of production for the inter-censal years for section II were not made for individual sub-groups. The separate estimates of sub-group totals at five-year intervals over the first twenty years were considered adequate to establish trends. The interpolation was made on the assumption that, after allowing for trend, the cyclical movement from year to year in this minor group would be determined by the same factors affecting the major group. Totals for section I were converted into series of five-year indexes and the differences in trend rates of growth of sections I and II eliminated by distributing the difference in census-year ratios uniformly over the interpolating index. For the period 1895-1900, half the ratio from 1890 to 1900 was assumed to reflect the change from 1895 to 1900.

In the discussion of the possible error in section II of the production estimates, it was assumed that the annual series were themselves reliable. The validity of this assumption may be checked by examining the data upon which they are based. The data are described fully below. Particular attention is given to the first sub-group of section I of the sample, because this series was the product of splicing two series derived from different sources. Furthermore, it accounted for about 55 per cent of the value of all construction materials produced in 1900.

The statistics on forest products were first compiled by a competent central authority in 1908, but it was not until 1910 that complete coverage was achieved.[22] The reports have been maintained on a consistent basis since that date. In 1908 many small mills in Quebec and all the mills in Prince Edward Island were not reported. There was improvement in 1909 when fewer mills in Quebec were missed and Prince Edward Island was included. The inclusion of the 26 mills in Prince Edward Island added less than one-tenth of one per cent to the national totals. The size of the output of the non-reported mills in Quebec has been estimated by Quebec authorities.[23] The value of output was raised 5 per cent in 1908 and 2.5 per cent in 1909 on the basis of their estimates.

The standards of measure of output of lumber varied in the different provinces. Appropriate conversion factors were secured from the Forestry Branch of the Department of Mines and Resources to put the volume of the cut from crown lands from 1895 to 1908 on a uniform basis. Average prices per thousand feet board measure of sawn lumber of the total cut in each province in 1908 were applied to the quantities cut in each province from 1895 to 1908. A similar procedure was followed for shingle production. National totals were converted from constant to current dollars by applying an index of wholesale prices of sawn lumber products which appeared in R. H. Coats, *Cost of Living Report*. This final series was then used as an index to run back the 1908 value of production of sawn lumber, lath, and shingles.

The adequacy of this procedure was supported by the fact that over 90 per cent of lumber produced in Canada originated on crown lands. The shift from crown lands to private ownership was negligible in this thirteen-year period. As late as 1945 in the leading timber-producing provinces, British Columbia, Ontario and Quebec, only 3.4, 6.0 and 7.2 per cent, respectively, of the productive forest lands was in private hands.[24] There may have been some illegal and hence unreported cutting, particularly in the western region during the settlement boom. It could not have been large, and since it probably moved in step with the total cut it would not affect the index.

A check on the results may be made with the indepdndent estimates reported in the federal census of forest products for 1900. The value of sawn lumber and square timber in 1908 was $54.3 million. The index derived from the cut on crown lands showed 1900 at 55.2 (1908-100.0) in current dollars. Thus after raising the 1908 value to 57.0 (the addition of 5 per cent explained above), we got $31.5 million as the value of sawn lumber and square timber in 1900. The census estimated the value of saw logs "when sawn into lumber" and square timber at $31.2 million. This is a remarkably close agreement. However, an examination of all the price-quantity data available indicated that if the present result were correct, then the census understated average prices and overstated quantities just enough to offset one another.

The price data in Dr. Coats's study of wholesale prices demonstrated that the census did indeed understate prices. It may also be shown that the extremely arbitrary method of the census resulted in an overstatement of quantities.[25] Dr. Coats[26] used the value of materials consumed by the "log products group" – chiefly saw mill products – reported in the censuses of manufacturing for 1900 and 1910, deflated by his wholesale index of lumber prices. In this comparison the real change was 54 per cent. Comparing the board-feet measure reported in the 1900 census of forest products with the quantity reported in 1910 to the Forestry Branch, which is regarded as accurate, the real change was 35 per cent. While Coats's approach provided only an approximate measure of the change, the difference was sufficiently great to demonstrate the contention that the census of 1900 overstates quantities. This examination of all the independent data available does not prove that the present estimate for 1900 is correct, but it suggests no reason for doubting its reliability unless one takes as reason the improbability of the "rule of

thumb" methods of the census resulting in two precisely compen-
sating errors. The discussion also illustrates the reason for not
accepting the census reports for 1890 and 1900.

Had the census been reliable it would have been possible to use
the crown lands data to interpolate rather than extrapolate. Despite
statements in the 1901 census to the contrary, the quantity data in
the 1891 census were compiled on a different basis which could not
be reconciled with the procedures of 1901 and 1908. According to
the census, "at the taking of previous censuses uniformity in measurement was provided by fixing a 'census stanard' of 100 feet b. m.
per log and on this basis the statistics of the four census years 1871
to 1901 are compared in table 48" (Introduction to Vol. 11, Census
of 1901). But in the accompanying table results secured by the
method described in footnote 25 were shown for 1901. The first
three were based on the "census standard"; but there were significant changes in the size of logs over this period. The statistics are
therefore misleading. The change shown from 1890 to 1900 appears
to be in the wrong direction.

Records of the commodities included in sub-group 2 of section
I of the sample were maintained continuously over the whole
period. These were published in *Annual Reports*, Mines Branch,
Department of the Interior prior to 1908, *Mineral Production of
Canada,* Department of Mines, 1908-20, and D.B.S. annual bulletins, *Non Metallic Minerals* and *Manufactures of Non-Metallic
Minerals* after 1920. Although some changes in classification
occurred, reconciliations were easily effected. Items like sand and
gravel, which presented peculiar difficulties owing to the impossibil-
ity of tracking down all producers, were omitted from the present
series.

For sub-group 3 and part of 4 this study has drawn upon
records of tonnage production published by the American Iron and
Steel Institute. Until the nineteen-twenties this organization secured
better coverage of Canadian iron and steel production than official
agents.[27] Certain arbitrary procedures were necessary in the earlier
years since three items were shown separately only after their output became significant. The item, "cast iron gas and water pipe and
fittings and cast iron soil and plumbers' pipe and fittings" was first
reported in 1914. Previously it was included under "all other finished rolled." The same was true of the second item, wrought iron
and steel pipes. There was no indication of their production in the
census of 1910. The procedure adopted was to assume zero output
in 1910 and interpolate the intervening years on a straight line. The
third item was finished angle-splice bars, tie plates, fish plates, rail
joints and fastenings, first reported in 1912. Information in the

Annual Reports of the Mines Branch on subsidies paid for domestic production of structural materials indicated that production of the material included in this third item began in 1905 and 1906. The outputs during the intervening years were interpolated on the assumption that "imports plus domestic production" followed the movement in the "production plus imports" of steel railway rails. This third item and steel rails (which alone constituted over 50 per cent of the entire output of finished rolled forms, structural and other, from 1902, when the large rail mills were first established, until the war of 1914) were included in sub-group 4. Structural shapes were shown separately from 1895 to 1905. Thereafter they were combined with wire rods. McLeish's records of wire rod production were used as an index to secure the desired breakdown.

Appropriate prices for nails and cast iron pipe and fittings were obtained from Coats, *Cost of Living Report,* and from issues of *Prices and Price Indexes,* D.B.S. Prices of wrought iron and steel pipe in the late twenties were secured from the latter source and run back on the index of wholesale prices of cast iron pipe. Wholesale prices of structural steel shapes were available in *Prices and Price Indexes* for 1926-30, run back to 1913 with an index of wholesale prices of iron and steel rolling mill products, and to 1895 with an index of wholesale prices of iron and steel products; both indexes appeared in late issues of *Prices and Price Indexes.* Steel rail prices from 1913 to 1926 were taken from *Prices and Price Indexes;* an index of prices paid by the federal government was assembled from *Sessional Papers,* and used to run the 1913 price back to 1901; a series of average import prices compiled from *Trade Reports* provided an index to carry the 1901 price back to 1895. Prices of finished angle-splice bars, tie plates, etc., appeared in *Prices and Price Indexes* after 1926, and were run back to 1905 on the index of steel rail prices.

Sub-group 4 of section I included the railway items from the American Iron and Steel Association records. Production of hewn and sawn ties and telephone and telegraph poles were given in the federal government bulletins cited above and the *Canada Year Book.* The value for 1908[28] was extrapolated to 1895 with an index of the value of ties and poles produced from crown lands. On the basis of this index, the value of ties and poles produced in 1900 was 28.1 per cent of their value in 1908, or $1,564,000. The census reports a value of $1,615,000 for ties and poles in 1900.

Imports and exports of construction materials. Statistics of Canadian trade were published in the *Annual Reports* of the Departments of Trade and Commerce and Department of Customs in the early years and by the Dominion Bureau of Statistics after its inception. Until 1920 "total imports" and "imports for home consumption" were both recorded. The latter classification, from which the data for this study were taken, was somewhat misleading in that it included some goods which were subsequently re-exported. "Exports of foreign produce" included these goods plus the difference between "total imports" and "imports for home consumption," a difference made up "almost wholly of wheat in bond from the United States, for re-export overseas."[29] After 1920 the single import designation "for home consumption" was used and included goods destined for re-export. These "exports of foreign produce" were shown separately. Bonded goods re-exported but not entered for home consumption were recorded in the statistics of "transit trade," a separate tabulation. Since values and duties collected for each commodity were shown separately, the average rate of duty could be calculated. This average rate in each case was applied to the value of the commodity re-exported to estimate the duty rebate used in the present tabulations.

F.o.b. invoice values were taken by customs officials as the import values, except in cases of obvious undervaluation when the value applied was "the fair market value of such goods when sold for home consumption in the countries whence, and at the time when the same were exported directly to Canada." Export values were their "value at the port of shipment." In this context "port" means simply the point of shipment inland or otherwise, and the value may be regarded as the value at producers' prices. The values of re-exports were probably overstated, since they included value added by storage and handling as the goods passed through the country; but the adjustment on this account was so small that it would not show in totals rounded to the nearest million.

The commodity classifications in the trade records were very detailed. In no instance was it necessary to devise procedures for breaking down mixed classifications. The values and, for imports, the duties for each item appearing in the commodity lists were transcribed for each year from 1895 to 1930. The calculation of domestic supply was carried out with production and trade totals rounded to the nearest thousand. An arbitrary procedure was used to adjust the trade totals to calendar years. Since detailed monthly reports were published by the Department of Trade and Commerce, a precise adjustment could be made. This adjustment would increase the tedious work of transcription sevenfold in the years before and fourfold in the years following 1907. Sample tests of recent data indicated that to adjust from fiscal to calendar years on the assumption of a uniform monthly distribution may introduce errors more serious for construction materials than for machinery and equipment because of a more pronounced seasonal variation in the former. But there was a tendency for the errors to partially offset one another so long as they cyclical movements endured over fairly long periods. For example, taking 25 per cent of fiscal 1930 added too much to 1930, but carrying back 75 per cent of fiscal 1931 was an under-allocation and offset the initial error. If a cyclical turning point occurred in the second half of the fiscal year this tendency would be weakened. In years of rising activity a corrective tendency was also at work. In these years the allocation of 25 per cent of a fiscal year was too much on seasonal grounds (shipments tended to fall off in January and February when building activity was low) but it was too little because of the cyclical factor.

A final rationalization on this point is that the possible error introduced by the procedure must be very small owing to the dominance of domestic production in determining the volume of the domestic supply of construction materials. From 1905 to 1930, exports as a percentage of production varied between 15, and, at the export peak in 1925, 30 per cent. Thus an error which, at the outside, might be 10 per cent of the export total would introduce less than a 3.8 per cent error in the peak export year. If exports were 10 per cent too low in such a year, the total of production minus exports would be 3.8 per cent too high. This error would be reduced, since imports, which were added in the next operation, would presumably err in the given year in the same direction as exports. The probable error arising from this source was small indeed. From 1900 to 1905 exports ran as high as 40 per cent, and from 1895 to 1900 50 per cent, of production. Imports varied between about 12 and 35 per cent of domestic supply.

Throughout the nineteenth century square timber and, especially after the American Civil War, sawn lumber had been Canada's leading staple exports. These forest products were replaced by wheat after 1900. One would expect a decline in the relative importance of exports markets for forest products from 1895 to 1905 as the domestic construction boom developed; but in view of the problem of the overstatement of quantities in the 1900 census of forest products discussed above, it is worth noting the sharpness of this decline. Perhaps it is too sharp, reflecting an understatement in our estimates for 1900 in the production of the important forest group.

The flow of construction materials at final prices. Before adjusting the apparent annual consumption of construction materials from producers' to final prices, it was necessary to eliminate the flow of construction materials to non-construction uses. The required estimates were made in the following way: construction materials used in wood-using industries were obtained from

P.I.C.F. for years after 1926, and from D.B.S., *Wood-Using Industries in Canada* (1926-27), and *Canada Year Book* from 1920 to 1925. The 1920 total was run back to 1900 for each census of manufacturing year on an index of the cost of all materials used in the same industries. Intercensal years were interpolated with an index of the production of furniture from the *Annual Census of Manufactures of Ontario.* Construction materials used in the production of iron and steel products were obtained in D.B.S., *Iron and Steel and their Products in Canada*, from 1926 to 1930 and run back to 1896 on a combined index of the value of production of agricultural implements, automobiles, railway rolling stock, and other vehicles from the production estimates of the present study. These industries accounted for 70 per cent ($11.4 million) of the construction materials used by all iron and steel industries in 1926.

To pass from value at producers' prices to value at prices paid by final users several operations should be carried through. As a first step the available domestic supply should be adjusted for changes in producers' and traders' inventories. The scattered, fragmentary data on these inventories were deemed insufficient to make these adjustments. Freight charges, sales taxes, and trade mark-ups should also be added. Lack of data forced the assumption that trade margins were a uniform percentage of the cost of sales over the period. Since the values were to be used in index form, no operation was required to implement this assumption. Dr. Kuznets adopted a similar assumption in respect to not only trade margins but also freight charges and taxes, in his overlapping decade estimates of capital formation in the United States from 1869 to 1919.[30] The Department of Reconstruction and Supply operated on the assumption that trade margins and freight charges were a constant percentage of value of construction materials at final prices in their study of capital formation in Canada, 1926 to 1941.[31] There were no marked changes in freight rates in Canada during this fifteen-year period. However, in the thirty-five years with which this study is concerned, freight rates were altered appreciably. Since the relevant data are available, the effect of this alteration upon final prices could be determined.

An index of freight rates was computed as follows: Geometric means of the commodity rates applicable to series of typical hauls were obtained from files in the Transportation Branch, Dominion Bureau of Statistics for each year from 1913 to 1930. These covered over a hundred rates and ten types of construction materials.[32] The means were converted to indexes (1926 – 100.0). A weighted average of these indexes was then computed using the relative tonnages hauled in 1926 as weights. This index covered the period of the

sharp rise in rates during the war and the downward movement
after 1920. The changes in the period before 1913 were scarcely
sufficient to affect the results. An index of freight rates compiled by
Professor Viner[33] was converted to 1913 base and used to run the
new index back to 1895.

Freight rates are on a tonnage basis. An approximate ad valorem freight rate for a single year in the early thirties used in the
Department of Reconstruction's study[34] was converted to a 1926
base by allowing for price and freight rate changes. Applying the
index of freight rates to this ad valorem rate provided an ad valorem rate in 1926 dollar terms for each year from 1896 to 1930.
Dividing by an index of construction material prices (1926 – 100.0)
yielded ad valorem freight rates in terms of current dollars. The
derivation of the index of construction material prices is explained
below.

Federal taxes on sales of construction materials by manufacturers and wholesalers, with separate rates for home-produced and
imported materials, were introduced in 1920 in an act amending the
Special War Revenue Act of 1915. The effective rates and subsequent changes in the rates and the nature of exemptions were
obtained from the statutes.[35] When changes became effective within
the year, the rate applicable to sales in the calendar year was calculated on the assumption that sales were distributed uniformly over
the year.

The results of these procedures are shown in Appendix table A.
The values of production, exports, and imports and duties less
re-exports and rebates, and the flows at producers' prices of construction materials to non-construction uses and to construction are
shown at producers' prices in current dollars. The totals at final
prices are also shown in current dollars.

The index of material prices mentioned above was derived by
linking two indexes: the D.B.S. weighted index of wholesale prices
of construction materials, 1913-30, and an index devised by combining the three unweighted indexes of wholesale prices of construction materials prepared by Dr. Coats, using weights for each index
based on the relative importance of the three groups of commodities in the domestic supply of 1908. Dr. Coats's indexes covered 48
commodities, 1890-1913. The D.B.S. index covered 32 commodities, 1913-25, and 97 commodities, 1926-31.

Reconciliation with P.I.C.F. commodity list. The *P.I.C.F.* list
of construction materials used to tabulate the production and trade
totals was altered in several respects. The following note indicates
the nature and amounts of the differences in the years from 1926 to
1930 when the two series overlap.

(a) Production

The total for 1926 in the official estimates was $371.8 million. The total of the commodities covered in the present study was $339.9 million. The components of the difference are shown in the following table.

Items excluded	Value in 1926 ($000)
Bolts, nuts, and rivets	4,596
Installations by contractors	19,055
Force-account materials	11,753
Tanks, storage	2,851
Glass fixtures	403
Piling wood	17
Total excluded items	38,675
Items added	
Unmanufactured products	6,792
Total adjustment	-31,883

The total adjustments in 1927, 1928, 1929, and 1930 were, respectively, 38.3, 43.6, 52.0, and 47.1 million dollars.

Detail of commodities excluded:

Installations by contractors: electrical instruments, anmeters, etc., fire fighting and protection equipment, lighting fixtures, hot air furnaces, builders' hardware and hardware n.e.s., heaters and water tanks (electric and gas), heating and ventilating equipment n.e.s., fire hose, boilers for heating, radiators and parts, refrigerators, (electric, domestic, and commercial), stoves (electric, gas, oil, and combination coal and electric and coal and gas), stoves and furnace pipe, super heaters and equipment;

Force-account materials: rail-welding parts, switches and accessories, switchboards, for light and power, telephone material n.e.s., transmission towers (electrical);

Glass fixtures: glass products n.e.s. including show cases, signs, and store fronts;

The unmanufactured products included were gypsum, crude and ground; slate; stone, rubble and crushed; hewn ties.

(b) Imports

The total for 1926 for construction materials in *P.I.C.F.* was $42.7

million. The total of the commodities covered in the present study was $34.2 million.

Items excluded	Value in 1926 ($000)
Sheets and plates, iron and steel	2,832
Bolts, nuts, rivets, iron and steel	417
Installations by contractors	3,156
Force-account materials	2,122
Total deductions	8,527

The deductions in 1927, 1928, 1929, and 1930 were 8.5, 11.8, 15.5, and 15.2 million dollars, respectively.

Details of commodities excluded:
Sheets, plates, hoop-band or strip coated with galvanized zinc n.o.p.;
Installations by contractors: hand fire extinguishers and automatic sprinkling systems, refrigerators (electric, domestic, or store), refrigerators n.o.p., stoves (gas, coal, oil, wood, spirits), electric heating and cooking apparatus, water pumps for domestic use, wire (iron and steel, zinc coated) and wire of all kinds n.o.p.;
Force-account materials: telegraph and telephone apparatus, transformers, wire of iron or steel n.o.p.

(c) Exports

The official estimate for exports of construction materials in 1926 was $98.6 million; that of the present study $96.4 million. The components of the difference are set forth in the following table.

Items excluded	Value in 1926 ($000)
Piling wood	315
Bolts and nuts of iron and steel	106
Installations by contractors	654
Force-account materials	1,137
Total deductions	2,212

The deductions in 1927, 1928, 1929, and 1930 were 2.0, 2.4, 2.9, and 2.2 million dollars, respectively.

3. The Value of Construction, 1896-1930

The procedures followed to raise the annual flow of construction materials to the value of total construction and the method of distributing total construction to new and repair construction were described in Section II. Kuznets assumed in his historical estimates of gross construction in the United States that the value of materials consumed was a constant percentage of the value of total construction (with both magnitudes expressed in constant dollars). The present estimates from 1896 to 1930 were based on the assumption that the ratio of wages to the material costs was 0.919, in 1913 dollars, from 1896 to the early twenties, declining thereafter to 0.647 (1913 dollars) in 1929. The result of this procedure was a fairly stable ratio of wages to materials in current dollars (see Appendix table A).

There are no reliable data to confirm or refute the assumption of a constant real ratio before 1920. Its chief support is the observation made in Section II that a series derived from the opposite assumption – a high degree of price substitution as opposed to rigid coefficients – differed by less than 5 per cent from the present one. Early construction records included a small sample of bridge building and interior decorating in 1900, to which some house building was added in 1910, and painting and glazing in 1915. These offered nothing to refute the assumption except in 1915 when the labour component reported for house building was very low. But since the overhead and profit component was correspondingly high, the adjustment implied if the data were representative would alter the components but not the level of the construction estimate for that year. The bridge company data supported the decline in the ratio from 1924 to 1929. The value of the output of these companies was relatively homogeneous and its distribution among building, engineering, and miscellaneous products fairly stable.

Until 1921 the index of materials costs was above the index of wage rates in the building trades in all years except 1913, the base year, and the two years of recession after the 1913 peak. The relative changes in the two indexes from year to year were similar. Exceptions were the two years following the peaks of 1907 and 1913 when material prices fell and slight wage gains were made, and the war years, when the material index rose somewhat more rapidly than the labour index. The index of material costs and the index of rates of wages both declined after the war, the material costs index declining more rapidly until in 1922 its relative change from the base period was the same as the relative change from the base of the wage index. Thereafter wage rates began to rise while material costs continued to fall. After 1922 the index of material costs, which had previously been above the index of wage rates, remained below the latter index for twenty years. The spread between the two, which was much more marked in the later period than the opposite spread in the earlier period, was at a maximum in 1930, with the wage index at 203.2 and the materials index at 135.5. The upward trend in wage rates was continuous throughout the whole period, but after 1920 there was a definite reversal in the trend of material costs.

The relatively higher wage rates in the late twenties may have been the result of an increased efficiency per unit of labour. If technological changes did not warrant the higher rates, and the higher rates were simply imposed by strong building trades, then it seems most likely that substitution of material input for labour would have occurred: a more economical use of labour may have been the result of higher wages. In either event the ratio of materials to labour would increase. In addition evidence may be adduced to support the impression that innovations raised the value of material costs relative to labour costs. Many materials were more highly fabricated when they reach the construction site in the later period. Higher standards of service with respect to electric lighting, refrigeration, heating and ventilating, elevators, plumbing, and so on, prevailed at the end of the period than at the beginning. The labour cost for the installation of these new construction materials was small relative to their costs as commodities.

Year-to-year comparisons of the ratios of material to labour costs in the construction census cannot be used as evidence of changes in the technological conditions governing the demands for these productive elements, because the requirements of different types of construction are different at any one time and changes in the ratio may merely reflect changes in the types of construction projects undertaken. This sort of change was evident in the censuses from 1934 to 1937 when shifts occurred from engineering to building construction and from public to private construction. Building construction required relatively less labour; and public construction was often designed to employ as many workers as possible on projects requiring few materials.

The procedure applied in this study was to establish relationships for the 1929 peak comparable to those for the 1937 and 1941 peaks – which was to assume, in effect, that technological conditions prevailing for construction in the late twenties were the same as those in the late thirties. The assumption that no improvement took place from 1930 to 1935 was plausible, in view of the inclination to return to primitive construction methods prevalent in official circles at the time and the lack of incentives to encourage investment in new equipment by contracting establishments.

8.
Investment in Machinery and Equipment

I. Definition and Classifications

ANNUAL GROSS INVESTMENT in machinery and equipment includes all expenditures made during a year by enterprise and government on new, movable durable goods for use in production. The following categories of finished durable goods exchanged during a year are excluded by the terms of the definition: existing durable assets transferred from one user to another, durable goods added to inventories of sellers, durable goods, including structures, bought by consumers, and structures bought by producers. Net investment in machinery and equipment measures the extent to which the gross additions to the stock of machinery and equipment in the possession of final users exceeds, or falls short of, the additions required to replace that part of the stock used up in the process of the year's production.

Two classifications of equipment expenditures are relevant in this study: (1) the flow of equipment to different levels of production distinguishing primary, secondary, and tertiary production and the sub-groups within each; and (2) the flow of equipment by types of equipment.

The second classification is employed in the present chapter. Although it cuts across the first to some extent, it also presents important parallels. For example, mining equipment and agricultural machinery and equipment go to sub-groups in primary production, and industrial machinery and equipment go into manufacturing. On the other hand, while the larger part of transport equipment flows to the transportation industry, much (e.g. producers' automobiles) is absorbed by other industries.

II Summary of the Method

The method employed to estimate gross investment in machinery and equipment was the supply method. The annual flow, at producers' prices, of the different types of machinery and equipment was secured from records of production, imports, exports, and re-exports. These values were adjusted to cost to final users by adding amounts for trade margins, freight charges, duties, and other taxes. The problem of setting up a classified list of machinery and equipment items was simplified by using the commodity list from P.I.C.F. as a starting point. Some minor items were dropped because they appeared to be intermediate goods or parts and some others were added because of a difference in handling machinery and equipment installed by construction contractors.[1]

The machinery and equipment items were distributed among the following classes to facilitate the tabulation of values and their adjustment to final cost:

1. Farm machinery and equipment
2. Mining and oil well machinery and equipment
3. Electrical machinery and equipment
4. Industrial machinery and equipment
5. Locomotives and railway cars
6. Vehicles and aircraft
7. Ships and boats
8. Office and store machinery and equipment
9. Professional and scientific equipment
10. Carpenters' and mechanics' tools
11. Miscellaneous durable equipment

A continuous record of imports, exports, and re-exports of machinery and equipment for the whole period was available in annual trade reports. (In this connection, it should be noted that a large proportion of the domestic consumption of machinery and equipment in Canada was imported.) Annual production records on the detailed commodity basis required were available for all years after 1920 either in publications of the Dominion Bureau of Statistics or in the files of the industrial census at the Bureau. Annual data from 1900 to 1920 were also available for the three major types of transport equipment in classes 5, 6, and 7, but not in the form required (e.g., ship production was reported to Department of National Revenue on a tonnage basis). In addition to these annual data, a production census, including all classes in its coverage, was taken in 1900, 1905, 1910, 1915, and from 1917 to 1920 inclusive. The difficulties here were, first, the problem of production in inter-censal years, and second, that the published and only available records of these censuses used a "chief product" classification.

An annual census of production for the period from 1900 to 1914 was taken in the province of Ontario. Since this province was the source of virtually all of the domestic production of the machinery and equipment in class 1 and most of the machinery and equipment in classes 2 to 4, its production records provided satisfactory interpolators. The difficulties in this census were a variation in coverage from year to year and the use of the chief-product method of classifying the output of reporting establishments.

The chief-product classifications used in the census of manufacturing from 1900 to 1920 were selected and grouped to correspond with the required classification. Values were then transcribed and tabulated for all groups. By this procedure a production series covering each census year from 1900 to 1920 was developed. It differed from the 1920 to 1930 series in scope by including an undetermined amount of consumers' and intermediate goods and repair work and by excluding some producers' durables. Furthermore, the equipment content in the various groups or classes in the earlier series matched the required classification in only four classes: 1, 5, 6, and 7. The remaining classes overlapped to some extent.

Since the two series overlapped in 1920 it was possible to determine the nature of the errors in that year. The net difference in the two estimates, the size and nature of excluded items, and the size and nature of unwanted items included in the early series were examined. Excluded items accounted for approximately 5 per cent of the total production of machinery and equipment in 1920 and were concentrated in classes 8 and 11. The net differences were large in all classes except class 1, farm machinery and equipment. They were largest in the three transport groups, (5, 6, and 7) owing to the inclusion of large amounts of repair work and repair parts. The differences were relatively great in the remaining classes owing to the inclusion of consumers' goods, especially durable consumers' goods, in the groups covering industrial and electrical equipment and semi-durable leather and rubber goods in the miscellaneous group.

Transportation equipment was the type of equipment on which the largest expenditures were made during the period of this study. The early census was abandoned as a source of data for the major items of transport equipment in classes 5, 6, and 7, because although the census estimates for carriages and wagons, small boats, and other minor vehicles were found satisfactory, for railway rolling stock automobiles, and ships, more reliable sources were available which had the additional advantage of providing annual estimates.

A wide variety of government and company records on railway development were used to make direct estimates of expenditures on railway construction, rolling stock, and other railway equipment (see Chapter XI). The direct estimates of expenditure on railway equipment were used in conjunction with series on imports and exports, which were prepared with the other trade series on equipment, to determine domestic production in this field.

Statistics on the total number and value of domestic production of automobiles were available in official sources for the years since 1904, when automobile production began. All trucks were included as producers' durables and, following the convention established in the official estimates of investment, 20 per cent of all passenger automobiles were assumed to be producers' goods.[2]

To estimate the annual production of ships, the series on tonnage of ship production mentioned above was converted to index form and an index of ship prices applied to obtain an index of the value of production. The Dominion Bureau of Statistics schedules on ship building were examined and, with the aid of a Bureau employee familiar with the records, a bench mark year was selected in which the reported data appeared most reliable. The value index was applied to the reported value of new production in the bench mark year to obtain a series covering all years from 1896 to 1930. The result was checked against the census of industry data and against imports and exports of ships. No marked discrepancy appeared in these checks.

Farm machinery and equipment comprised the largest of the remaining classes in 1920, and, by the evidence of the early census, the relative importance of this class was greater in earlier years. The error in 1920 was small, owing to the homogeneity of the early census classifications of agricultural implements. The net adjustment required to make the estimate conform to the 1920 estimate of the 1920-30 series was applied to the value of production in each year of the series from 1900 to 1919.

The same procedure was followed to adjust the remaining classes (2 to 4 and 8 to 11) in the earlier series. This method yields a tolerable result if the estimates for these smaller classes are not used separately. The method is based on an assumption (which is more likely to hold for the combination than for any one of the classes in it) that the pattern of output of the establishments covered in earlier census years was the same as in 1920.

Thus a complete picture was obtained for the three transport groups from 1900 to 1930, and for other groups in 1900, 1905, 1910, 1915, and annually from 1917. There remained the problem of interpolating inter-censal values for these other groups.

The annual census of manufacturing taken in Ontario from 1900 to 1914 provided appropriate interpolators in this period. Establishments were classified in this census by chief products and, on this basis, they were selected and arranged in groups corresponding to the grouping in the early census series described above. The problem of the variation in the coverage was partially solved by the fact that in each census the values of production both in the current year and in the preceding year were given for each reporting establishment. Two-year links were calculated for each year, and these were chained for the three periods, 1900-5, 1905-10, and 1910-14. The agreement of these indexes with the Ontario data in the national census was very close after 1905. Indexes were prepared for classes 1 to 4 and for the minor transport items, carriages and wagons. Ontario indexes were appropriate interpolators for these commodities since the bulk of the domestic production originated in that province. The differences in the quinquennial rates of change reflected in the Ontario indexes and similar rates in the national totals were distributed uniformly over the indexes. The application of these indexes provided series which, when added to the major transport series, completed the production estimates from 1900 to 1915 in all classes from 1 to 7. The remaining classes were a relatively small part of the total, and, on the assumption that their cyclical variation would correspond in direction and relative amplitude with that of classes 1 to 4, the implicit indexes for each quinquennium derived from these major classes were adjusted for the difference in trend in each case and applied to interpolate intercensal values for classes 8-11. The values of production in 1916 for all classes except 5, 6, and 7 were interpolated by prorating the relative changes in imports for each class in 1915, 1916, and 1917 over the relative change in production for each class from 1915 to 1917. This completed the production picture for all years from 1900 to 1930.

Production less exports plus imports less re-exports provided the series of domestic disappearance at producers' prices. No adjustment was made for changes in inventories. The duties paid on imports were taken off with the value of the imports. Ad valorem sales taxes appropriate to each class of equipment were secured from government statutes cited in Chapter VII. Where changes in the tax rate became effective during the year, the average effective rate for that year was calculated, on the assumption that the monthly distribution of the annual total sales were uniform.

Indexes of freight rates were obtained from D.B.S. for four important classes of durable equipment from 1913 to 1930. These were extrapolated to 1900 with an index of iron and steel freight rates calculated by Viner. Price indexes were prepared to convert the freight indexes from a weight to a value basis. The final indexes were then applied to "percentage of value" rates secured from the

Department of Trade and Commerce. (These were prepared in connection with the estimates of P.I.C.F.)

Trade mark-ups for each class of equipment were calculated in P.I.C.F. for all years after 1925 on the basis of information from the decennial census of merchandising in 1931 and 1941, and from annual surveys of the Dominion Bureau of Statistics. The average gross margins and cyclical deviations from average for each class of equipment from 1926 to 1933 were computed from these data. On the assumption that there had been no change in these averages from 1900 to 1930, the upper and lower deviants of these margins were assigned to trough and peak years, respectively, and other years were interpolated on a straight-line basis.

The components of the flow of machinery and equipment at producers' prices from 1900 to 1925 are shown in Appendix table C on an annual basis. The production estimates from 1896 to 1899 are not firm enough to be shown annually. The estimates at final prices cannot be used on an annual basis because they are not adjusted for inventory and assume a flat trend in margins. The estimates of gross investment in machinery and equipment, by major types, are shown quinquennially from 1896 to 1930 in Appendix table D.

III. Sources and Procedures

In this section the sources and procedures which were outlined in Section II are given in detail, beginning with production and proceeding through imports and duties, exports, re-exports and duty rebates, sales taxes, freight charges, and trade margins.

1. Production of Machinery and Equipment

Production statistics, 1920 to 1930. The records, with the exception of ship production, were available either in publications of the Dominion Bureau of Statistics or in the files of the General Manufactures Section of the Bureau where the results of the census of industry are kept in the form of summary schedules. It was necessary to consult these schedules for all industries except iron and steel for all years before 1926. For subsequent years the information was already tabulated and available in the files of the Department of Trade and Commerce.

Iron and Steel and their Products in Canada, published by the Dominion Bureau of Statistics since 1920, provided detailed alphabetical lists of commodities produced each year for each of twelve or thirteen industries classified under iron and steel. A single alphabetical list covering the products of all these industries was added in 1923. In early issues the production of commodities within each industry for two successive years was shown. Later a cross-classification by commodities and industries was introduced.

The iron and steel reports were the only satisfactorily detailed reports published on the census of industry in the nineteen-twenties. The summary schedules at the Dominion Bureau of Statistics had to be consulted for the following data: manufactures of non-ferrous metal products; manufactures of wood-using industries, including the boat building industry, carriages and wagons, the furniture industry, and miscellaneous wood industries; the container industry; manufactures of leather goods, of rubber goods, and of cordage, rope, and twine. The importance of these industries was relatively small. Iron and steel predominated in all classes except the electrical equipment class, in which non-ferrous metal products were more important, and the miscellaneous class. Wood products entered into class 6 (carriages and wagons), into class 7 (small boats), and into class 8 (office furniture and store fixtures). Leather harness and saddlery were prominent in class 1, and items from the schedules on leather, rubber, and cordage, rope, and twine accounted for more than half the value of class 11 (in 1925).

All iron and steel and part of leather saddlery was allocated to farm equipment. It was assumed that 50 per cent of leather harness and saddlery was allocable to consumer durables prior to 1920, and that this percentage declined uniformly to zero through the decade of the twenties as the automobile came into common use. The same convention was applied to buggies and pleasure carts, which, although largely farm equipment, were included in class 6. Twenty per cent of passenger automobiles were classified as producers' durables. This was the allocation made in the official estimates of capital formation on the basis of information in the decennial census of 1931 and 1941.

The Dominion Bureau of Statistics records of iron and steel ship production were inconsistent and incomplete owing to a change in classification of the industry and to the loss of some records. The summary schedules for 1920 covered iron and steel as well as wooden ship building in considerable detail and the value of finished ships was taken for that year. The volume of production of ships, in numbers and total tonnage, was reported in *Shipping Reports of the Department of National Revenue*. According to officials of the Department, this series, which covered the period from 1900 to 1930, was accurate and consistent. The tonnage series was converted from fiscal to calendar years, on the assumption of uniform monthly production, and applied in index form on a 1920 base to the value of ship production in that year to obtain a value series in constant dollars for all years from 1900 to 1930. An index of ship prices covering this period in the United States was taken from Shaw's *Commodity Output since 1869* and adjusted for variations in Canadian duties on recorded ship imports. The coefficient of variation was calculated for each year from the following formula: one plus the ratio of the duty paid to the value of recorded ship imports. Shaw's index was multiplied by this coefficient and the resulting index applied to the tonnage ship production series.

Production statistics, 1900 to 1920. Annual estimates were made for the major transport items in classes 5, 6, and 7. Since the series on railway equipment is included among the direct estimates described in Chapter XI it need not concern us here. The minor items, including small boats, drays, wagons, carts, buggies, etc., were adequately treated in the quinquennial census and are dealt with in part (b) below. Part (a) deals with automobiles. Ships and vessels before 1920 were based on the National Revenue series described above. Part (c) covers the use of the Ontario census and the interpolation of inter-censal years for the remaing classes.

(a) Automobiles

Automobile production began in Canada in 1904. Complete records from 1917 on a calendar year basis were reported in early issues of *Iron and Steel and their Products* for passenger automobiles and trucks. Both numbers and values were given. The total number produced prior to 1917 and an estimate of their total value were also given, but an intensive search failed to turn up the annual distribution of these aggregates. Production in this early period was not large and a variety of data was available to make a reliable allocation of the totals. (The quinquennial census reported automobiles separately for the first time in 1910. Their value of production in that year was $6.3 million, of which less than 2 million would be producers' durables.)

The following data were taken from issues of *Iron and Steel and their Products in Canada*: total numbers of cars registered each year in Canada since 1906; numbers and values of cars imported, exported, and re-exported since 1904; numbers withdrawn from use annually since 1917; and numbers produced annually since 1917. Since use of automobiles was negligible before 1904, the oldest car in the country in 1917 would be twelve years old. Withdrawals were assumed zero before 1912 and calculated for subsequent years on the basis of a straight-line interpolation from 1912 to 1917. From these data the number of cars produced in each year was easily determined (assuming that all car owners complied with registration laws). An annual average price per unit of production was calculated by running back the average unit price for 1917 with an index of the average price of exported units. This price was then applied to the volume series to estimate the annual value of production.

The total number and total value of production obtained for these early years in this way were 134,792 and $96.1 million, respectively, which compared closely with the 135,000 and $100 million reported in *Iron and Steel and their Products*. The close agreement in numbers suggests that the Dominion Bureau of Statistics figure was not a record but an estimate made by the same method as the one described above. The reliability of the estimates depends largely on the reliability of the series on registrations. Withdrawals were a small component, and a large relative error in their estimation would have a small absolute effect on the totals. One would expect considerable evasion of registration laws in any one year, but the possibility of any one car escaping registration throughout a period of ten years is so small, as to be negligible. This implies that the total for the period is reliable but its annual distribution questionable. An index of car production based on the quinquennial census was compared with an index based on the annual estimates: indexes of output by the former for 1920, 1915, and 1910, respectively, were 100.0, 23.4, and 5.0; and by the latter, 100.0, 23.7, and 2.9. The annual series was adjusted from 1912 back by redistributing the annual totals in the following way: an amount taken from 1911 (which appeared too high relative to 1912-13) was allocated to 1910, 1909, and 1908 in the proportions 3:2:1. This arbitrary adjustment raised 1910 to the level indicated in the quinquennial census and made the rate of change from 1908 to 1913 conform to the rate of change in exports through this period. An adjustment was also made in the earlier estimates to correct for the bias in registration statistics, but these changes were too small to show in results rounded to millions and need not be described.

The number of trucks produced before 1918 was estimated on the bases of (i) the number of trucks and passenger cars registered in 1920, (ii) the number of trucks and passenger cars produced from 1917 to 1920, and (iii) interpreting the series on withdrawals as though the average length of life of trucks were the same as that of other cars. On the assumption that the ratio of trucks to all cars produced was the same each year as for all years prior to 1918, the annual totals before 1918 were broken down between truck and passenger cars. The flat percentage applied was 9 per cent. (Truck production was approximately 9, 7.5, and 9 per cent of total production in 1918, 1919, and 1920, respectively.)

(b) The census of manufacturing, 1900 to 1920

The census of manufacturing was taken quinquennially for calendar years from 1900 to 1915 and annually from 1917 to 1920. It was the primary source of the estimates of production of all types of machinery and equipment before 1920, except the major items of transport equipment. The implications of the degree of reliability of the census for the estimates of production may be judged by a consideration of the value of the part of total production derived from it. The following table shows the breakdown for 1920.

Value in 1920 of Components Derived from the Census

Class	Type of equipment	Value of production ($000,000)
1	Farm	41.8
2	Mining	1.5
3	Electric Power	11.1
4	Industrial	29.7
8	Office and store	14.3
9	Professional and scientific	.5
10	Minor tools	6.0
11	Miscellaneous	16.4
5, 6, and 7	Producers' transport equipment (minor items)	6.1
	Total	127.4

All other Producers' Machinery and Equipment

Class	Type of equipment	Value of production ($000,000)
5	Railway	34.1
6	Vehicles	24.3
7	Ships and vessels	30.9
	Total	89.3

(The value of production of consumers' automobiles in 1920 was $64.5 million.)

Thus of a total production of machinery and equipment of $216.7 million in 1920, the equipment items that are estimated from the census in earlier years account for $127.4 million, or just under 60 per cent. The earliest year for which accurate statistics are available for making this comparison is 1920, but in that year the output of motor vehicles and ships almost certainly comprises a greater proportion of the total production than it did before the war. Since the earlier estimates are themselves in question a similar comparison based upon them to indicate the extent of this shift would be of little value.

It has already been observed that the classification in the early census was by chief products. As a result the totals reflected in the initial estimates from this source were too high. The amount and components of the error were precisely known for 1920, the terminal year in the early series. Furthermore, a distribution of products among the eleven classes was impossible in the early period, with the result that group sub-totals in the initial estimates did not match the classes followed in tabulating the import, export, and later production statistics. Some classes did match: class 1, for example, and also the minor and major components of classes 5, 6, and 7. (The major components were also taken off to serve as rough checks of the annual estimates made from other source material.)

The most satisfactory classifications in the early census were of farm equipment. With a product of $41.8 million, farm equipment was the most important class in 1920, accounting for almost 20 per cent of all machinery and equipment produced in that year, and for 33 per cent of that part of the total based on the early census (cf. table above). In years prior to 1920 its relative importance was even greater. The adjustment to the early census estimate for 1920 was $5.9 million (47.7-41.8). The excess was made up of unfinished goods, repair parts, and some custom repair work performed by establishments in the agricultural implements industry. The same relative adjustment was applied to the initial estimates for 1900, 1905, 1910, and 1915. Detailed commodity statistics were available for 1917, 1918, and 1919, for approximately 80 per cent of total output (basis 1920) in issues of *Iron and Steel and their Products*, and the summary schedules at Dominion Bureau of Statistics supplied data to complete the estimates in these years.

Of the remaining classes, 3, 4, 8, and 11 were the most important, and the adjustment in these for 1920 averaged 40 per cent. To make the adjustments in years before 1920, the components of the various classes were reclassified to fit the early census groups: the iron and steel components of classes 3, 4, 8, 10, and 11 were combined; the non-ferrous metal components of classes 3 and 4 were combined; and the leather, rubber, and cordage components of class 11 were treated separately. The adjustments for the wooden component of class 8 and for the rubber goods component of class 11 greatly exceeded 50 per cent; the census series applicable to these were therefore abandoned. They were extrapolated on the assumption that their relative position in their class in 1920 reflected their relative importance in the previous six census years. Production of professional and scientific equipment, class 9, was negligible before 1917. Its value in 1920 was only $.5 million, which was extrapolated to 1917 on a basis of exports.

The combination of the various components of the different classes necessary to this stage of the procedure explains the classification presented in Appendix tables C and D. It was necessary to use the elevenfold classification to estimate freights and trade margins,[3] but such detailed estimates are too weak to stand alone. The broader estimates of production for these classes combined are weak enough. Fortunately, they comprised less than half of the total production of machinery and equipment, and domestic production of these classes is less important than imports in the total domestic supply.

The product classifications in the early census were much more detailed at the end of the period than at the beginning. In the various census reports, the items included in the product categories were listed in appendixes. To ensure a consistent coverage in the initial series from 1900 to 1920, the broad categories in the 1900 census were taken as the standard and subsequent reclassification in the census was related to it by careful analysis of the changes in classifications as these occurred. It would have been possible to work back from 1920 and break down the values reported under the broadening categories on the basis of the nearest – always a later – census instead of making all adjustments on the basis of 1920. However, it is doubtful whether this time-consuming procedure would greatly improve the results. It implies the assumption of a variety of patterns instead of the simple assumption of one. The detail in 1920 was so much greater than in any earlier year that its pattern would dominate throughout. In other words the multiplicity of assumptions would imply greater variety of pattern than could be actually achieved. In any event, the procedure would not have altered the estimates for agricultural implements and transportation equipment and, since these are the only components in the total which are used separately in this study, the simpler method was adopted.

(c) Interpolations: use of the Ontario census

The Ontario census covered production of classes 1, 2, 3, 4, and carriages and wagons, employing a product classification which corresponded to their coverage in the national census. The application of the chain indexes computed from the Ontario census is illustrated in the following table which shows the index of production of agricultural implements in Ontario for the three five-year periods from

1900 to 1915, an index of national production in the first and fifth years of the same periods, and the final indexes used to interpolate the inter-censal values of production of agricultural implements.

Agricultural Implements

Year	Chain indexes for Ontario	Indexes of national production	Indexes used
1900	100.0	100.0	100.0
1901	121.7	—	116.6
1902	144.8	—	134.6
1903	158.0	—	142.7
1904	161.0	—	140.6
1905	156.0	130.5	130.5
1905	100.0	100.0	100.0
1906	108.4	—	108.4
1907	111.4	—	111.4
1908	113.7	—	113.7
1909	156.9	—	156.9
1910	165.7	165.8	165.8
1910	100.0	100.0	100.0
1911	102.1	—	102.1
1912	126.1	100.0	126.1
1913	160.0	—	160.0
1914	124.6	—	124.6
1915	—	62.0	62.0

The Ontario establishments reporting to the national census produced approximately 95 per cent of all production of agricultural implements in 1905 and 1910. Two observations may be made respecting the very close agreement in the change in the Ontario and the national indexes from 1905 to 1910 and the wide disparity from 1900 to 1905. The latter is due to the small coverage of the Ontario census before 1905 (according to the national census the trend in output in Ontario did not differ greatly from the national trend). The bias in the Ontario index was assumed to emerge by a uniform annual increment through the period: the series 5.1, 10.2, 15.3, 20.4, 25.5 was deducted from the Ontario index from 1901 to 1905.

Since the change in the Ontario index from 1905 to 1910 was very nearly the same as the change reflected in the national estimates, no adjustment was made to the Ontario index either for the intervening years or for the years following 1910.

The carriages and wagons indexes for Ontario were similarly

Carriages and Wagons

Year	Ontario index	National index
1900	100.0	100.0
1905	166.0	118.3
1905	100.0	100.0
1910	148.6	149.5

biased in the period before 1905 and representative in the period from 1905 to 1910:

Classes 2, 3, and 4 were interpolated together, using an Ontario index covering production of foundries and machine shops from

Industrial, Mining, and Electrical Equipment

Year	Ontario index	National index
1900	100.0	100.0
1905	199.8	162.0
1905	100.0	100.0
1910	196.1	201.7

1900 to 1905, and an index covering producers of "engines and machinery" thereafter. Again the change in the Ontario index was close to the national index from 1905 to 1910 and divergent, although relatively less so, from 1900 to 1905.

The differences in both periods were distributed uniformly over the Ontario index to secure the interpolators.

Classes 8, 10, and 11 accounted for 4.0, 4.7, and 7.2 per cent, respectively, of machinery and equipment production in 1900, and their relative importance was only slightly increased in 1905, 1910, and 1915. These minor classes and small boats were the only ones for which no direct material for interpolation could be found. Small boats were interpolated with the larger items in their class, and 8, 10, and 11 were interpolated on the basis of the total of classes 1 to 4 plus producers' carriages and wagons. The method applied in each case was, first, to determine the ratio of production of the minor group in question to the production of the appropriate major group in each national census year. Inter-censal ratios expressed as percentages were then interpolated on a straight-line basis and applied to the major series to derive the required values for the minor group for inter-censal years. For example, the value of production of office and store equipment was 7.48 per cent of the total value of production of classes 1 to 4 plus minor vehicles in 1905, and 7.86 per cent in 1910. Its relative values in the intervening years were assumed to increase from the former to the latter percentage by uniform increments. This same method was used to break down the annual values of classes 2, 3, and 4, which were interpolated as a single group from 1900 to 1915. It will be noted that only the distribution among these classes of a known total value in each year was effected by this method. This breakdown was made because, owing to rather wide differences in freight rates and trade margins appropriate to different classes of machinery and equipment, an improvement in the final results could be obtained by even a rough approximation to the relative size of the different classes in each year. No such arbitrary device was required with imports of machinery and equipment because these were available by classes throughout the whole period. The breakdown of production for those classes which were combined to effect the adjustments which comparison of the national census series from 1900 to 1920 with the accurate series beginning in 1920 seemed to indicate were necessary was made on the basis of the distribution of the components in the production of 1920.

2. Imports and Duties, Re-exports and Duty Rebates, and Exports of Machinery and Equipment

The description of the Canadian trade statistics in Chapter VII need not be repeated. The practice of mixing parts and machinery in the tariff classifications is the matter requiring attention here. The following notes indicate the importance of imports of machinery and equipment and describe the extent of mixed classifications in the trade reports and the methods adopted to separate them.

The importance of imports in the domestic supply of machinery and equipment is indicated in the following table which shows imports less re-exports as a percentage of the domestic disappearance of machinery and equipment at producers' prices.

Years	Percentage imports of domestic supply
1900	34.2
1910	39.4
1920	34.0
1930	44.0

All trade statistics were tabulated for fiscal years. Duty rebates on re-exports were calculated by applying the ratio of duty paid to value of imports for the appropriate type of equipment to value of re-exports. Imports plus duty less re-exports plus duty rebates and exports were converted to calendar years on the assumption of uniform monthly distribution of fiscal year totals. Seasonal variations were much less marked in these series than in construction materials. Tests of the method, with data for the late twenties and thirties when totals on both bases were available, indicated a very small error in all years except the turning points. The error was as high as 4 and 6 per cent in 1933-34 and 1929-30. This suggests that such interpolations should be used with caution in the discussion of cycles. However, even in these unusual years, the method did not shift the turning points.

The values reported for all classifications of machinery and parts were taken off and three totals obtained in the initial tabulations: machinery and equipment, parts, and machinery and parts. The following table shows the value of the first of these totals in 1900 and 1920 as a percentage of the final estimate of the total of all imports of machinery and equipment. The difference between this percentage and 100.0 per cent indicates the proportion of the final totals derived from mixed classifications in the trade reports.

Year	Percentage of total imports classified on required basis
1900	66.2
1920	66.6

Fifty per cent of the mixed classification of machinery and parts was taken to be finished machinery in all cases except one. The single exception was the tariff classification "all other machinery of iron and steel and parts thereof" of which 75 per cent was taken, owing to the wide variety of equipment included (cf. tariff classification 453 in *Annual Report*, Department of Trade and Commerce, 1910). These simple procedures were found to approximate the breakdown of machinery and parts for those classifications which were broken down in later years in the trade reports.

Total exports were not large and the extent of mixed classifications was of about the same relative magnitude as in imports. Mixed classifications in earlier years were broken down into the categories established in the earliest year for which the trade reports provided a breakdown. If a breakdown had never been made, 75 per cent of the total was taken as finished machinery: this percentage corresponded to the typical breakdowns made on the basis of later detail for other exports. The range of possible adjustment was never broad enough to affect the final estimates of the flow of machinery and equipment appreciably.

Of the mixed classifications only one was large enough to affect the totals significantly; this classification, vehicles (chiefly automobiles), was not broken down into producers' and consumers' until the final flow of vehicles was determined. Two mixed classifications were ignored in the earlier years: wooden and metal office and store furniture, which accounted for perhaps 10 per cent of totals of furniture imports never exceeding two million dollars.

3. From Producers' Prices to Cost to Final Users

Taxes. Import taxes were reported with the values of imports and were included in estimates at producers' prices. The statutes covering other taxes were cited in the previous chapter. Mr. A. F. MacMillan, Chief of the Excise Division of the Department of National Revenue, was kind enough to check the writers interpretations of the statutes. The effective ad valorem sales taxes, expressed as percentages of values at producers' prices, on automobiles beginning with 1918 were as follows: 6.7, 10.0, 14.0, 15.0, 7.5, and in 1923 and thereafter to 1930, 5.0 per cent; on all other domestically produced and non-exempted machinery and equipment beginning with 1920: 1.5, 3.7, 5.3, 6.0, 5.3, 5.0, 5.0, 4.0, 3.0, 3.0, and 1.3 per cent. The following exemptions were made: boats for use in the fisheries, and fishermen's supplies from May 24, 1922; all mining machinery, virtually all agricultural implements, and professional and scientific equipment from April 11, 1924.

Freight charges. The study of freight rates in Canada, available in the files of the Transportation Branch, Dominion Bureau of Statistics, covered that part of the period after 1900 during which marked changes in the level of freight charges took place. Among the various components of this study were four classifications related to producers' durables: iron and steel manufactured products; automobiles and trucks; agricultural implements; and furniture, including wooden and metal office and store furniture. Geometric means of commodity rates applicable to a series of typical hauls for a wide range of commodities in each of the four classifications were calculated annually from 1913 to 1930. These series were converted to index form, base 1913, and run back to 1900 with the index of freight rates prepared by Viner.[4] The four series were then converted to a 1926 base. Since each index of freight rates was based on weight, appropriate price indexes were needed to convert the indexes to an ad valorem basis. The following price indexes were devised:

(a) Automobiles and trucks

The series on numbers of trucks and automobiles produced, exported, imported, and re-exported, described above in part 1 of this section, were revalued using the average prices of production of exports, of re-exports, and of imports (value plus duty) in 1926. Application of the supply formula (production less exports plus imports less re-exports) yielded two series in 1926 prices. Dividing these series into the series of domestic disappearance of trucks and automobiles yielded two indexes of prices: one for trucks, another for passenger automobiles.

(b) Agricultural implements

Quantities and average unit prices of domestic production of 24 principal farm implements from 1917 to 1930 were reported in issues of *Iron and Steel and Their Products*. The implements represented 63 per cent of total production of finished agricultural machinery and equipment in 1926: three types of harrows, eight types of plows, binders, reapers, threshers, cultivators, hay mowers, seed drills, scufflers, corn planters, hay loaders, hay rakes, manure spreaders, windmills, and fanning mills. Two series, one with current unit prices and one with 1926 unit prices, were calculated and the implicit price index derived. An index of prices of imported agricultural implements was used to extrapolate this index to 1900.

The extrapolator was devised by splicing two indexes. The first of these covered the period from 1900 to 1913 and was calculated from an index of the value of imported agricultural implements in current prices and an index of their value in constant prices appearing in Taylor, *Statistical Contributions to Canadian Economic History*. Taylor's indexes were adjusted from fiscal to calendar years by straight-line interpolation. This index of import prices was extended to overlap the index of prices of domestically produced agricultural implements by using an index of United States prices of farm implements adjusted for variations in the ratio of duty paid by Canadian importers to the declared value of farm implements imported. The United States index appeared in December issues of *Wholesale Prices*, Bureau of Labour Statistics, Washington, D.C.

(c) Producers' equipment

An index of wholesale prices of producers' equipment, 1913 to 1930, appeared in the annual Dominion Bureau of Statistics publication *Prices and Price Indexes*. It was spliced to a similar index, 1900 to 1913, from R. H. Coats, *Cost of Living Report*. These indexes covered some finished producers' goods but a great many unfinished commodities were also included.

This last index was used for classes 2 to 4 and 8 to 11. The freight index for iron and steel manufactures was used in all these classes except 8, where the freight index for furniture was applied. The first and second price indexes were combined with the freight indexes for trucks and automobiles and agricultural implements in classes 1 and 6. No freight charges were added in classes 5 and 7 (railway rolling stock and ships and vessels). Indexes of freight rates were divided by the assigned price indexes to yield indexes of ad valorem freight charges for each class. The freight charges appropriate to each class in 1926 were secured from the files of the National Income Unit, Dominion Bureau of Statistics, and these, expressed as percentages of the 1926 values of domestic disappearance at producers' prices, were extended to all years by applying the indexes of ad valorem freights. Freight charges were then calculated by applying these percentages.

The price indexes devised for vehicles and farm implements reflect variations in unit prices with reasonable accuracy. The quality aspect of the index number problem is not relevant here. It is the weight of the average unit in different years which matters. If an index of the variations in the weight of the average unit could be combined with an index of the variations in the price of the average unit, the resulting index would meet the demands of the present problem. The method employed assumes that the variation in weight was not an important factor, and for automobiles and the major types of farm implements some evidence could be adduced to support this assumption. There are detailed data on tonnage hauled by the railroads which could be incorporated in the estimates, but the effort involved in incorporating them would scarcely be repaid since the freight component is a small part of the final total. It may be noted that estimates for freight in classes 1, 5, 6, and 7 are not affected by the Dominion Bureau of Statistics-Coats index of producers' equipment, which is the least appropriate of the price indexes used.

Trade margins. Effective gross margins for each class of equipment were taken from a study made by the National Income Unit, Dominion Bureau of Statistics, for the period from 1926 to 1941. The average gross margins from 1926 to 1933 were applied to the respective classes for all earlier years, on the assumption that the range of cyclical deviations from 1926 to 1933 would hold for the whole period. The latter assumption is not of great importance since the deviations, relative to the margins, do not exceed plus or minus five per cent. The average margins, which are shown below were small in all major classes except 1 and 5. The assumption of a flat trend is more important to the reliability of the result, and in this connection nothing can be said either to support or to refute the assumption. The margins give some indication of the size of the component handled in this arbitrary fashion.

Class	1	2	3	4	5, 6, 7	8	9	10	11
Average gross margin (%)	31.5	10.5	9.0	14.0	26.5	36.0	37.5	39.0	19.5

These averages conceal the complexity of their components. The study from which they were taken analysed decennial census material for 1930 and 1940 and a variety of sample data collected by the Merchandising and Services Branch, Dominion Bureau of Statistics, to determine the various trade channels between domestic producers and importers, on the one hand, and final users, on the other. The same sources provided information on trade mark-ups, commissions, and other selling costs appropriate for each type of intermediary active in the various trade channels. Allowance was also made for trade discounts. The results of these calculations are taken here in gross margin form. In each class and in each year the derived margin was subtracted from 100.0 per cent and the result divided into the sum of three estimates to yield investment at cost to final users. The three estimates that were combined before this final step were the value of the equipment at producers' prices, the sales taxes paid by manufacturers, wholesalers, importers, and other dealers, and the charge for freight. It is the arbitrariness of this final adjustment for margins which precludes reliance on annual estimates of gross investment in machinery and equipment. In Appendix table D these estimates are shown for five-year periods only.

9.
Investment in Inventories

I. Definitions and Classifications

THE ADDITION of net investment in inventories to total expenditures on structures and machinery and equipment yields gross domestic capital formation. Inventories are the stockpiles of goods held throughout the country by producers and governments in the form of raw materials, goods in process, or finished good. Inventories in the hands of consumers are excluded by the definition of investment followed in this study.

Inventories may be conveniently subdivided into the following categories:

    (a) Farm inventories
        (1) Livestock on farms
        (2) Grain on farms
    (b) Grain in commercial channels
    (c) Business inventories
        (1) Manufacturing
        (2) Wholesaling
        (3) Retailing
        (4) Miscellaneous

The volume of inventories is defined as the total book value of these stocks at any point in time. "Investment in inventories" is commonly used to mean either the change in value or the value of the physical change in inventories. The latter definition is used here. Investment or disinvestment in inventories is the physical change, in the sense of actual additions to or subtractions from the physical stock in a given period, valued at current prices.

II. Summary of Methods

The definition of investment in inventories required end-of-year inventories in either physical quantities or constant dollars and the average prices prevailing during the period for which the estimate of the investment outlay was made. These data were secured on an annual basis for the bulk of the inventories over a large part of the period from 1900 to 1930. Estimates for the remaining inventories were made on a quinquennial basis.

The estimates of inventory investment are the least reliable of the four major components of gross investment. Some records of farm inventories were available before 1915; but the manufacturing inventories from 1900 to 1910 were secured by a crude assumption with respect to their share in working capital, and the trade inventories were assumed to bear a constant relation (over a period of twenty-five years) to the total of export and import commodity trade. (It is worth noting that before 1915, when the inventory records were least satisfactory, inventories accounted for 20 to 22 per cent of the estimated gross capital formation. They were relatively less important after 1915). Furthermore, some complex questions are necessarily ignored by the methods employed; e.g., the role of speculation in agricultural inventories, and the valuation methods of manufacturers.

1. Livestock on Farms

Annual records of the numbers of the various types of livestock on all farms and of average farm prices were available from 1907 to 1930 inclusive, and for 1891 and 1901, in federal government sources. Provincial records covering over half of the inventories and the prairie census for 1905 were used to interpolate the national totals in the other years. The several series were adjusted from census dates to December 31 by straight-line interpolation and appropriate prices applied to the annual physical changes.

2. Grain on Farms

Annual data on stocks of wheat, rye, barley, oats, and flax on farms, from 1909 to 1930, and average farm prices appeared in official sources. The stocks were for March 31 in each year. Marketings of grain by farmers in the first three months of each year were obtained from records back to 1919. The only record of farm grain stocks before 1909 was for wheat in 1905. Year-end stocks of all grains in 1895 and 1900, and for coarse grains in 1905, were estimated from production of each type of grain for those years. Annual physical changes after 1909 were valued by the average farm prices for each year. The physical changes from 1895 to 1900, 1900 to 1905, and 1905 to 1908 were valued with an average of the annual prices (weighted by the annual crops in the case of wheat) in each interval.

3. Grain in Commercial Channels

Bushels of wheat, oats, barley, flax, and rye in store at the several terminal points (country elevators, interior terminals, Vancouver terminals, Lakehead terminals, eastern terminals, United States lake and Atlantic ports) were given in an official source back to 1920. Annual data back to 1910 were obtained from various official sources. Information on wheat was available back to 1905. Estimates of all grains in store in 1895 and 1900 and of coarse grains in 1905 were made on the basis of production statistics and the relationship between annual production and the December 31 stock in later years.[1]

Two adjustments were necessary in the price series for wheat. The prices were adjusted for the freight differentials prevailing each year between the several terminals and for the annual variations in the average quality of the crop.

4. Manufacturing Inventories

Total book values of manufacturing inventories at December 31 appeared in the *Census of Manufacturing* or were obtained in D.B.S. files for 1915 and each year from 1917. These values were assumed to represent the lower of cost or market price and were therefore revalued to December 31 market prices in all years when prices were rising during the last months of the year. Following the method of P.I.C.F., the average length of life in days of the inventory was estimated as the ratio of the inventory to the average of raw materials costs and the value of gross output times the number of days in the year. The book value was then raised by the relative increase in prices during this turn-over interval in each year requiring adjustment. With all book values expressed in year-end prices, the end-of-year book values were deflated, by using an index series based on December 31 prices, and the annual changes were expressed in current values by applying an index series based on average annual prices.

Appropriate price indexes were not available. The year-end price index used was an average of D.B.S. December and January indexes of wholesale prices. These monthly index numbers were also used to calculate the relative price increases in revaluing inventories from cost to market in years of rising prices. The annual price index used to convert the values of the changes from constant to current dollars was the D.B.S. annual index of wholesale prices (simple averages of their monthly series).

The investment in manufacturing inventories from 1900 to 1915 was estimated for each five-year period. The census of manufacturing reported only total working capital (inventories plus cash and receivables) for 1900, 1905, and 1910. The ratio of inventories to working capital apparent in the 1915 census (about one-half) was applied to estimate the earlier stocks. Wholesale price series were used to deflate the book values, and simple quinquennial averages of annual wholesale price indexes were used to express the change in each five-year period in current prices.

5. Coverage of the Estimates Based on Records

All the estimates of inventory investment described thus far were based on records of some kind. The trade and miscellaneous inventories are much less reliable. In view of this fact their relative importance at the end of the period under review is worth noting. They were probably of less relative importance with respect to total inventories in the early years because of the dominance of farming among all industries.

Relative Size of Inventories, by Types, 1926-30
(percentages of total book values)

	1926	1927	1928	1929	1930
Livestock on farms	24.6	25.0	25.3	24.5	23.8
Grain on farms	8.2	9.8	8.4	5.0	4.8
Grain in commercial channels	5.7	5.7	6.7	9.1	4.9
Manufacturing	27.6	27.5	27.4	28.1	31.9
Sub-total (1 plus 2 plus 3 plus 4)	66.1	68.0	67.8	66.7	65.4
Trade	29.7	28.4	28.5	29.5	29.7
Miscellaneous	4.2	3.6	3.7	3.8	4.9
Sub-total (6 plus 7)	33.9	32.0	32.2	33.3	34.6
Grand total	100.0	100.0	100.0	100.0	100.0

(*Source:* P.I.C.F.)

6. Wholesale, Retail, and Miscellaneous Inventories

It was assumed that wholesale and retail inventories would vary with the general level of trade activity. Their relation to the sum of commodity imports and exports in each year from 1926 to 1930 was fairly stable. The average relationship in this five-year period was applied to the average of the sum of calendar year imports and exports in 1900-1, 1905-6, 1910-11, 1915-16, and 1920-21 to secure year-end estimates of trade inventories for 1900, 1905, 1910, 1915, and 1920. These values were deflated with year-end wholesale price indexes, and the five-year differences converted to current prices with a simple average of annual wholesale price-index numbers for each quinquennia. Book values for miscellaneous inventories were assumed to bear the same relation to the total book values of all inventories in the earlier years as on the average from 1926 to 1930 (about 4 per cent).

Appendix table E shows the investment in inventories, by types, from 1895 to 1930. Table F shows the total book values of inventories at December 31, by types, for selected years from 1900 to 1930.

III. Sources and Procedures

1. Livestock on Farms

Numbers of milk cows, other cattle, horses, sheep, and swine, as estimated by crop correspondents at June 1 appeared in *Monthly Bulletins of Agricultural Statistics,* D.B.S., 1919-26, and in *Livestock and Animal Products,* an annual publication included in Dominion Sessional Papers from 1909 to 1918. Slight revisions were made to bring these series into closer conformity with decennial census records in *Quarterly Bulletins of Agricultural Statistics,* D.B.S. A recent edition (1944) gave totals for 1907-11.

Provincial sources included *Annual Reports,* Department of Agriculture and Immigration, Manitoba, from 1892 to 1907, and *Annual Reports of* (Ontario) *Bureau of Industry,* 1890-1911. Interpolations for the prairie were based on censuses of 1891, 1901, and 1905 and the annual series for Manitoba, and, for the rest of the country, on the decennial census of 1891 and 1901 and the annual series for Ontario.

Price series back to 1911 were "average values per head, on the farm" as reported by crop correspondents. (Cf. *M.B.A.S.,* February 1927, 51, and *L.A.P., 1911-141*) These series were run back to 1895 using Ontario farm prices as indexes (values per head of stock on farms at June 15, from *Annual Reports*, Statistics Branch, Department of Agriculture, Ontario).

2. Grain Inventories

(a) In commercial channels

Quantities of wheat, oats, barley, rye, and flax in store at the several terminals for the week ending nearest December 31 were taken from January issues of *Monthly Bulletin of Agricultural Statistics*, D.B.S., back to 1920.

Negligible Vancouver stocks before 1920 were ignored. Stocks at interior terminals back to 1916, at Lakehead terminals back to 1904, and at eastern terminals back to 1909 for December 31 were published in *Weekly Reports*, Commercial Intelligence Branch, Department of Trade and Commerce, 1906 to 1920. The first interior terminal was built in 1915. Stocks of a small group of "private" elevators at Lakehead, not available at December before 1920, were determined for December 31 on the basis of relative stocks in March of each year (cf. below) and monthly shipments and receipts.

Stocks in store at country elevators prior to 1920 were for March 31, reported in *Census and Statistics Monthly* (Ottawa, annual) to 1916 and M.B.A.S., 1917 to 1920. No records of monthly receipts and shipments could be found. The following technique was used to adjust these March stocks to December 31: *Net* receipts of western terminals for January, February, and March were taken as gross shipments of country elevators. Their first-quarter receipts from farms were estimated by applying an average of "first-quarter receipts to crops" in later years to current crops. March stock plus first-quarter shipments minus first-quarter receipts yields inventories at December 31.

No attempt was made to get annual series before 1910. A November wheat stock for country elevators and an April stock for terminals for 1905 were obtained from *Weekly Reports*, June 11, 1906. Earlier wheat stocks and stocks of coarse grains for 1895, 1900, and 1905 were taken as a fraction of the respective crops, the fraction in each case being the average of the total year-end stock over crop in each year from 1910 to 1914. The total stocks were then distributed to the various points – farm, country, and terminals – on the basis of the December distribution of total stocks in later years.

The cost of freight on wheat shipments between the various points in the distributive channels were taken from Mackintosh, *Economic Problems of the Prairie Provinces*, Appendix A, Table 5. A table on page 26 of the same source gave the percentage of the wheat crop which graded No. 3 or better in each year. Average price differentials between grades were secured from the Farm Management Department, University of Saskatchewan. Using the No. 1 Northern price, Fort William and Port Arthur, as base, the differentials were applied taking the average of the crop as No. 2 if 80 per cent were grade 3 or better, No. 3 if 50 to 80 per cent were grade 3 or better, and No. 4 if under 50 per cent were grade 3 or better.

Prices of wheat (No. 1 Northern), oats (No. 2 C.W.), barley (No. 3 C.W.), flax (N.W. Man. No. 1), and rye (Ont. No. 2) are from D.B.S., *Prices and Price Indexes,* annual issues, for years since 1913, and from Coats, *Cost of Living Report,* for 1895-1913.

(b) Grain on farms

Stocks of all grains on farms at March 31 each year appear in April issues of M.B.A.S. from 1916 to 1930, and C.S.M. from 1909 to 1915. Marketings in January, February, and March from 1920 to 1930 are reported in *Grain Trade Year Books,* S. Evans Statistical Service, Winnipeg, for wheat, barley and oats. Flax and rye stocks are not large. March figures were taken as nearest year-end.

In both 1915 and 1920, 78 per cent of the total wheat crop was marketed by March 31 of the following year. It was therefore assumed that the percentage of the crop marketed in the first quarter in 1921 could be used to adjust the March 31, 1916, stock back to December 31, 1915. The same method of adjustment was used for 1910. The total change for each five-year period was then prorated to each year in the period on the basis of the annual changes in the March 31 series covering the same five years.

For oats, March stocks in 1911, 1916 and 1921 were adjusted for December 1910, 1915, and 1920 by adding back rough estimates of the amounts used for feed from January through March. These estimates were made with an index of numbers of horses in these years. The total five-year changes were prorated to an annual basis using the series on annual changes from the March series. March changes in barley and other stocks were taken as calendar changes.

Wheat stocks on farms for 1905 were reported in the *Weekly Reports* cited above. The stocks of coarse grains in that year and of all grains in 1900 and 1895 were secured as part of the estimate of total grain stocks already described.

Prices applied to the series of annual physical changes beginning with 1910 were "average prices received by farmers" as reported by crop correspondents in January issues of M.B.A.S. and C.S.M. These price series were extrapolated to years before 1910 with indexes of Lakehead terminal prices for each type of grain.

3. Manufacturing Inventories

The following table of the steps in estimating the investment in one year illustrates the method adapted from P.I.C.F. Lines 2 and 3 indicate whether prices are rising or falling. Line 4 indicates by how much. If they are rising (line 4>unity), then the inventory is valued at cost and is raised to market; line 5 is inventory valued at current market prices. If prices are falling (line 4<unity), the value of line 1 will be repeated in line 5. Values in line 5 are expressed in constant prices in line 6; then changes are revalued.

	1924	1925
1. Book value, Dec. 31 ($000,000)	677.	695.
2. Relative price, Dec. 31 (1913 – 100)	163.2	163.7
3. Relative price, Aug. 31	156.8	158.9
4. Line 2 divided by line 3	1.041	1.03
5. Line 4 times line 1	705.	716.
6. Line 5 divided by line 2 (X 100)	432.	437.
7. Change in 1925, in 1913 prices		5.
8. Price index (average for the year)		160.3
9. Line 8 times line 7		8.

Book values were obtained from D.B.S. files. Average length of life of inventory was calculated at four months. Price indexes were taken from D.B.S., *Prices and Price Indexes.* The annual series in millions of dollars from 1916 to 1925 inclusive was as follows: 25, 68, 34, -13, 146, 27, -53, 18, 14, and 8. The decline from the war-time peak in 1917 was obscured in the book-value series which reflected a steady rise to 1920. The positive increment in the recession of 1921 was also obscured in the book-value data (Manufacturing inventories show a similar lag in the recession of 1930.) The limitations of the price indexes used should be borne in mind. For example, although grains were included in the inventories of flour mills, their weight in total manufacturing inventories was not so great as the weighting for grains in the price indexes. This sort of distortion increased the inappropriateness of applying a wholesale price index to manufacturers' stocks.

The following table shows the data from the census of manufacturing and the relationship used to estimate manufacturing inventories in 1900, 1905, and 1910.

	Inventory ($000,000)	Cash and receivables ($000,000)	Total working capital ($000,000)
1915	337	369	706
1910			593
1905			379
1900			238

The procedure amounted to taking half the change in working capital as the change in book values of total inventories. The possible error introduced by this arbitrary procedure would not be very large relative to total inventory investment. In later years inventories were relatively higher—between 55 and 60 per cent of total working capital.

10.
Balance of International Payments, Current Transactions

THE ADDITION of the net change in claims against foreign assets to gross domestic capital formation yields total gross investment. The net change in foreign assets – foreign investment or disinvestment – is measured by the net balance of payments on all current international transactions. Professor Knox applied the concepts and methods developed at the Dominion Bureau of Statistics to extend the official estimates of Canada's balance of payments, which begin with 1926, back to 1900.[1] One revision was made in his estimates to allow for a bias recently discovered in the methods used to estimate credits on tourist transactions.[2] Also the gold items as treated by Professor Knox were excluded and the total Canadian production of gold was entered as a credit item in their place. This adjustment eliminated the necessity of adding the net change in the monetary gold stock as a fifth component of gross investment.[3]

The quinquennial estimates of net foreign and British investment from 1901 to 1930 appear in Appendix table G. Gross credits and debits as well as the net balances on current transactions, by major types, are shown in the table. It should be observed that the estimates of external investment were based upon the concept used in *Public Investment and Capital Formation*. The concept differs from the one used in the current official estimates of foreign investment through its inclusion of migrants' capital and inheritances as current transactions.[4]

11.
Transportation, Housing, and Direct Government Investment; and Indexes of Building and Real Estate Activity

1. Introduction

THE GLOBAL ESTIMATES of real investment developed in the last four chapters provided aggregates of significance for the analysis of economic development in Canada from 1896 to 1930. Some useful breakdowns of the investment in machinery and in inventories were also established by the methods employed. But the estimate of the volume of construction masked so many heterogeneous activities that it appeared worthwhile to secure direct estimates of its major components.

No single aspect of Canada's development as a continental economy has been more fundamental than transportation. The total investment in this field and its division among railway road and equipment, canals, harbours and river work, highways and bridges, producers' and consumers' automobiles, are a primary concern in this chapter.

Another concern is direct investment outlay by governments. The various levels of government have taken an active role in the investment field. Public finance statistics in their published form do not indicate the extent of this direct participation by governments. Apart from their intrinsic interest, estimates of direct investment and deficits and surpluses of governments were also necessary to determine the relative importance of domestic saving and foreign borrowing in the capital development of Canada since 1900.

Another obviously fundamental aspect of the capital formation process was the provision of housing to meet the demands of a rapidly growing population. The mere question of the relative size of the housing component is an important one.

In addition to estimates of investment in housing, several supplementary series were developed. These include new series on mortgage loans, property transfers, subdivision activity, and urban building activity. An attempt was also made to determine the approximate level of the gross national product from 1900 to 1930.

The next section is a summary of the methods employed and the following section gives greater detail on sources and procedures.[1]

II. Summary of Methods

1. Investment in Transportation

Steam railways. The estimates covered gross investment and repair expenditures of steam railways, excluding inventories, with a breakdown between road construction and rolling stock. Detailed estimates of this kind were available for 1926 to 1930 in an official study. Annual records of the two maintenance accounts – ways and structures and equipment – appeared in D.B.S. publications beginning in 1920 and in *Sessional Papers* for the earlier years. These records were given in sufficient detail for most of the period to permit the subtraction of certain items which were neither replacement nor repair. It was possible to secure a sound breakdown of replacement charges and repair for the equipment account and to adjust the former from a "charge" to an "expenditure" basis. A satisfactory approximation of the same breakdown was achieved for the road account. The determination of the net investment expenditures[2] offered greater difficulty.

In 1926 there were two large systems, the Canadian Pacific and the Canadian National (hereafter C.P.R. and C.N.R.), accounting for 91 per cent of the total mileage, and a group of minor roads. The history of the lines was examined and the status of the constituents of the major systems was established for each year back to 1895. Only two of the minor roads, the Temiskaming and Northern Ontario (T.N.O.) and the Pacific Great Eastern (P.G.E.), were covered. Provincial records provided most of the data for these two minor lines. The C.P.R. offered little difficulty. Its expenditures on road and equipment were published in fair detail in annual reports.[3] Similar detail on the C.N.R. was published after 1923. The C.N.R. report for that year covered several major groups – the Grand Trunk and the Grand Trunk Pacific, the Canadian Northern system, and the government railways group including the National Transcontinental. The last two groups were combined for coordinated operation in the closing months of 1918. The Grand Trunk Pacific, including the Saskatchewan Branch Lines Co. (G.T.P.), was added in September 1920. The Grand Trunk (G.T.), which had been acquired by the federal government in 1920, was added in 1922. Thus the C.N.R. emerged in a "period of transition" from 1917 to 1922. The total expenditures during this period were not too difficult to determine and the total was allocated to the different years with the help of *Auditor General's Reports*, federal *Public Accounts*, annual reports of the companies, and several monographs and official documents on Canadian railways.

The annual expenditures of the Grand Trunk were adequately reported in the company's reports back to 1895. The required data for the government railways group appeared in *Auditor General's Reports*. There remained only the G.T.P. and the Canadian Northern system. Reports on the former were never published and the annual reports of the latter were unreliable.

The total actual expenditure on the construction of the G.T.P. from 1903 to 1917 was a matter of public record since certified costs were reported by the G.T. to the government during construction. Non-investment costs, e.g. the large interest payments during construction, were easily eliminated from the itemized account of the cost. The final problem was to distribute the total cost to appropriate years. There was an independent estimate of the cost of the road prepared by a group of engineers under the direction of Professor Swain for the Royal Commission on Railways and Transportation, 1917 (*Drayton-Acworth Report*). Swain's report gave complete details of the estimates for each section of the G.T.P. and Saskatchewan Branch Lines. A complete history of the road was worked out from various sources and the dates of beginning and completion of each section were tabled chronologically. Swain's cost data were then applied to secure an index of annual construction appropriately weighted for the wide variations in cost in different parts of the country.[4] The index was used to distribute the total real investment over the years.

The Canadian Northern was made up of over twenty lines. The Drayton-Acworth Commission determined the total receipts of cash by sources for all these companies and accounted for their disposition by types of expenditure. The total expenditures on road, terminals, and equipment were established in these data. The ratio of equipment investment to total investment in studies by Swain and Buchanan[5] provided the required breakdown. This left only the problem of distributing totals to appropriate years from 1896 to 1917. The method used rests on the probability that annual cash outlay on road and equipment must have varied closely with annual cash inflow. From various official and private sources the annual cash inflow from security sales (less discounts), equipment trust securities, net proceeds of land sales, short term loans, government advances (when not reflected in bonded liabilities), and cash subsidies was determined for the group as a whole. A three-year moving average of a two-year moving average of this series was taken to interpolate from June fiscal to calendar years and to smooth the series. An index of this series was then used to allocate the total real investment to years. As a first approximation, equipment expenditures were taken as a constant ratio of the total. Then an index based on annual changes of the numbers of rolling stock (the different types were weighted with their relative prices in the early twenties) was used to redistribute the equipment expenditures and make the final adjustment between road and equipment investment in each year.

Other transportation. Other major transportation structures – highways and bridges, canals, harbours, docks, and river work – were products of direct government investment and are included in the following sub-section. Investment in automobiles by producers and consumers, and investment in ships have been dealt with in Chapter VIII. Detailed estimates of the investment in electric railways were not made: a series on capital liabilities was used as a rough index of their development. Municipal streets and sidewalks are part of municipal investment which is described below.

2. *Direct Government Investment*

Federal government. Definitions, sources, and general procedures were derived from those employed in *Public Investment and Capital Formation* (P.I.C.F.). The official estimates covered investment and repair expenditures on construction, resource development, and machinery and equipment. A considerable proportion of these was charged by the government to current account and also many items included in government capital expenditures were not investment in the economic sense.[6] However, the records of annual expenditures available in the *Auditor General's Reports* were sufficiently detailed to allow the appropriate reclassifications.

The examination of annual *Auditor General's Reports* was limited to the four federal departments most active in the construction field: Public Works, Railways and Canals, Marine and Fisheries, and, although less important than the others, Trade and Commerce. In 1926 these departments accounted for $27.1 million of the total new construction outlay by the federal government of $28.6, that is, for 94.6 per cent of the total reported in P.I.C.F.

The official estimates published in P.I.C.F. were made for six spot years from 1926 to 1941 by an examination of each item of expenditure shown in the detailed *Reports*. A ten-dollar expenditure on sawn lumber by the smallest department would not be overlooked. Such care was neither practicable nor warranted for the present study. However, since the estimates were made for each year from 1900 to 1926, the present estimates are consistent over the whole period. A comparison with the official estimates for 1926 showed a remarkably close agreement. For that year the present estimate of new construction by the four major departments was $26.5 million which is $0.6 million or less than 2 per cent below the P.I.C.F. estimate for the same departments, and $2.1 million or 7.3 per cent below the official estimate for all new construction. The $2.1 million difference was run back, as miscellaneous construction, on an index of federal building construction.

The present method gave a less satisfactory result for repair construction. The method accounted for $3.6 of the $4.3 million spent by the four major departments in 1926. There was an additional expenditure of $1.3 million by other departments not covered at all. These $2 million of repair unaccounted for were run back with an index of building construction along with the $2.1 million of miscellaneous new construction.

The final results were a reliable total for new construction, with component estimates for railways, canals, harbours, and river work, etc., new building construction, and a small miscellaneous category; and less reliable but, in view of their size and significance, satisfactory repair totals. Expenditures on railway repairs were made in connection with the railway estimates. Capital expenditures through the Harbour Commissions were secured from reports of the Commissions and, where these were lacking, by direct correspondence with harbour officials.

No effort was made to measure federal expenditures on machinery and equipment other than railway rolling stock. The total in 1926 was $3.8 million which included certain duplications already covered in construction.[7] Important elements in this expenditure were automobiles and office machinery and equipment, and both, especially automobiles, would be less important in the earlier years covered here. Another excluded item was investment in resource development (reforestation, topographical surveys, etc.) which accounted for one million dollars of federal investment in 1926. Again some part of this was duplicated in construction and therefore covered. The pattern of government construction in the twenty-five years under review was heavily weighted by railway construction before the first war. The peak values in 1913 and 1914 were twice the 1926 expenditure. The expenditures on machinery and equipment and resource development would hardly follow this pattern. Since they could hardly have reached a million dollars in the pre-1920 era, it was safe to ignore them.

Provincial governments. Here again the pattern established by P.I.C.F. was followed. The most careful attention was given to highways which predominated in provincial investment. It was the rapid emergence of the automobile during the first war that raised provincial investment from relatively low levels before the war to levels comparable with federal expenditures during the twenties. In 1926, for example, when the federal government spent $27 million on new construction, the provinces spent $24 million; when repair was added, provincial expenditures were raised to $39 million which, owing to the large provincial highway repair account, was $5 million more than the federal government spent on new and repair construction that year.

The general method was to make an estimate for 1926 (from the *Public Accounts* of the provinces) that conformed as closely as possible with the P.I.C.F. estimate, then to make comparable estimates for several spot years and fill in the intervening years with appropriate interpolators. Annual series on highway expenditures were obtained for all provinces except Manitoba and the Maritimes. These were reliable total series but, while in some (for example, the estimates prepared for the Ontario Royal Commission on Transportation, 1938) the distinction between new and repair was sound, in others this breakdown was made more or less arbitrarily.

Since the soundest parts of the present estimates are of highway construction and new public buildings, the relative importance of these two components of total provincial investment expenditures is worth indicating. In the P.I.C.F. estimates for 1926, 80 per cent of provincial construction expenditures was on highways and bridges. Public buildings absorbed 16 per cent, and less than 4 per cent went to harbour and river work, dams, ferries, etc.

Provincially owned public utilities were treated as autonomous corporations in P.I.C.F. An independent effort was made to measure the gross investment in certain utilities (Ontario Hydro Electric Power Commission and the Prairie Telephone Companies). Two major railways developed by direct provincial investment (P.G.E. and T.N.O.) were included with the railways. Apart from these, provincial activity in the railway field was virtually limited to subsidies in cash, some land grants, and bond guarantees.

As a result of the absence of complete provincial records in most libraries, the procedures and reliability of the estimates varied among the different provinces. This point is covered in more detail in Section III. On the whole the estimates of new construction of highways and public buildings are good. Records for the Maritimes and Manitoba were scanty, but these provinces accounted for a small part of the total (16 per cent in 1926). Large relative errors in their expenditures would not affect the total for all provinces appreciably. The minor construction category (noted above as 4 per cent of the total in 1926) was covered by records back to 1914 for three provinces and estimated for the remaining six provinces by projecting their expenditure in 1926 back to 1914 on an index of their building construction. Since the whole category amounted to less than a million dollars in 1914, it was ignored in earlier years.

The present highway estimate for 1926 checked precisely at $31.2 million with the P.I.C.F. estimate for that year. The differences by provinces did not exceed $0.1 million. Provincial grants to municipalities for highway construction were included in the municipal expenditures described below. The smaller investment in public buildings of $3.4 million also checked closely with the official estimate for 1926. The present method was again inadequate with respect to building repair: only 45 per cent of the 1926 P.I.C.F. total was accounted for. This coverage was assumed to be a sufficient sample to blow up the series to conform with the more comprehensive P.I.C.F. series.

Municipal governments. Information on municipal expenditures was scarce. There were series on new and repair highway construction by local governments in Ontario. These appeared in a historical table in *Report of the Royal Commission on Transportation* (Toronto, 1938), which gave highway expenditures by all levels of government in that province annually from 1889. The table included an estimate of expenditures on urban streets based on a sample of municipalities. In addition there was information on expenditures of British Columbia municipalities on roads, sewers, street lighting, and parks from 1914, with no breakdown between new and repair. This appeared in the British Columbia submission to the Royal Commission on Dominion-Provincial Relations and in *Annual Reports* of the British Columbia Department of Municipal Affairs. A similar series for Ontario from 1892 to 1911 appeared in *Annual Reports of the* (Ontario) *Bureau of Industry.*

These series were of some use in the discussion of transportation development, but they fell far short of providing a full picture of municipal activity in the investment field. Extremely rough estimates were made of total new construction expenditures of municipalities by extrapolating the estimate for 1926 in P.I.C.F. with an index of gross annual sales of municipal bonds.[8] This bond series was compiled by various editors of the *Monetary Times* and appeared in *Monetary Times Annuals* from 1904 to 1926. It covered sales in all markets. Viner's estimates of private sales in London from 1900 to 1905 and from 1905 to 1909 were used to extra-polate the bond series from 1905 to 1901.[9]

The P.I.C.F. repair estimate for 1926 was extrapolated to 1922 and 1913 by an index of the repair expenditures given by H. C. Goldenberg in his study *Municipal Finance in Canada* (Ottawa, 1939). The 1913 outlay was run back to 1911 with the Ontario repair series cited above. The years 1914 to 1921 and 1923 to 1925 were interpolated using a series on municipal tax revenues. Repair estimates were not attempted for the years before 1911.

The crudity of these municipal estimates can hardly be over-emphasized. The most certain bias (among several) in the bond series is the varying proportion of the annual proceeds used for refunding. Five-year totals may offset some of this, but it is proba-ble that the large number of expanding new cities in the West in the earlier years introduced a trend from less to more refunding opera-tions. Western cities were relatively greater borrowers before 1914-20 than after.

3. Investment in Housing

The method employed to estimate investment in housing was simi-lar to that employed in the official estimates prepared under Dr. O. J. Firestone's direction. The gross additions to the stock of dwelling units in each decade from 1891 to 1931 were secured from Fire-stone's study.[10] There were marked changes in building costs over the period. Consequently it was necessary to distribute the volume data to an annual basis before applying price series to obtain the required value estimates. This distribution of the gross decade changes in dwelling units was made with a deflated index of the annual domestic disappearance of construction materials.

Independent estimates of the gross decade changes in farm units were made with a breakdown between prairie farm and other farm units. Since a quinquennial census was taken in the prairie provinces, it was possible to secure the gross quinquennial changes in prairie farm units. The two farm series were distributed to an annual basis and deducted from the annual series of all dwelling units to secure an annual series for the non-farm sector.

In the final step the three volume series were valued by apply-ing estimated annual average prices of the units in each sector. A weighted average of the cost of non-farm dwelling units erected in 1921 taken from the official estimates was projected to 1895 with the implicit index of construction costs derived in Chapter VII. The trend in annual unit values secured in this manner was checked against other information on housing costs. A similar procedure was used to obtain unit prices for non-prairie farm dwellings. This non-prairie farm price series was adjusted to allow for a regional factor and also a trend factor to secure a series of lower prices appropriate to the prairies. There were data to confirm the adjustments.

4. Miscellaneous Estimates

Building and real estate activity, 1865-1948. The various series were based on information secured directly from records of Registry and Land Titles Offices in Winnipeg and Toronto, vault records of Hugh C. MacLean Publications Ltd., Toronto, various municipal offices in Toronto and the surrounding suburbs, and several government publications. Only very simple methods of estimating were involved, since the material obtained from these records was comprehensive. Indexes of the following annual series were made for greater Toronto: numbers of real estate instruments registered, 1867-95; numbers of mortgages registered, 1894-1948; numbers of deeds registered, 1894-1948; numbers of mortgages discharged, 1894-1948; numbers of sub-divisions recorded, 1880-1948; value of building permits, 1886-1948; numbers of permits, 1886-1948; numbers of residential permits, 1920-48. In addition to these Toronto series, indexes of real estate activity for Winnipeg, 1872-1948, based on deeds, mortgages, and discharges of mortgages, and of urban building in Canada, 1860-1948, based on deflated values of permits issued were prepared.

Gross national product. The current D.B.S. estimates of the gross national product begin with the year 1926. The old D.B.S. series began with an earlier year, but, since neither its components nor the methods employed in its estimation were ever published, one cannot do much with it. A more reliable series, prepared by D. C. MacGregor, was available for the period from 1921 to 1930.[11] J. J. Deutsch published an admittedly rougher series for the period from 1911 to 1920.[12] Both series used the same general method: estimating value added by each branch of primary and secondary industries on the basis of D.B.S. and other federal records and estimating the tertiary component with the sample series including railways, government, and certain service industries. There was no apparent inconsistency in the adjacent terminal estimates (1920 and 1921) for the primary and secondary components of the two series and perhaps a slight shift in the tertiary component. The two series – called national income produced – were taken together as a reasonably consistent series from 1911 to 1930. Depreciation was included by the methods employed by both writers. Certain adjustments were required to make the series conform conceptually with G.N.P.: (1) deduct investment income paid abroad; (2) add investment income from abroad[13]; (3) add indirect taxes less subsidies; (4) add an imputed rent for owner-occupied dwellings. A sample for (3) covering 72 per cent of the total in 1926 was available over the period. MacGregor's estimates of (4) were projected back from 1921 with a rent index and a rough series on numbers of owner-occupied dwellings based on the housing estimates of the present study. The net values added by the construction industry in both the MacGregor and Deutsch series were based on MacLean's contracts awarded.[14] The estimates of construction in Chapter VII above provided a better basis for this purpose and accordingly the net value added series for construction was adjusted.

An estimate was made of income produced in 1900 following Deutsch's method and similarly adjusted to a G.N.P. basis. The adjusted series for 1900 and 1911-30 inclusive was used as an index to extrapolate the official estimates of G.N.P. to 1911 and to 1900.

The years from 1901 to 1910 were interpolated on the basis of the stable relationship observed in each year from 1911 to 1920 between the estimated G.N.P. and the volume of the money supply (cash in the hands of the public plus total domestic deposits: annual averages of month-end figures). This ratio resembles Angell's circular or income velocity which he called "one of the stablest magnitudes in the economic universe."[15] Professor MacGregor established that the same relation was only slightly less stable in Canada from 1911 to 1930.[16]

A check of the annual series against the best index of economic activity available in Canadian records, the sum of exports and imports, did not reveal any obvious discrepancies in the crude estimates.

III. Sources and Procedures

1. Railways

General. Procedures followed to obtain net expenditures of the C.P.R., G.T., the C.N.R. after 1923, the National Transcontinental and other federal lines, the P.G.E. after 1918, and the T.N.O. require little comment. Annual reports of the first three companies furnished exhibits itemizing capital expenditures. *Exhibits of Evidence,* the *Thirty Per Cent Case,* the *Twenty Per Cent Case,* and the *Mountain Differential Case,* were an additional source.

Care was taken to exclude cost of land, hotels, office buildings, and other non-railway items. The provincial public accounts and federal sessional papers provided records of the other lines: Auditor General reports were the basic source for federal lines; British Columbia public accounts for P.G.E.; Reports on T.N.O. in sessional papers of Ontario for T.N.O.

The C.P.R. switched from calendar to June fiscal years after 1900 and back to calendar years after 1916. The same problem arose with maintenance accounts, which were all June fiscal until 1918. The G.T. reports, published every six months from 1902 to 1913, provided a solution. Four series of half-year expenditures – net road, net equipment, maintenance of road, maintenance of equipment – were tested for seasonal factors. Equipment series were uniform, but, as one would expect in view of Canada's climate, both construction series reflected a pronounced seasonal influence. From 1902 to 1903, an average of 65.3 per cent of new construction, 67.3 per cent of maintenance of road and structures, and 50.3 per cent of equipment expenditures came in the July to December intervals. Averages of the deviations – ignoring signs which were evenly distributed – were 4.4 per cent for equipment and 3.1 per cent for ways and structures. The G.T. ratios were accordingly used to effect adjustments from June fiscal to calendar years where these were required. Government construction series were on March fiscals after 1907. Since less than one-sixth of an annual construction total would come in the severe first quarter of the year, no adjustment was made. Uniform monthly distribution was assumed for government equipment expenditures.

A series on annual net changes in bonded liabilities for all minor roads was examined and rejected as a basis for estimating their net expenditures. Over the period 1896-1925 perhaps $30 or $35 millions of expenditure were therefore omitted. This omission was offset in total (but probably not in its timing) by the inclusion of net expenditures of the G.T. and C.P.R. on their American lines. The replacement and repair expenditures of the minor roads were included in the maintenance accounts which covered all Canadian lines.

Canadian Northern system before 1918. The cost of road and equipment published in the annual reports of this system had been written up to cover about $100 million of "water-stock." It also included large discounts on bond sales (about $21 million, most of it arising in 1914-15) and interest, etc. (ef. *Drayton-Acworth Report*). The history of control, mergers, and amalgamations of the constituents of the system appeared in Robert Dorman. *A Statutory History of Steam and Electric Railways of Canada, 1836-*

1938 (Ottawa, 1938). Sources of funds were given in Drayton-Acworth Report, p. xlii. The annual proceeds from these sources were calculated for the following companies: Bay of Quinte; Brockville, Westport and S. S. Marie; Central Ontario; Great Northern; Irondale Bancroft and Ottawa; Inverness and Richmond; Lake Manitoba Railway and Canal; Manitoba and South Eastern; Montford Colonization; Montford and Gatineau; Northern Pacific and Manitoba; Nova Scotia Central; Central Nova Scotia; Ontario, Belmont and Northern; Quebec and Lake St. John; Hudson Bay (Winnipeg Great Northern), Canadian Northern; C.N. Ontario; C.N. Quebec; Halifax and South Western. In some cases, e.g. subsidies, a flow basis was used; in others, e.g. bond sales, a net change (in liabilities) basis was used. The large discounts of 1914 and 1915 were deducted and the balance of total discounts distributed uniformly. (Fournier states discounts were the same on both guaranteed and unguaranteed sales.) The problem of shifts in bond liabilities between members of the group was avoided by combining totals. Government loans before 1914 showed up as changed in bond liabilities, since bonds were used as collateral. Sources of data were: "Railway Statistics" in *Annual Reports,* Department of Railways and Canals (D.R.C.); *Statistics of Steam Railways of Canada,* D.B.S.; "Accountant's Report," *Annual Reports,* D.R.C.; *Drayton-Acworth Report; Federal S. P. No. 20, 1920; Annual Reports,* Canadian Northern; D. B. Hanna, *Trains of Recollection* (Toronto, 1924); Robert Dorman, cited above; L. T. Fournier, *Railway Nationalization in Canada* (Toronto, 1935); N. Thompson and J. H. Edgar, *Canadian Railway Development* (Toronto, 1933).

Grand Trunk Pacific and Saskatchewan Branch Lines. The data on certified cost reported to the federal government and Swain's cost study appeared in *Drayton-Acworth Report,* 24-25 and 48-55. Dates of surveys, initial construction, and completion were given in *Annual Reports,* G.T., and Thompson and Edgar, *Canadian Railway Development.* Since the original contracts were let by sections, the chronology fitted well with the sectional breakdown employed by Swain except for Prairie Branch Lines, and these were built so rapidly that little difficulty was encountered in handling them. Swain divided the 2,780 miles of road into 23 sections for this study. There may have been a bias in the index derived from Swain's values. Swain stated that "it is quite likely that prices used are at variance, on certain lines or in some localities, with actual prices paid." (*Drayton-Acworth Report,* 65). However, he did attempt to estimate original cost, not reproduction cost as with the C.N. study.

Equipment expenditures were a relatively small part of the total investment. An act of 1906 authorized a special bond issue for equipment purchases. Some part of the proceeds was used for other purposes. From 1906 to December 1916, $31 million were raised under this act (cf. *Drayton-Acworth Report*, 24). The timing of sales of this bond issue provided a rough guide to the timing of the expenditures. According to *S. P. No. 282*, 1916, $22.5 million had been spent on equipment (probably to the end of 1915), with interest accounting for $2.6 million of the total. It was assumed that $2 million of the remaining $8.5 million (31-22.5) was spent on equipment in 1916 and that the balance went to interest and other purposes.

Railway accounting methods and the maintenance accounts. Until 1930 the C.P.R. used what is sometimes called replacement accounting. Under this method when rolling stock becomes obsolete or is destroyed, the current cost of the actual or anticipated replacement (without allowance for any change in either capacity or price) is charged to the maintenance account. The Canadian National used retirement accounting. Under this method the charge to operating expenses is the original cost of the equipment item retired, and the difference between the costs of the replacement and of the retirement is charged to capital account. The Canadian Northern also used the retirement method. The Grand Trunk used it too but, in addition, employed special renewal and suspense accounts to spread the charge for so-called extraordinary replacements over several years. The government lines employed something like a depreciation method, making renewal charges on a uniform basis and charging replacements to a renewal reserve. (Cf. "Classification of Revenue etc.... Construction, Equipment etc. ... " C.P.R. handbook for accounting employees (Montreal, 1907); *Report of the Royal Commission on Railways and Transportation (Duff Report)*) (Ottawa, 1931); *Annual Reports*, Grand Trunk Railway, December 1901, 7; December 1905, 7; December 1907, 7; and the expenditure accounts of D.R.C. in *Auditor General's Reports* prior to 1919.)

The details of maintenance accounts for all railways operating in Canada appeared from 1907 to 1920 in "Railway Statistics," *Annual Reports*, D.R.C., and after 1920 in *Statistics on Steam Railways in Canada*, D.B.S. Expenses for printing, injuries to persons, snow removal, and the like were deducted from both accounts. The road account from 1895 to 1907 was not given in detail. The unwanted items were estimated on the basis of their relative size in 1907-10. Before 1907 two accounts, maintenance of cars and cost of motive power, appeared instead of the single equipment account. Again unwanted items, somewhat larger here, were eliminated using the 1907-10 comparison base. Renewal charges included in the equipment account were totalled back to 1907 and projected to 1895 on the basis of data from *Annual Reports* of the C.P.R. and G.T. These lines provided a large sample for that period. The renewal series was subtracted from maintenance to secure a series on equipment repair expenditures.

As often as not the renewals charged were an actual replacement expenditure in the same year. However, in some cases, the renewals were accumulating over several years, and in other, although the timing of renewals and replacements was more closely related, rather large changes appeared in the equipment reserves. The equipment or renewal reserves were obtained for the C.P.R., C.N., G.T., and C.N.R. from annual reports, and for government lines from the relevant D.R.C. reports. The annual net changes in these reserves were applied to the renewal series to get the required expenditure series.

A temporary expedient was employed to secure a breakdown of repair and replacement expenditures on road account. Actual replacements from 1926 to 1930 averaged 31.7 per cent of the total of replacement plus repair. A flat 30 per cent was applied to five-year totals throughout the earlier period. This is a crude expedient. But while the error in the replacement total may be large, the relative error in the total of net plus replacement will not be great, and the relative error in the repair total is likewise smaller because repair is over twice as large as replacement. However, it should be borne in mind that, while the total net and the total gross plus repair are reasonably sound, the breakdown of the latter to gross and repair is not precise. One would expect repair to be understated in the early years because the roads were newer. Also, all companies were attempting to show as much "profit" as possible, hence renewals charges were held to a minimum. The relative size of the components may be seen in the following table.

2. *Federal Government*

Most of the sources have been given. The following notes indicate the chief problems and procedures established to deal with them. *Auditor General's Reports* are referred to as *Reports*.

A discrepancy appeared with P.I.C.F. in harbour and river work, attributable to a higher allowance made here for work of Harbour Commissions. Detail of the P.I.C.F. estimate on this was not available, but it appeared to have excluded the St. Lawrence Ship Channel which should be included as investment in this category.

Railway Road Construction and Repair
($000,000)

Years	Net	Replacement	Repair	Total
1896-1900	42	13	31	86
1901-05	95	22	52	169
1906-10	341	33	77	450
1911-15	478	47	110	636
1916-20	126	94	220	440
1921-25	129	115	269	513
1926-30	220	132	284	635

(Note: Slight apparent errors in the total are the result of rounding components to nearest million. Expenditures of T.N.O. and P.G.E. are not included in this table.)

Avoiding the analysis of detailed lists of individual expenditures in the *Reports* made it necessary to follow arbitrary rules in the determination of several new:repair breakdowns. Altogether $5.0 million of the total of $30 million of new and repair were affected by these rules. For example, "harbour and rivers, improvement," an extremely detailed item, was approximately half new in two years that were checked. Therefore 50:50 was assumed to be the ratio in all years. An item called "staff and repairs, canals" was checked in two years and 40 per cent was taken in all years to be repair. The remainder was neither new construction nor repair.

The St. Lawrence Ship Channel involved annual expenditures by Marine and Fisheries, but these were confused in *Reports* with expenditures on the Sorel Shipyard. A detailed historical table was given in *Report of the Department of Marine and Fisheries, 1927,* and although this didn't check precisely with Auditor General's data, it was nevertheless used for this item. Cost of dredging was always taken as new construction.

There were three Harbour Commissions receiving government funds in the period of this study. Amounts of advances shown in *Auditor General's Reports* in later years checked closely with capital expenditures shown in the Commissions' reports. It was not possible to determine advances in all years from *Auditor General's Reports.* The series was completed with data on capital expenditures obtained from Commissions' Reports and by correspondence with National Harbours Board.

With respect to capital items charged current: 25 per cent of total new construction was so charged in 1926; $17 million or less than 20 per cent at the peak of railway activity in 1913 and 1914; and about 35 per cent of new construction before 1905. These percentages indicate one aspect of the weakness of estimates based on federal capital account totals. However it should be observed that that part of the present totals taken from the current account contains whatever errors may have been introduced by the arbitrary practices mentioned above. This would imply that railway and canal investment expenditures are the most reliable of all the components because they appeared almost entirely in the capital account. Buildings and harbour and river work data are somewhat less reliable since they were subject to the effect of the allocations of current account items between new and repair. The small miscellaneous new building category and all the repair estimates are the components most subject to error.

3. Provincial Governments

Highways and Bridges

Quebec. Direct estimates were made from *Public Accounts* for 1902, 1907, 1915, 1920, 1925, and 1926. Interpolations were made with series of total capital expenditures under the Good Roads Act and total expenditure on colonization roads (source: Quebec Statistical Year Books). Interpolations for maintenance and repair construction were made with series on total current expenditures of the Department of Roads from 1913 to 1926. Expenditures by the province were negligible before 1913.

Ontario. Estimates were made for spot years with interpolations based on the complete historical record of highway expenditures, new and repair, published in *Royal Commission on Transportation,* Province of Ontario (Toronto, 1938).

Saskatchewan. Estimates were prepared from Public Accounts for all years.

Alberta. Direct estimates were made from Public Accounts for 1908, 1912, 1914, 1919, 1921, 1925, and 1926. Intervening years were interpolated on the basis of (1) capital expenditures on highways for new, and (2) current expenditures of highway department for repair after 1919. The change in highway debt from 1915 to 1918 was distributed as new construction using provincial capital expenditures as an index. Repair from 1915 to 1918 was distributed as new construction using provincial capital expenditures as an index. Repair from 1915 to 1918 was interpolated on a straight line. The small expenditures from 1907 to 1912, the initial peak, were interpolated on a straight line, and the expenditure for 1906 (the first full year of the province's existence) was inferred from the change in the expenditures in Saskatchewan from 1906 to 1907.

British Columbia. Direct estimates were made from *Public Accounts* for each year from 1919 to 1926. The Public Accounts in this period provided historical tables on total highway expenditures back to the beginning of the period of this study.

Manitoba and the Maritimes. Public Accounts were not used for these provinces. Fairly satisfactory estimates were made, with the expenditures reported for 1913, 1921, 1925, and 1926 in *Public Accounts Inquiry,* Royal Commission on Dominion-Provincial Relations (Ottawa, 1938) providing bench-marks. Highway debt statistics from the same source, and a mimeographed study "Transportation in Manitoba" (Winnipeg, 1938), provided information to interpolate the missing years. The small totals in the earlier period were extrapolated back from 1913 using Ontario road expenditures as an index.

General. The Manitoba and Maritimes estimates are only fair. The estimates for the other five provinces are firm and together they accounted for 84 per cent of total highway expenditures in 1926. Another factor contributing to the reliability of the estimates is that data for British Columbia and Ontario were excellent in all years. These two provinces accounted for about 50 per cent of expenditures on highways.

One limitation in the scope of the estimates should be borne in mind. The procedures of P.I.C.F. involved treating grants to municipalities for road construction as municipal investments. This exclusion gives a misleading picture of provincial activity in this field, especially in the early twenties and before 1920 when a great deal of road construction was carried out by local governments with provincial governments sharing the cost. These grants were not an important factor in the West, or in the Maritimes, but in Quebec, for example, the grant in 1920 was four times the size of the direct expenditure by the province. Grants were also important in Ontario. In 1920 the total provincial grant to municipalities in Ontario and Quebec was $9 million; in 1926 it was $6 million. The grants are included in municipal expenditures below and in the estimates of total transportation investment that appear in Chapter III.

Building Construction

These estimates are probably less reliable than the highways estimates. It has been pointed out that this component was only 16 per cent of the total provincial construction in 1926, but in earlier years its relative importance was greater (it was about 50 per cent of the total in 1913).

New construction was fairly easy to estimate because it was reported largely among capital expenditures. Repair work, with which we are not so greatly concerned, was included with general maintenance and operation of public buildings.

Again the *Public Accounts* were available for five provinces. Estimates were made for spot years comparable in coverage with the P.I.C.F. estimate for 1926. The intervening years were interpolated using capital expenditures of departments of public works (or the comparable department) to fill in the new construction series, and current expenditures of the same departments for the repair series. The *Public Accounts Inquiry* was used for the other provinces. Useful material appeared in S. Bates, *Financial History of Canadian Governments* (Ottawa, 1939). Repair services were frequently interpolated on a straight-line basis. In general, the repair total is weak but satisfactory if used only on a five-year total basis.

4. Municipal Governments

The sources and methods employed in estimating total municipal investment and repair expenditures have been indicated. These are the most unreliable of the estimates made. The new and repair series on Ontario highway expenditures from the Royal Commission of 1938 and the series on municipal highway expenditures in British Columbia were the only firm municipal series discovered. These fragments served a useful purpose; but the rough character of the estimates of the total municipal investment should be borne in mind in assessing the discussion of public investment in Chapter V.

5. Housing Investment

The investment in non-farm dwelling units from 1921 to 1930, and average prices per unit in 1921 for the different types of units were taken from *Residential Real Estate*. Gross additions to the total numbers of dwelling units in the earlier decades were secured from the same source.

The numbers of available farm units in 1941, 1931, and 1921

were projected to 1911, 1901, and 1891 on the basis of the numbers of farms reported in each census from 1891 to 1941. The number of farms and the number of available farm housing units were virtually the same in recent census records when both were specifically enumerated. Series of net changes in the numbers of available units in each decade were calculated for prairie farm and other farm. These were raised to gross additions by applying replacement rates. (A replacement rate is the ratio of the number of dwellings demolished and destroyed during a period to the number of units existing at the beginning of the period.) Preliminary estimates of these rates for three types of locality – urban, small urban, and rural – were prepared for decades from 1871 to 1931 by Firestone. His rural rate was used as an index, base 1921-31, to run back the 1921-31 replacement rate for "other" farm units.

Special care was required in the estimation of prairie demolitions from 1901 to 1921 owing to the pattern of housing development peculiar to the frontier. Many homesteaders, with no alternative, erected sod huts upon their arrival on the frontier and later replaced them with the more substantial wooden frame houses characteristic of western farms. The sod dwellings were eliminated from the totals reported in the census. The rural replacement rates, which would take into account losses through fire, other natural hazards, and normal demolitions, were applied to the remainder. The decade gross changes in prairie farm units from 1901 to 1931 were then prorated to quinquennial changes on the basis of net changes in farm units reflected in quinquennial censuses for each of the prairie provinces.

The elimination of sod houses from census totals for the prairies followed the assumption that the "other" category of dwellings shown in the census classification by types of materials of construction was wholly of the sod variety. These declined from 23.7 per cent and 27.9 per cent in Saskatchewan and Alberta, respectively, in 1901 and 2.0 per cent and 1.6 per cent of total dwellings in these provinces in 1921.

The price series were checked for bias in the cost index against unit prices calculated for spot years from issues of *Canadian Architect and Builder* available at Hugh C. MacLean Publications Ltd., Toronto. The value of farm buildings erected in Manitoba from 1893 to 1918 recorded in *Annual Reports,* Department of Agriculture and Immigration, and data on numbers and values of farm dwellings and other farm buildings, Kindersley district, Saskatchewan, from 1907 to 1930, given in R. W. Murchie *et al., Agricultural Progress on the Prairie Frontier* (Toronto, 1936), were used to check the prairie farm-price series.

The total number of rooms and the average number of rooms per dwelling were calculated for each province from each census from 1891 to 1931. The national average of rooms per dwelling was fairly stable (5.91 in 1891, 6.07 in 1901 and 1911, 5.97 in 1921, and 5.91 in 1931). The trend was slightly downward in all provinces except the prairie provinces where the pioneer influence was very apparent and necessitated two adjustments. From 1901 to 1921 the average size of prairie dwelling units increased by approximately 40 per cent, then remained stable through the twenties. In Manitoba, Saskatchewan, and Alberta, the average numbers of rooms per dwelling in 1931 were 5.05, 4.39, and 4.3, respectively. To allow for these two factors, prairie farm units built in the twenties were priced 15 per cent lower than eastern farm units, and the trend in size was allowed for by reducing the annual price in 1896 by a further 25 per cent and reducing this discount by 1 per cent per annum until 1920.

Both the Kindersley and the Manitoba series confirmed the use of the value of the wheat crop to distribute five year changes in prairie farm units to an annual basis. The same sources, recent studies in the Agricultural Statistics Branch, D.B.S., and also recorded experience in the United States (see, for example, N. Buchanan, *International Investment and Domestic Welfare* (New York 1946), 12 and 13), confirmed the assumption that farmers tended to spend an amount on other farm buildings equal to, or only slightly less than, the investment in dwellings. Where a rough estimate of total farm construction was required, as in Chapter II, expenditures on other buildings were estimated as 90 per cent of the farm housing expenditures in each five-year period.

The allocation of the decade gross changes in non-farm and non-prairie farm units was made with a series based on the annual domestic disappearance of construction materials. Since there are no records of materials that go exclusively into dwellings, this type of index is inevitably biased by movements in other types of construction activity. Furthermore, inventory adjustments were not made. However, the prices were applied to the volume series and the annual values were combined in five-year totals. The method appeared sufficiently sound to approximate the desired quinquennial estimates.

Housing repair and maintenance expenditures from 1921 to 1930 were available in *Residential Real Estate*. These estimates were projected to 1896 on two independent bases, and an average of the results was then taken to secure the required quinquennial estimates from 1896 to 1920.

The first projection was based on the assumption that annual repair expenditures were determined solely by the housing stock. An annual series of the available dwelling units, with a farm:non-farm breakdown, was prepared. An average cost of repair for each type of unit in the early twenties was applied to secure the estimates of annual repairs in constant dollars. The two series were added and converted to current dollars with the cost of construction index from Chapter VII.

The second projection was based on the assumption that repair expenditures reflected the annual domestic disappearance of building materials (secured from the data of Chapter VII). The 1921 repair bill from *Residential Real Estate* was projected to 1896 on an index of this series valued in current dollars.

An average of the two variants was then taken and the annual estimates summed to obtain quinquennial totals. The estimates were used along with other estimates of repair expenditure to break down the global estimates of total construction into new and repair.

6. Building and Real Estate Activity

Index of urban building activity. The values of permits issued were deflated from 1896 to 1948 with a cost of construction index, and from 1886 to 1896 with a cost of construction materials index. These cost indexes are described below. A cost index for earlier years was not required because the only data available before 1886 are of numbers of buildings erected in Montreal. The final building index is the product of splicing several indexes, each of which utilizes the permit data available for the several periods. The following table indicates the coverage in each period.

Period	Cities	Source of data
1865-86	Montreal	Montreal Archives
1886-90	Montreal, Toronto	Hugh C. MacLean Publications Ltd., Toronto
1890-1900	Montreal, Toronto, Hamilton	
1900-14	Increases from 7 to 80 cities	Hugh C. MacLean Publications Ltd., *Labour Gazette,* and R. H. Coats, *Cost of Living Report*
1915-19	35 cities	D.B.S.
1920-40	63 cities	D.B.S.
1940-48	204 cities	D.B.S.

The changing sample from 1900 to 1914 was chained in a single index. Splices of the several series were made by working back from 1943. This method introduces a distortion which does not affect the purpose of the index, which is merely to indicate the approximate timing of urban building cycles.

An index of material prices, 1890-1948, was made by linking the D.B.S. weighted index of wholesale prices of construction materials, 1913 on, and an index devised by combining the three indexes of wholesale prices of construction materials prepared by R. H. Coats (see Chapter VII). The 1890 value was extrapolated to 1886 on a general wholesale price index. The material price index was combined with the D.B.S. index of wage rates in the building trades with weights derived from Chapter VII.

Building and real estate activity in Greater Toronto. The numbers of plans of subdivisions of lots registered in York County, 1880-1948, in East Toronto, 1889-1948, and in West Toronto, 1905-48, were taken from records at York County Registry Office in Toronto and the Toronto Registry Office. It may be noted that the term "York" designates various localities. The York County Registry Office, however covers all the suburban regions of Toronto whether incorporated urban or not. Greater Toronto includes the city of Toronto; York, East York, North York, Etobicoke, and Scarborough townships; Leaside, Mimico, New Toronto, Weston, all towns; Forest Hill, Swansea, and Long Branch villages.

Three series covering York (East and West) and East and West Toronto on numbers of transfers, new mortgages, and mortgage discharges annually from 1894 to 1948 were obtained from the Toronto and York Registry Offices and from Ontario, *Sessional Papers,* annual reports of the Inspector of Registry Offices. Annual registrations in the Land Titles Office in Toronto of deeds 1921-48) and of mortgages (1922-48) were secured from Economics Research Division, Central Mortgage and Housing Corporation. York (East and West) in the registry divisions covers the southern part of York Country except the City of Toronto. The other division, York North, is largely rural and not to be confused with North York, which is urban although treated as rural in census classifications. A single series on total instruments registered in the same registry divisions from 1867 to 1894 was secured from the annual reports of the Inspector of Registry Offices.

The city of Toronto has detailed records on permits issued back to 1920 and total numbers and values of permits back to 1900. Numbers and values for most years back to 1886 were obtained from vault records of Hugh C. MacLean Publications Ltd., Toronto. Local newspaper files were also consulted. Numbers were not found for 1886, 1887, 1905, and 1906 and were inferred from values of permits issued in those years. An estimate for 1890, for which neither values nor numbers could be found, was interpolated. The series was also adjusted for certain anomalies in 1891 and 1892. For example: "in 1891 and 1892 . . . the totals (value) were swollen by inclusion of the new Parliament Buildings and the City Hall" (*Toronto the Prosperous,* Mail and Empire, Toronto, 1906); also: "The record of building permits . . . is very incomprehensible. Permits (numbers) taken out . . . show a considerable increase over . . . last year. But where is the work?" (*Canadian Architect and Builder,* April 1892, 36).

Numbers and values of building permits for localities in Greater Toronto appear in the annual reports of the Ontario Bureau of Labour from 1906 to 1914. Records from 1920 to the present were obtained directly from local building inspectors in the suburban municipalities. Estimates of dwellings erected in the period after 1930 appear in the useful study by Humphrey Carver, *How Much Housing Does Greater Toronto Need?* (Toronto, 1946).

A population series for Greater Toronto was developed by interpolating decennial census figures with an annual series based on estimates made by local assessment commissioners.

Two indexes of building for Toronto and suburbs were made: number of permits per capita, 1886-1948, and number of residential permits per capita, 1920-48. The problem of gaps in the building data was dealt with by adjusting the population coverage in the denominator of the ratio to conform with the permit coverage in the numerator.

One would judge from reading contemporary commentaries that the peak came in 1889. The series on registrations of real instruments and subdivision plans show an 1889 peak. However, the value of permits show a peak value in 1891, with 1892 also above 1889. The peak shown in American studies varies from 1890 to 1892. The Montreal peak in both numbers and values came in 1887, with a secondary peak in 1889. This question of the precise date of the turning point in Toronto building is not a crucial one for the conclusions of the present study.

Winnipeg real estate activity. The real estate data for Winnipeg were taken directly from the property records in the Land Titles Office in Winnipeg. The totals of transfers, mortgages, and discharges of mortgages were obtained annually from 1886 to 1948 and the total number of all instruments registered under the old registry system was obtained for each year from 1872 to 1894. The Torrens system was enacted in 1885 and introduced the following year.

7. Tables of Estimates

The estimates described in this chapter are shown in the Appendix. the rough estimates of G.N.P. appear in table I. Tables J and K present all the data on transportation investment for which firm estimates could be made on an annual basis. The only significant transport expenditures not included are municipal streets and high-ways, and the electric railways. Table L presents federal and provincial investment expenditures, annually, from 1901 to 1930, and table M shows gross investment by all governments, quinquennially, from 1901 to 1930. The housing estimates appear in table N. The various series on building and real estate activity are shown in tables O and P.

Appendix:
Tables of the Estimates

THE first part of Table A shows the annual flow of construction materials to construction uses, at producers' prices. This series was converted to an index with 1921 equal to 100.0 and applied to the value of the material component of total construction in 1921, the benchmark year, to obtain the material component of total construction in each year from 1896 to 1930. The material component was expressed in constant (1913) dollars using the cost of construction materials index described in Chapter VII. Annual real wage costs were obtained by applying the ratios of real wages paid to material costs in 1913 prices. The derivation of these ratios is explained in Chapter VII. The material series was converted into current dollars by applying the index of material costs mentioned above. The wage component was also expressed in current dollars, using the Department of Labour index of construction wage rates, 1900 to 1930. (The trend of this index was extrapolated to 1896 to obtain a rough index for the four years before 1900.) The sum of the two series – material costs and wage costs – was then divided by 85.7 to incorporate the 14.3 per cent of total construction attributed to overhead and profit (see Chapter VII). The estimates of total construction appear in column 1 of Table A2. Column 2 shows the percentage relation of the cost of materials component, in-current prices, to estimated total construction. Column 3, the implicit cost of construction index, was obtained by dividing the sum of the materials and wage components in current dollars by their sum in constant dollars.

TABLE A
1. Annual Flow of Construction Materials, 1900-30
(millions of dollars)

	1900	1901	1902	1903	1904	1905
1. Production of construction materials	67	68	81	94	95	112
2. Exports of construction materials	27	29	32	33	30	33
3. Imports plus duties less re-exports and duty rebates	16	16	18	22	25	25
4. Available supply at producers' prices	55	55	67	83	90	104
5. Flow to non-construction use at producers' prices	12	13	13	14	14	16
6. Flow to construction	43	42	54	69	76	88
7. Freight charges	5	5	6	7	8	9
8. Sales tax	—	—	—	—	—	—
9. Flow to construction adjusted for tax and freight	48	47	59	76	84	97

	1906	1907	1908	1909	1910	1911	1912	1913	1914	1915
1.	143	163	149	174	188	208	213	214	186	160
2.	38	39	35	39	39	36	36	36	37	46
3.	26	28	21	23	31	40	56	57	35	21
4.	131	152	135	158	180	212	233	236	184	135
5.	19	23	21	22	26	31	37	39	29	27
6.	112	130	114	136	154	181	197	197	156	109
7.	10	11	10	13	15	16	17	17	13	10
8.	—	—	—	—	—	—	—	—	—	—
9.	122	141	124	148	169	197	214	212	169	118

TABLE A (Continued)

1. Annual Flow of Construction Materials, 1900-30
(millions of dollars)

	1916	1917	1918	1919	1920
1. Production of construction materials	180	241	277	338	489
2. Exports of construction materials	55	54	61	97	109
3. Imports plus duties less re- exports and duty rebates	26	34	36	40	54
4. Available supply at producers' prices	151	221	252	281	435
5. Flow to non-construction use at producers' prices	36	48	44	52	66
6. Flow to construction	115	173	208	229	368
7. Freight charges	9	11	13	14	20
8. Sales tax	—	—	—	—	—
9. Flow to construction adjusted for tax and freight	123	183	221	243	388

	1921	1922	1923	1924	1925	1926	1927	1928	1929	1930
1.	300	295	345	327	333	340	354	409	455	360
2.	74	86	109	99	101	96	87	78	78	58
3.	35	33	41	34	33	34	37	44	51	36
4.	261	242	278	262	265	278	304	375	428	338
5.	45	39	50	44	44	51	53	62	71	53
6.	217	203	228	218	221	226	251	313	357	286
7.	15	15	16	16	17	17	20	24	27	23
8.	6	9	11	11	11	11	11	9	7	3
9.	238	227	254	244	249	255	281	347	392	312

TABLE A (Continued)
2. Annual Estimates of Total New and Repair Construction, 1896-1930

Year	Total construction (millions of dollars)	Percentage of material component	Implicit cost of construction index (1913 – 100.0)
1896	78	47.4	58.8
97	67	46.5	57.5
98	75	45.7	57.4
99	87	46.8	60.2
1900	119	49.8	66.6
1901	118	48.7	66.8
2	150	48.1	70.1
3	194	47.9	73.2
4	220	47.4	74.7
1905	253	46.7	76.9
1906	316	47.3	82.2
7	360	47.8	86.9
8	322	47.1	86.7
9	396	45.9	85.7
1910	453	45.6	88.9
1911	535	45.1	91.2
2	597	44.0	94.4
3	583	44.7	100.0
4	480	43.1	97.1
1915	344	42.2	95.7
1916	336	44.9	103.1
7	464	48.3	120.7
8	558	48.4	138.7
9	618	48.2	162.2
1920	986	48.3	198.7
1921	631	46.2	177.1
2	624	44.6	162.4
3	697	44.7	166.7
4	692	43.3	164.2
1925	697	43.8	161.3
1926	703	44.3	159.5
7	783	44.1	158.8
8	940	45.2	161.9
9	1,046	46.0	167.3
1930	928	41.3	165.5

TABLE B
New and Repair Construction, Quinquennially, 1896-1930
(millions of dollars)

	New construction	Repair construction	Gross and repair construction
1896-1900	269	156	425
1901-5	681	254	935
1906-10	1,439	408	1,847
1911-15	2,007	531	2,538
1916-20	2,122	841	2,963
1921-25	2,271	1,070	3,341
1926-30	3,109	1,290	4,399

There is one omission in the estimates of the annual and quinquennial flows of machinery and equipment which appear in Tables C and D: the value of the unrecorded imports of ships from 1914 to 1925. The figures were recently obtained through the courtesy of Professor F. A. Knox. They have not been incorporated in the estimates since the amounts were too small relative to totals to warrant revising all the tables of investment. However they are fairly large relative to the totals for classes 5, 6, and 7 in the two tables. The amounts involved are given below in millions of dollars:

1914—1	1917—1	1920—	1923—
1915—1	1918—5	1921—4	1924—
1916—1	1919—	1922—	1925—2

TABLE C
Annual Flow of Machinery and Equipment at Producers' Prices, 1900-25
(millions of dollars)

	1900	1901	1902	1903	1904	1905	1906	1907	1908	1909	1910	1911	1912
Class 1 (Farm Machinery and Equipment)													
Production	10	12	14	14	14	13	14	15	15	20	21	21	26
Exports	2	2	2	2	2	2	2	3	3	4	5	5	5
Imports and duties less re-exports and duty rebates	3	3	4	4	3	3	4	4	4	6	9	13	15
Flow at producers' prices	11	13	16	17	16	14	16	16	15	22	25	29	36
Classes 2, 3, and 4 (Industrial, Electrical, and Mining Machinery and Equipment)													
Production	4	5	6	7	7	7	9	11	11	12	14	16	18
Exports	—	—	—	—	—	—	—	—	—	—	—	—	—
Imports, etc.	6	6	7	8	8	9	11	14	11	13	18	23	31
Flow at producers' prices	10	11	13	15	15	16	20	25	22	24	32	39	49

Classes 5, 6, and 7 (Railway Rolling Stock, Other Land Vehicles, and Ships)

Production	9	10	12	13	11	14	22	34	28	23	22	32	42
Exports	—	—	—	—	—	—	—	—	—	—	—	1	1
Imports, etc.	1	1	2	10	3	5	3	4	2	4	5	7	18
Flow at producers' prices	10	11	14	23	14	19	25	38	30	27	27	38	59

Classes 8, 9, 10, and 11 (Office and Store, Professional and Miscellaneous Machinery, and Equipment)

Production	4	5	6	7	7	7	9	9	9	11	12	15	19
Exports	—	—	—	—	—	—	—	—	—	—	—	1	—
Imports, etc.	4	4	5	5	6	6	6	7	6	6	8	9	11
Flow at producers' prices	8	9	11	12	13	13	15	16	15	17	20	23	30

Total (Classes 1 to 11)

Production	27	32	37	42	39	42	54	70	63	66	69	84	106
Exports	2	2	2	3	3	3	3	4	4	5	6	7	7
Imports and duties less re-exports and duty rebates	13	15	18	28	20	22	24	29	23	28	41	52	75
Flow at producers prices	38	44	54	67	56	61	75	95	82	89	104	129	173

TABLE C (Continued)
Annual Flow of Machinery and Equipment at Producers' Prices, 1900-25
(millions of dollars)

	1913	1914	1915	1916	1917	1918	1919	1920	1921	1922	1923	1924	1925
Class 1 (Farm Machinery and Equipment)													
Production	33	26	13	20	33	33	36	42	31	16	23	21	21
Exports	7	7	9	5	5	7	10	11	6	5	7	9	11
Imports and duties less re-exports and duty rebates	9	4	4	8	14	20	14	18	10	7	9	6	10
Flow at producers prices	35	23	8	22	42	46	40	49	35	17	25	19	20
Classes 2, 3, and 4 (Industrial, Electrical, and Mining Machinery and Equipment)													
Production	19	15	9	20	27	28	28	42	40	26	36	40	38
Exports	1	1	1	2	3	5	6	4	2	2	3	3	2
Imports, etc.	31	21	22	29	32	32	34	43	30	25	28	26	30
Flow at producers' prices	49	35	30	47	56	54	55	81	68	49	62	63	66
Classes 5, 6, and 7 (Railway Rolling Stock, Other Land Vehicles, and Ships)													
Production	57	39	19	31	64	82	106	108	73	37	73	57	47
Exports	1	2	3	14	10	20	47	37	13	9	12	10	11
Imports, etc.	17	6	3	5	7	8	11	11	7	7	8	6	7
Flow at producers' prices	73	44	20	22	61	70	70	83	67	36	68	53	42

Classes 8, 9, 10, and 11 (Office and Store, Professional and Miscellaneous Machinery and Equipment)

Production	24	21	12	18	22	28	29	37	24	22	27	24	25
Exports	—	1	1	1	2	3	2	2	1	1	1	2	2
Imports, etc.	11	9	7	10	11	11	14	17	12	11	12	12	13
Flow at producers' prices	35	29	19	27	31	36	41	52	34	32	37	34	36

Total (Classes 1 to 11)

Production	133	100	54	90	146	171	199	230	168	101	159	142	131
Exports	9	10	14	22	19	35	65	54	23	17	24	23	26
Imports and duties less re-exports and duty rebates	68	40	36	51	64	70	73	90	59	50	57	50	60
Flow at producers' prices	193	131	77	118	190	206	207	265	204	135	192	168	164

TABLE D

Quinquennial Estimates of Gross Investment in Machinery and Equipment, 1896-1930
(millions of dollars)

	1896-1900	1901-5	1906-10	1911-15	1916-20	1921-25	1926-30
Class 1 (Farm Machinery and Equipment)							
Flow at producers' prices	39	76	94	131	199	116	207
Taxes	–	–	–	–	1	3	–
Freight	4	7	7	10	18	14	25
Mark-ups	20	37	48	63	96	63	107
Gross investment	62	120	149	204	314	196	339
Classes 2, 3, and 4 (Industrial, Electrical, and Mining Machinery and Equipment)							
Flow at producers' prices	29	69	124	202	293	308	576
Taxes	1	–	–	–	1	14	15
Freight	1	3	6	9	13	15	31
Mark-ups	5	12	22	37	53	63	94
Gross investment	35	84	152	248	361	400	716
Classes 5 and 6 (Railway Rolling Stock and Other Land Vehicles)							
Flow at producers' prices	28	58	120	202	284	236	395
Taxes	–	–	–	–	6	15	16
Freight	1	1	1	3	8	10	22
Mark-ups	5	7	11	21	46	46	84
Gross investment	34	65	132	227	344	307	516

Class 7 (Ships and Boats)

Flow at producers' prices	8	24	26	31	23	30	113
Taxes	–	–	–	–	–	–	–
Freight	–	–	–	–	–	–	–
Gross investment	8	24	26	31	23	30	113

Classes 8, 9, 10, and 11 (Office and Store, Professional, and Miscellaneous Machinery and Equipment)

Flow at producers' prices	31	56	81	136	187	173	262
Taxes	–	–	–	–	1	8	7
Freight	2	3	4	7	8	9	14
Mark-ups	15	28	42	59	84	88	131
Gross investment	48	87	127	202	280	278	413

Total (Classes 1 to 11)

Flow at producers' prices	135	283	445	702	986	863	1553
Taxes	–	–	–	–	9	40	38
Freight	8	14	18	29	47	48	92
Mark-ups	45	84	123	180	279	260	416
Gross investment	187	380	586	912	1,322	1,211	2,097

TABLE E

Quinquennial Investment in Inventories, by Types, 1896-1930

(millions of dollars)

Type	1896-1900	1901-5	1906-10	1911-15	1916-20	1921-25	1926-30(a)
Farm inventories							
Livestock on farms	17	100	63	112	98	-3	-46
Grain on farms	3	18	23	168	-18	20	
Grain in commercial channels	3	10	5	65	-43	101	50
Business inventories							
Manufacturing	19	61	95	-27	260	14	
Trade	40	23	63	25	308	5	621
Miscellaneous	4	10	13	16	-17	22	
Total investment	86	222	262	360	589	159	625

(a) The figures for 1926 to 1930 are from D.B.S., *National Accounts, Income and Expenditure* (Ottawa, 1952). The value of the physical change in business inventories was obtained by deducting the reported inventory revaluation item from the change in the book value of business inventories. Investment in other inventories included in the National Accounts is the value of the physical change.

TABLE F

Book Values of Inventories, by Types, Selected Years, 1900-30
(millions of dollars at December 31)

	1900	1905	1910	1915	1920	1925	1930(a)
Farm inventories							
Livestock on farms	241	397	535	888	803	641	634
Grain on farms	45	63	94	266	311	209	128
Grain in commercial channels	14	24	34	115	118	213	130
Business inventories							
Manufacturing	119	190	296	337	873	695	849
Wholesaling	119	151	223	306	878	275	291
Retailing						417	498
Miscellaneous	22	34	49	80	124	119	129
Total inventories	560	859	1,231	1,992	3,107	2,569	2,659

(a) The figures for 1930 are from P.I.C.F., 45.

TABLE G

Balance of International Payments, Current Transactions, 1901-30

(millions of dollars)

	1901-5	1906-10	1911-15	1916-20	1921-25	1926-30
Credits						
1. Merchandise exports	944	1,307	2,062	6,366	4,962	5,886
2. Net exports non-monetary gold	95	49	74	81	138	178
3. Tourist and travel expenditure	37	65	105	223	440	870
4. Interest and dividends	24	34	56	171	208	239
5. Freight, shipping, and all other current credits	142	257	360	616	648	856
6. Total credits	1,242	1,712	2,657	7,457	6,396	8,029
Debits						
1. Merchandise imports	1,151	1,727	2,705	5,062	4,120	5,484
3. Tourist and travel expenditure	42	94	170	210	314	497
4. Interest and dividends	208	360	711	1,033	1,211	1,442
5. Freight, shipping, and all other current debits	142	315	586	1,414	679	1,169
6. Total debits	1,543	2,496	4,172	7,719	6,324	8,592
Net Balances						
1. Merchandise trade	-207	-420	-643	1,304	842	402
2. Net exports non-monetary gold	95	49	74	81	138	178
3. Tourist and travel expenditure	-5	-29	-65	13	126	373
4. Interest and dividends	-184	-326	-655	-862	-1,003	-1,203
5. Freight, shipping, and other	0	-58	-226	-798	-31	-313
-30- Total net balance	-301	-784	-1,515	-262	72	-563

TABLE H
Domestic Capital Formation and Gross Investment, 1901-30
(millions of dollars)

	1901-5	1906-10	1911-15	1916-20	1921-25	1926-30
1. Construction	681	1,439	2,007	2,122	2,271	3,109
2. Machinery and Equipment	380	586	912	1,322	1,211	2,097
3. Inventories	222	262	360	589	159	625
4. Gross domestic capital formation (1 + 2 + 3)	1,283	2,287	3,279	4,033	3,641	5,831
5. Foreign investment	-301	-784	-1,515	-262	72	-563
6. Gross investment (4 + 5)	982	1,503	1,764	3,771	3,713	5,268

TABLE I
Rough Estimates of Gross National Product, 1901-30
(millions of dollars)

	Five-year totals
1901-5	5,650
1906-10	8,482
1911-15	12,178
1916-20	20,923
1921-25	22,589
1926-30	28,758[a]

(a) The total for 1926-30 is from D.B.S., *National Accounts, Income and Expenditure* (Ottawa, 1952).

TABLE J
Annual Gross Investment and Repair, Steam Railways, 1896-1930(a)
(millions of dollars)

Year	Net(b)	Road construction Replacement(c) and repair	Net(b)	Equipment Replacement	Repair	Gross investment and repair
1896	3.2	8.1	.9	.6	5.6	18.4
1897	6.4	7.8	1.4	.6	5.8	22.0
1898	12.6	8.3	2.9	.7	6.2	30.7
1899	8.4	9.3	3.9	.8	7.1	29.5
1900	11.4	10.3	3.4	.9	8.1	34.1
1901	12.6	11.7	4.6	1.0	9.0	38.9
1902	12.4	13.8	6.6	1.2	10.6	44.6
1903	19.2	14.7	8.2	1.4	12.4	55.9
1904	25.0	16.1	6.3	1.5	12.4	61.3
1905	33.0	17.4	8.5	1.6	14.7	75.2
1906	42.5	19.1	13.3	1.9	17.3	94.1
1907	72.2	19.6	23.8	2.0	18.9	136.5
1908	75.5	19.8	18.7	2.9	18.1	135.0
1909	69.6	23.9	14.8	1.3	21.4	131.0
1910	88.1	26.9	11.8	1.5	23.3	151.6
1911	93.4	29.1	20.4	2.7	25.1	170.7
1912	110.3	32.8	34.1	2.8	30.2	210.2
1913	115.7	34.1	46.7	2.8	33.1	232.4
1914	91.9	29.8	23.1	2.7	29.5	177.0
1915	78.9	31.5	7.9	1.5	28.5	148.3
1916	29.7	36.5	6.4	2.0	35.4	110.0
1917	27.1	44.3	28.9	6.8	45.9	153.0
1918	26.6	59.9	37.1	4.9	69.5	198.0
1919	32.4	79.0	31.5	7.6	79.2	229.7
1920	42.3	94.7	36.6	8.3	107.3	289.2
1921	33.2	84.9	37.7	2.7	87.7	246.2
1922	15.0	76.6	6.2	6.1	83.7	187.6
1923	35.0	78.4	30.1	13.4	86.1	243.0
1924	32.1	74.0	19.1	9.1	77.9	212.2
1925	22.6	70.4	2.8	5.6	77.3	178.7
1926	30.5	76.4	14.1	7.8	82.9	211.7
1927	39.3	82.2	30.9	8.3	84.4	245.1
1928	55.4	93.5	12.4	9.5	91.3	262.1
1929	79.1	89.4	55.4	9.1	89.9	322.9
1930	53.2	74.3	32.8	13.7	67.6	241.6

(a) Government investment in railways is included in the estimates.
(b) This is "net" as the railways use the term.
(c) A reliable breakdown of this component on an annual basis has not been made.

TABLE K

Annual Gross Investment in Non-Railway Transportation Structures, Equipment, and Construction Repair, 1901-30

(millions of dollars)

| Year | Construction Gross investment | | | | Automobiles | | Gross investment, repair, and consumers' outlays on automobiles |
	Provincial highways and bridges	Canals	Harbour and river work	Repair	Producers	Consumers'	
1901	.6	2.2	2.5	1.6	—	—	6.9
1902	1.0	2.0	3.5	1.8	—	—	8.3
1903	.9	2.0	4.6	2.0	.1	.3	9.9
1904	.4	2.2	5.3	2.3	.2	.6	11.0
1905	.4	1.7	6.1	2.6	.3	.9	12.0
1906	.8	1.0	4.8	2.6	.4	1.0	10.6
1907	1.8	1.9	8.1	3.7	.5	1.5	17.5
1908	2.6	2.1	9.1	4.5	.7	1.8	20.8
1909	2.7	1.8	7.6	3.8	1.8	4.8	22.5
1910	3.8	2.4	9.2	4.4	3.3	8.8	31.9
1911	4.8	2.7	11.2	4.9	5.0	13.5	42.1
1912	8.1	2.4	12.7	5.3	6.8	18.2	53.5
1913	9.9	2.6	18.2	6.7	7.4	20.3	65.1
1914	8.8	5.4	18.6	6.3	6.8	18.8	64.7

Year							
1915	6.9	6.2	13.7	4.9	7.5	21.6	60.8
1916	4.2	4.5	10.5	4.7	10.5	29.4	63.8
1917	4.2	1.9	8.3	4.4	25.6	69.4	113.8
1918	4.5	2.4	4.4	4.9	29.7	76.0	121.9
1919	10.0	4.9	6.9	6.8	32.1	82.2	142.9
1920	16.5	6.1	9.8	8.7	40.7	103.5	185.3
1921	20.3	6.2	9.8	8.9	29.0	82.9	157.1
1922	21.2	7.2	10.7	10.1	29.9	80.6	159.7
1923	24.6	8.0	14.9	12.3	31.3	82.1	173.2
1924	15.6	10.2	15.9	12.8	28.0	77.5	160.0
1925	18.7	12.3	14.6	14.0	38.3	97.0	194.9
1926	19.1	13.5	9.3	13.8	55.7	140.0	251.4
1927	(not available)			59.4	59.4	145.7	
1928	(not available)				82.8	183.7	
1929	40.8	51.7(a)			81.5	184.4	358.4
1930	54.3	56.5(a)			51.6	106.2	268.6

(a) These include canals, harbour and river work, new and repair, and highway repair.

TABLE L
Annual Gross Investment, Federal and Provincial Governments, 1901-30
(millions of dollars)

Year	Federal government				Provincial government	Total federal and provincial
	Railway	Other transportation	Buildings and other	Total		
1901	3.2	4.7	1.7	9.6	.8	10.4
1902	2.7	5.5	1.3	9.4	1.2	10.6
1903	1.8	6.6	1.4	9.7	1.1	10.8
1904	3.6	7.5	2.5	13.6	.7	14.3
1905	3.9	7.8	3.5	15.2	.6	15.8
1906	6.2	5.8	2.1	14.1	1.3	15.4
1907	21.0	10.0	3.3	34.4	3.0	37.4
1908	27.5	11.2	4.6	43.3	5.0	48.3
1909	21.0	9.4	2.7	33.2	5.8	39.0
1910	23.6	11.6	2.1	37.3	9.1	46.4
1911	22.4	13.9	3.1	39.3	11.2	50.5
1912	17.6	15.1	4.8	37.5	15.7	53.2
1913	20.7	20.8	9.2	50.6	19.5	70.1
1914	19.6	24.0	10.4	54.0	17.3	71.3
1915	17.6	19.9	5.7	43.1	14.5	57.6
1916	15.3	15.0	3.8	34.1	9.4	43.5
1917	9.1	10.2	3.4	22.7	6.9	29.6
1918	6.4	6.8	8.1	21.3	8.6	29.9
1919	3.8	11.8	9.6	25.3	15.8	41.1
1920	1.7	15.9	5.4	23.0	25.0	48.0
1921	1.5	16.0	3.8	21.3	32.3	53.6
1922	1.0	17.9	2.0	20.8	30.2	51.0
1923	—	22.9	2.5	25.4	34.8	60.2
1924	—	26.1	5.0	31.1	24.8	55.9
1925	—	26.9	4.9	31.7	26.6	58.3
1926	2.7	22.8	3.1	28.6	24.1	52.7
1927				36.9	31.6	68.5
1928	(breakdown not available)					
				40.2	41.2	81.4
1929				45.9	51.5	97.4
1930				63.2	67.7	130.9

TABLE M
Gross Investment, All Governments, 1901-30
(millions of dollars)

	Federal	Provincial	Municipal	Total
1901-5	57.5	4.5	32.0	94.0
1906-10	162.3	24.2	61.4	247.9
1911-15	224.6	78.1	137.0	439.7
1916-20	126.3	65.7	100.1	292.1
1921-25	130.3	148.7	159.8	438.8
1926-30	214.8	216.1	171.1	602.0

TABLE N
Gross Investment, Residential Housing, 1896-1930
(millions of dollars)

	Non-farm	Prairie farm	Other farm	Total
1896-1900	85.9	10.4	7.3	104
1901-5	164.4	41.7	15.6	222
1906-10	372.0	64.4	31.2	468
1911-15	524.3	26.5	16.8	568
1916-20	555.3	66.9	18.8	641
1921-25	709.6	16.9	15.1	742
1926-30	967.1	72.0	20.8	1060

TABLE O
Urban Building and Real Estate Activity, Selected Series, 1867-1945

Year	Winnipeg — No. of instruments registered	No. of property transfers, mortgages, and discharges of mortgages registered (Torrens system)	Montreal — No. of permits for new buildings	Index of permits for new buildings per capita (1900-100.0)	Toronto — Index of residential permits per capita (1920-100.0)	National index of urban building activity (1900-100.0)
1867	—	—	281	—	—	28.0
8	—	—	351			55.3
9	—	—	490			49.7
1870	—	—	603			61.1
1	401	—	1,060			107.5
2	502		728			73.8
3	1,914		724			82.5
4	840		850			86.2
5	920		732			74.2
6	920		463			46.9
7	1,230		349			34.4
8	1,903		241			25.1
9	1,886		240			24.3
1880	2,623		209			21.2
1	10,787		248			25.2
2	11,804		231			23.4

3	4,963	—	260	—	—	26.4
4	2,814	—	317	—	—	32.2
5	1,630	—	429	—	—	43.5
6	2,166	424	699	89.3	—	70.9
7	1,824	873	1,076	80.3	—	123.2
8	1,400	1,082	933	114.9	—	112.2
9	1,545	1,391	1,032	142.3	—	125.6
1890	3,079	1,341	937	122.8	—	115.3
1	2,733	1,574	778	111.8	—	111.1
2	2,931	2,063	640	86.8	—	104.1
3	2,611	2,688	561	77.7	—	97.5
4	2,354	2,455	382	67.3	—	66.2
5	2,426	2,294	277	61.6	—	68.7
6	2,295	2,159	315	67.5	—	55.2
7	2,349	2,330	408	55.1	—	64.1
8	2,410	2,912	351	88.4	—	92.7
9	3,259	3,735	357	108.0	—	110.7

Table 0 (Continued)
Urban Building and Real Estate Activity, Selected Series, 1867-1945

Year	Winnipeg No. of instruments registered	No. of property transfers, mortgages, and discharges of mortgages registered (Torrens system)	Montreal No. of permits for new buildings	Index of permits for new buildings per capita (1900=100.0)	Toronto Index of residential permits per capita (1920=100.0)	National index of urban building activity (1900=100.0)
1900	4,104	4,510	331	100.0	—	100.0
1	4,505	5,191	443	139.8	—	120.3
2	5,844	8,109	467	210.6	—	136.5
3	4,984	10,616	581	271.0	—	192.7
4	4,221	12,268	799	322.7	—	249.5
5	4,487	17,396	1,145	379.4	—	332.8
6	4,549	22,605	1,484	418.0	—	409.4
7	4,338	21,409	1,472	438.9	—	388.2
8	3,827	20,909	1,283	425.3	—	299.0
9	4,447	25,295	1,702	472.1	—	467.2
1910	4,154	27,829	2,726	548.1	—	608.3
1	4,457	32,453	2,811	586.4	—	797.4
2	4,530	36,511	2,845	496.7	—	1,106.3
3	4,535	37,304	2,698	450.5	—	817.7

Year						
4	4,576	36,227	2,520	438.0	—	520.8
5	3,924	17,121	(a)	288.9	—	183.5
6	3,618	14,136	1,492	254.7	—	201.6
7	3,332	12,904	(a)	281.8	—	147.0
8	3,215	11,492	(a)	264.8	—	138.9
9	3,820	17,126	(a)	507.5	—	248.8
1920	3,988	23,143	(a)	540.2	100.0	262.1
1	3,648	19,774	(a)	680.6	168.6	296.5
2	4,038	19,507	3,742	794.0	382.4	410.8
3	3,552	18,894	3,951	702.4	305.7	360.6
4	3,159	16,793	4,445	544.8	215.1	347.0
5	2,839	17,749	4,124	529.3	224.6	348.9
6	2,870	19,180	4,003	481.3	166.8	441.6
7	2,512	20,069	4,595	523.8	185.4	522.8
8	2,519	20,445	4,940	494.8	191.5	609.1
9	2,397	19,822	4,116	463.2	162.9	632.1

(a) Breakdown of new and repair not available in these years. Total permits for both new and repair from 1914 to 1922 were: 3,626, 2,081, 2,843, 1,579, 1,481, 2,133, 2,699, 4,577, 5,338.

TABLE O (Continued)
Urban Building and Real Estate Activity, Selected Series, 1867-1945

Year	Winnipeg No. of instruments registered	No. of Property transfers, mortgages, and discharges of mortgages registered (Torrens system)	Montreal No. of permits for new buildings	Index of permits for new buildings per capita (1900=100.0)	Toronto Index of residential permits per capita (1920=100.0)	National index of urban building activity (1900=100.0)
1930	2,243	17,005	3,275	395.7	128.0	462.2
1	1,925	13,657	3,173	350.1	117.7	335.3
2	2,061	10,197	1,307	235.5	41.0	136.3
3	1,953	8,517	875	191.5	29.4	73.5
4	2,064	8,412	813	185.5	40.8	90.7
5	2,515	9,418	776	217.4	53.6	153.1
6	3,350	10,328	926	229.7	65.6	131.7
7	2,960	11,309	983	251.4	60.4	165.9
8	4,185	12,241	950	233.2	57.9	185.0
9	2,935	12,120	1,151	289.2	90.3	182.0

1940	1,971	14,005	1,254	280.8	101.8	229.5
1	2,008	16,336	1,105	278.4	109.8	249.6
2	2,216	—	—	212.6	76.5	179.9
3	2,306	—	—	190.3	63.4	130.3
4	2,261	—	—	207.4	78.2	202.1
5	2,583	—	—	294.9	107.1	308.1
6	2,718	—	—	—	—	560.7
7	2,276	—	—	—	—	—
8	2,115	—	—	—	—	—
9	2,011	—	—	—	—	—

TABLE P
Real Estate Registrations, Toronto, 1869-1948

Year	Subdivision plans registered Toronto (a)	York	All instruments registered Toronto	York	Property transfers registered Toronto	York	Mortgages registered Toronto	York	Discharges of mortgages registered Toronto	York
1869	—	1,574	2,433							
70	—	1,705	3,497							
1	—	1,791	3,968							
2	—	1,321	4,155							
3	—	1,277	4,511							
4	—	2,640	5,939							
5	—	2,549	5,200							
6	—	1,399	4,888							
7	—	1,641	5,272							
8	—	2,675	4,880							
9	—	2,855	5,000							
1880	21	3,105	5,815							
1	10	3,409	6,805							
2	40	3,796	6,610							
3	28	3,382	7,136							
4	43	3,277	8,921							
5	33	3,722	9,847							
6	56	5,230	14,243							
7	89	7,387	17,639							
8	78	7,366	18,854							
9	49	115	9,583	24,420						

Year										
1890	42	97	20,572	8,708						
1	34	36	17,594	6,892						
2	13	23	14,035	5,764						
3	12	16	10,549	3,438						
4	7	10	8,790	2,984	2,198	1,080	2,133	665	1,991	648
5	5	16	—	—	1,674	815	1,674	588	1,669	534
6	3	6	—	—	1,606	689	1,374	488	1,328	451
7	4	9	—	—	1,415	713	1,241	375	1,248	376
8	5	7	—	—	1,696	716	1,470	405	1,505	438
9	7	7	—	—	2,524	872	1,847	409	1,773	448
1900	13	9	—	—	2,812	838	2,108	442	1,795	498
1	21	8	—	—	3,388	1,160	2,614	527	2,315	543
2	14	10	—	—	3,790	1,332	3,132	614	2,432	553
3	13	10	—	—	4,255	1,320	3,576	727	2,711	617
4	15	13	—	—	6,004	1,731	4,932	898	3,496	765
5	39	20	—	—		(not available)				
6	69	32	—	—	8,127	2,318	6,999	1,369	4,227	875
7	59	30	—	—	8,192	2,619	7,836	1,617	4,538	1,099
8	40	36	—	—	6,671	2,243	6,969	1,661	4,205	1,057
9	47	42	—	—	9,102	2,974	9,328	2,132	5,663	1,251

(a) East Toronto only before 1905.

TABLE P (Continued)
Real Estate Registrations, Toronto, 1869-1948

Year	Subdivision plans registered		All instruments registered		Property transfers registered		Mortgages registered		Discharges of mortgages registered	
	Toronto	York	Toronto	York	Toronto	York	Toronto	York	Toronto	York
1910	58	38	—	—	12,669	2,713	12,186	1,819	7,221	1,313
1	56	114	—	—	13,653	4,245	13,267	2,777	8,352	1,686
2	46	129	—	—	17,508	6,072	16,922	3,960	9,877	2,334
3	44	89	—	—	15,883	5,569	16,265	4,007	9,885	2,193
4	19	71	—	—	12,111	5,665	13,443	4,096	9,744	2,430
5	9	17	—	—	6,829	4,176	7,143	2,222	6,965	1,752
6	6	4	—	—	6,001	3,179	4,846	1,176	6,065	1,260
7	11	10	—	—	7,166	3,419	6,176	1,567	7,154	1,511
8	7	15	—	—	7,944	3,391	6,799	1,863	6,827	1,407
9	11	32	—	—	17,656	6,329	16,468	4,007	11,375	2,438
1920	20	35	—	—	19,833	6,829	18,707	4,783	12,545	2,694
1	22	41	—	—	15,011	6,880	14,626	5,369	10,986	2,630
2	20	63	—	—	15,728	7,901	17,699	6,993	12,163	3,236
3	25	61	—	—	14,431	7,687	17,513	7,063	12,597	3,698
4	14	25	—	—	11,263	7,096	15,678	6,386	13,982	3,752
5	12	20	—	—	10,637	6,929	16,127	6,156	14,352	4,150
6	10	23	—	—	9,451	6,536	13,787	5,406	12,741	3,818
7	11	21	—	—	9,042	6,434	12,958	5,634	12,867	4,076
8	13	19	—	—	9,179	6,738	12,012	5,950	11,654	4,335
9	10	29	—	—	9,429	6,842	11,245	6,006	10,792	4,018

Year										
1930	16	32	—	—	8,405	6,445	10,340	5,417	9,437	3,681
1	4	21	—	—	7,476	5,795	8,955	4,885	8,197	3,324
2	14	9	—	—	5,160	4,358	4,621	2,517	4,760	2,045
3	6	5	—	—	4,237	3,323	2,531	1,475	3,132	1,533
4	4	6	—	—	4,073	3,234	2,535	1,614	3,146	1,523
5	5	3	—	—	4,278	3,407	2,966	1,913	3,550	1,708
6	2	14	—	—	4,544	3,949	3,124	2,399	3,813	2,081
7	7	4	—	—	5,157	4,185	3,596	2,733	4,064	2,242
8	7	10	—	—	5,147	4,301	3,256	2,630	3,785	2,101
9	6	17	—	—	5,187	4,789	3,123	3,128	3,502	2,073
1940	4	33	—	—	5,814	6,250	3,222	4,152	3,900	2,245
1	0	38	—	—	7,364	7,622	4,795	5,259	4,603	2,811
2	7	27	—	—	9,728	8,264	6,759	5,791	5,647	3,182
3	5	29	—	—	9,209	7,748	6,427	4,953	6,238	3,440
4	5	48	—	—	12,137	10,257	8,574	6,227	8,104	4,570
5	2	37	—	—	11,697	12,165	7,966	6,858	9,069	5,840
6	3	93	—	—	13,656	17,264	9,365	9,671	11,055	7,647
7	4	112	—	—	11,776	16,123	9,500	10,880	11,144	7,995
8	2	94	—	—	12,129	18,171	10,598	14,177	10,964	8,530

Notes

Chapter One

[1] In its broadest conception, suggested by Knight, the community's capital is simply its capacity to produce economic goods and services quantified at a point in time. Investment is the growth in productive capacity through time. (F. H. Knight, "Diminishing Returns from Investment," *Journal of Political Economy*, March 1944, 26-47,) By this definition real capital would include – in addition to physical durable assets and inventories held by producers and governments, housing, and the net stock of claims against foreign assets – all commodities held by consuming units, all natural resources, and the numbers and the qualities of that part of the population which contributes in any way to production. Qualities, here, refer to the health and energy of the members of the labour force as well as the knowledge applied in their activities as producers. Expenditures on the development and extension of health services, expenditures on education which spread knowledge of technical ways and means over a large number of people, and expenditures on research and experimentation which raise the level of technological knowledge, are undoubtedly investment expenditures, but these are all excluded from the present definition unless they are reflected in outlays on structures and machinery and equipment. Resource development is treated in the same way. The conventional concept of investment is far from satisfactory from the point of view of capital planning of underdeveloped countries.

[2] There are two possible interpretations of the term "real" depending upon the meaning attached to "production." Production may be defined as activity which ends with the commodities produced when these are in the hands of their final users, or, in accordance with the economic theory of value, as activity undertaken to satisfy consumers' wants. On this second view, if it is held consistently, all commodities would be regarded as productive agents administering want-satisfactions. (Cf. Knight, "Diminishing Returns from Investment," 35.) Consumption would then be defined as a flow of subjective services. If subjective or psychic incomes were regarded as the object of economic activity, it would imply that, by some means, these individual real incomes be aggregated into social real income, that capital be expressed in terms of its power to yield this fundamental income, and that investment be a measure of the size of variations in this power per units of time. Professor Knight has pointed out that we cannot define

real income in this sense in any meaningful way because it is impossible to distinguish economic activity from life in general. Even if this difficulty could be overcome, the concepts of income, capital, and investment involved would not be statistically operative. "Real" is therefore defined at the commodity level in order to apply quantitative methods and to avoid the difficult question of the nature and formation of tastes.

3 *Ibid.*, 34.

4 Cf. *Public Investment and Capital Formation* (Ottawa, 1945), 12-20. Resource development was defined as expenditures "designed to improve or maintain the material fabric of the country." The expenditures in 1926, including duplications of certain construction and equipment outlays, were $1 million by the federal government and $2.3 million by provincial governments. The total for both levels of government excluding duplications was $2 million. (Cf. Table 9, *Private and Public Investment in Canada, 1926-1951* (Ottawa, 1951). The latter study also included small amounts for exploration and developmental expenditures by mining companies. For a detailed discussion of the concepts employed in these two studies and their relation to the estimates used in D.B.S., *National Accounts Income and Expenditure* and to the estimates of the present study, see "Capital Formation in Canada," *Studies in Income and Wealth,* XIX, forthcoming publication of the National Bureau of Economic Research, New York.

5 The value of a specific capital item at any point of time is determined by the series of future services anticipated at that time, the expected future prices of these services, and the rate of discount. These are all subject to change over the life of the instrument, enhancing or reducing its value as the case may be. It is only that rate of depreciation and obsolescence which is consciously or implicitly anticipated as part of the future economic life of the instrument at the time of purchase which is regarded as a "normal" charge against gross receipts of operations. After purchase, when the process of valuing the capital is a matter of imputation within the enterprise and independent of the course of reproduction costs, the anticipated useful life, which along with various other factors entered into the formation of the price at the time of purchase, remains the basis for comparison by which imputed changes in value are reckoned normal or otherwise. When these changes are "otherwise," they are charged to capital account as revaluations. Depreciation, in the sense outlined above, is assumed to cover the using up of capital which takes place despite the expenditures on repairs and maintenance necessary to keep the capital in efficient operation. Replacement expenditures exceeding current expenditures on repair and maintenance by an amount equal to current depreciation would be required to maintain capital intact under this definition. The remaining types of capital change are allocable either to net capital investment (or disinvestment) or to capital revaluations, which include any other change in the value of the stock which may arise as a result of unanticipated obsolescence, windfall gains, or fortuitous change of any kind, as well as, in particular cases, the growth of earning power

through the creation of good will or other forms of monopolistic, intangible capacity. For the full discussion of capital consumption from which this description was taken, see Solomon Fabricant, *Capital Consumption and Adjustment* (New York, 1938).

6 From a typical budget speech in the early seventies, in which the minister is justifying federal investment expenditures on canals and railways. (Quoted by W. A. Mackintosh, *The Economic Background of Dominion-Provincial Relations* (Ottawa, 1939), 16.)

7 These earlier booms are discussed in Chapter IV which treats building and real estate activity in urban centres.

8 In 1900 and 1901, gross home investment in the United Kingdom reached the highest levels achieved from 1870 to 1913. This boom even attracted foreign, particularly American, capital to the United Kingdom in the finance of the underground tubes. (See A. Cairncross, *Home and Foreign Investment in Great Britain, 1870-1913* (Doctoral thesis, Cambridge University), 246-7 and Table 21.)

9 The pattern of Canadian economic experience appears to conform with Schumpeter's schema, wherein the second long "Kondratieff" cycle from 1843 to 1897 reaches a peak about 1870. (J. A. Schumpeter, *Business Cycles* (New York, 1939).) Because of the importance of international prices and price trends to a simple staple-producing and exporting economy and the fact that Kondratieff derived the shape of his cycles from data heavily weighted by prices, this conformity is not surprising. However, the relative secular stagnation in Canada from the seventies to the nineties was not the product of any rhythm in general international business activity, but of a closed frontier in the east and the absence of resources in the West. The relative flatness in the trend in Canadian activity from the seventies to the nineties, evident in the chart, reflects the status of the prairies in those years when, like other parts of the continental plain before they became resources, they were vacant.

10 See W. A. Mackintosh, *Economic Problems of the Prairie Provinces* (Toronto, 1935), Chapter 1, for trends in transportation costs and the cost of borrowing through this period.

11 Birth and mortality rates have played an important role, and in recent years the principal role, in determining the rate of growth of Canada's population, but in the period from 1870 to 1930 migration was chiefly responsible for the wide *variations* in the decade rates.

12 The population increased from 5.4 million in 1901 to 10.4 million in 1931, Net migration in this period was 1,928,000. (Cf. *Monthly Review*, Bank of Nova Scotia, July 1954.)

13 Including buildings, equipment, trucks, inventories, but excluding passenger cars.

14 W. A. Mackintosh, *Economic Background of Dominion-Provincial Relations* (Ottawa, 1939), 35.

15 If unskilled workers not allocated were all treated as manufacturing, the increase in manufacturing would still be lower than the national average. Actually these unallocated workers were working in construc-

tion and transportation as well as in manufacturing. (Cf. D.B.S. *Census Bulletin,* No. 0-6, *Occupations and Industries* (Ottawa, 1944).

[16] V. C.. Fowke, "The Distributive Pattern in the Prairie Provinces," *The Commerce Journal*, 1945, 70.

[17] *Ibid., 71.*

[18] The capacity of country elevators increased from 12.8 million bushels in 1900 to 192.9 million bushels in 1930. The cost of constructing these at 1930 prices would exceed $70 million, with no allowance for those destroyed or demolished during the period. Capacities are from *Canada Year Book* and unit costs from D. A. MacGibbon, *The Canadian Grain Trade* (Toronto, 1932), 93.

[19] Terminal capacity increased from 5.6 million bushels in 1900 to 201.7 million bushels in 1930.

[20] Cf. Fowke, "The Distributive Pattern in the Prairie Provinces," for a description of the institutional pattern of the typical market centre in the western provinces.

[21] One example will illustrate the need for caution in the use of the annual construction figures. The basic flow of materials series was not adjusted for changes in inventories. In years when construction was rising or falling continuously, the error introduced would be small, but in some turning-point years the error in the final estimate would be large. For example, there was almost certainly a large, unplanned accumulation of lumber, lath, shingle, and other material inventories in 1920. The estimate of the volume of construction for that year would be too high by some multiple – more than twice – of this investment. For 1921, and perhaps 1921 and 1922 also, the estimates would be correspondingly low, but not by an equal amount, owing to changes in prices and in the ratio of material cost to final cost.

Chapter Two

[1] Chester Martin, *Dominion Lands Policy* (Toronto, 1938), Chapters 9 and 10.

[2] *Ibid.,* 232. Townships were laid down containing 36 sections in 6 rows of 6 sections each and numbered horizontally beginning with the southeast corner. All even numbered sections were available as homesteads, except 8 and three-quarters of 26, which were Hudson's Bay lands. In every fifth township all of 26 went to the Hudson's Bay Co. All odd numbered sections were reserved for railway grants except sections 11 and 29, the school lands. Each section was bounded on three sides by a 66-foot allowance for road construction.

[3] *Ibid.,* 431.

[4] *Ibid.,* 499.

[5] See Chapter IV, Section II.

[6] For a discussion of the physical factors see W. A. Mackintosh, *Prairie Settlement: The Geographical Setting* (Toronto, 1934).

[7] By 1886 "Red Fife had replaced other varieties on the prairies after a circuitous migration from Ontario down the Ohio, into Minnesota, and back to Canadian territory." Marquis ripened faster than Red Fife but it came too late to contribute to Manitoba's settlement. "The settlement after 1900 was essentially that of Palliser's triangle . . . and here the problem was not of frost but of drought." V. C. Fowke, *Canadian Agricultural Policy* (Toronto, 1946), 234-6.

[8] *Ibid.*, 237.

[9] *Ibid.*, 239.

[10] Historical tables of wheat prices and freight rates from the West to Liverpool are available in the statistical appendices of W. A. Mackintosh's study, *Economic Problems of the Prairie Provinces* (Toronto, 1935).

[11] *Ibid.*, 13.

[12] *Ibid.*, 283.

[13] D. B. Hanna, *Trains of Recollection* (Toronto, 1924), 112-13.

[14] Compare N. J. Silberling, *The Dynamics of Business* (New York, 1943), 188-9, with the data shown in Chapter IV, Section II below.

[15] Silberling, *The Dynamics of Business*, Chapters 9 and 10.

[16] H. Hoyt, *One Hundred Years of Land Values in Chicago* (Chicago, 1933), Chapter 4.

[17] D.B.S., *Agriculture, Climate and Population of the Prairie Provinces of Canada* (Ottawa, 1931), *passim*. Hereafter called *Statistical Atlas*.

[18] *Statistical Atlas*, 41.

[19] Various issues of *Canada Year Book*.

[20] D. A. MacGibbon, *The Canadian Grain Trade* (Toronto, 1932), 55.

[21] *Decennial Census*, 1931, VIII, 29.

[22] Extensive investment accompanies population growth and the discovery of new resources; intensive investment is related to technological change. (See A. H. Hansen, *Fiscal Policy and Business Cycles* (New York, 1941), Chapter 2.) The degree of "capital intensity" in agriculture, in the sense of the ratio of equipment to product, appeared to change very little, if at all during the period under review (see below).

[23] See Table II, Chapter I.

[24] Of 390,000 homestead entries made from 1901 to 1914, 110,000 were made by Americans, 107,000 by Canadians (including many returning from the United States), and 69,000 by British immigrants. A tendency to excessive speculation characterized these groups with the result that tenancy was much higher among them after inflation subsided than among the continental European settlers with whom farming was more a "way of life." By 1930 the continental European "is preeminently the owner-operator of the Canadian West. The United States immigrants are at the other extreme." (R. W. Murchie, *Agricultural Progress on the Prairie Frontier* (Toronto, 1936), 119.)

[25] The source of plotted product and acreage data and of yields referred to in the text is "World Wheat Crops, 1885 to 1932" in *Wheat Studies of the Food Research Institute* (Stanford University, 1932-33), IX, 239-274. The series on the average annual selling price of land is from

Canada Year Book, 1930. The price series from D.B.S. is for No. 1 Northern, Fort William-Port Arthur.

[26] See Figure 2 above.

[27] Farm operators did not make impressively rational decisions. For example, W. A. Mackintosh suggests that at the peak of the boom western farms capitalized land values on the basis of the record yields of 1915 and the record prices of 1918-20 (*Economic Background of Dominion-Provincial Relations* (Ottawa, 1939), 39).

[28] D.B.S., *Indexes of Prices of Farm Products and of Commodities Farmers Buy*.

[29] The numbers of physical housing units added in the six quinquennia from 1901 to 1930 were, in thousands, 62.9, 85.3, 24.2, 42.4, 5.0, and 45.0, successively.

[30] That Canadian urban building has followed cycles 15 to 20 years in length is demonstrated in Chapter IV below.

[31] The most important innovations were the tractor, the automobile, and later the combine. At the same time field implements were greatly improved for use with the tractor. Estimates of the increased efficiency of some twenty standard implements over this period appear in *Special Committee on Farm Implements* (Ottawa, 1937), Chapter 8. For a fairly comprehensive study of technology and western agriculture see A. Stewart, *The Economy of Machine Production in Agriculture* (Montreal, 1931). Also Barger and Landsberg, *American Agriculture, 1899-1939* (New York 1942), Chapter 5.

[32] The first refinery on the prairies was built at a cost of $2.5 million in Regina in 1916. It began processing crude oil from Wyoming at a rate of 1,500 barrels a day. The early gasoline-powered tractors were large, difficult to handle, and inefficient. Radical changes in design and performance were made in 1918. In Saskatchewan alone 3,500 were sold in the following year. (Cf. Imperial Oil Co. booklet *Power for the Prairie*, 1954.)

[33] Annual sales in each province, 1918-30 are reported in the trade journal *Canadian Farm Implements*. (See December 1930 issue.) Reports on the sales of combine are available from 1926 on in the same journal.

[34] Murchie, *Agricultural Progress*, 27.

[35] The more rapid movement of grain off farms placed severe strain upon interior elevator capacity. (See D. A. MacGibbon, *The Canadian Grain Trade*, 115-17.)

[36] In 1921, 73.4 of the 157.0 thousand; and in 1931, 21.5 of the 48.4 thousand trucks and 133.5 of the 321.3 passenger cars. (Sources: *Decennial Census* and D.B.S., *Iron and Steel Industry*.) To allow for the probability that farm automobiles are not on the average of the more costly varieties, 25 per cent of the total expenditure on automobiles was allocated to farm. No effort was made to break down the expenditure on passenger cars by farmers between consumer and investment outlay. Official estimates show 50 per cent of the expenditure as producer investment.

[37] W. A. Mackintosh, *Economic Problems*, 18.
[38] R. H. Coats, *Report of the Board of Inquiry into Cost of Living* (Ottawa, 1915), II, and D.B.S., *Prices and Price Indexes*, 1930.
[39] Barger and Landsberg estimated the increase in the product per worker in United States agriculture in the neighbourhood of 50 per cent from 1900 to 1930 (*American Agriculture*, 251, 295). Greater gains were registered in field crops than in dairying and livestock (*ibid.*, 295). Since the former predominate in western Canada, the 100 per cent gain suggested by the rough measures in the text is probably not much too high. The indexes of efficiency of farm implements cited above registered a 60 per cent improvement from 1910-14 to 1932.
[40] See, for example, the treatment in W. A. Mackintosh, *Economic Problems*, 17-18.

Chapter Three

[1] H. A. Innis, Introduction to Glazebrook's *History of Transportation in Canada* (Toronto, 1938); H. A. Innis, *History of the Canadian Pacific Railway* (Toronto, 1923); O. D. Skelton, *The Railway Builders* (Toronto, 1921); *Report of the Royal Commission to Inquire into Railways and Transportation* (Ottawa, 1917); *Report of the Royal Commission on Railways and Transportation* (Ottawa, 1931), hereafter referred to as Duff Report; and W. T. Jackman, *Economic Principles of Transportation* (Toronto, 1935).
[2] Fowke, *Canadian Agricultural Policy*, (Toronto, 1946) 220-2.
[3] *Duff Report*, 92.
[4] *Ibid.*, 92.
[5] It is for this reason that Silberling has suggested that Schumpeter's theory of development would be sounder if limited to innovations in transportation. (N. J. Silberling, *The Dynamics of Business* (New York, 1943), 213-15.)
[6] Even public capital resources have been inadequate to realize the full potential of the waterways from Fort William to the Gulf of St. Lawrence. At each step in their development the economic result has never fulfilled the hopeful expectations based on the dream of the complete unit.
[7] D. A. MacGibbon, *The Canadian Grain Trade* (Toronto, 1932), 118. Capacity was developed to move the grain in the fall. During the other seven or eight months of the year up to 60 per cent of all cars were idle.
[8] An interesting account of construction practices during the extensive phase is given by the first president of the C.N.R., Mr. D. B. Hanna (*Trains of Recollection* (Toronto, 1924), 273-5). For example, wooden tressels were installed because they were cheaper and more quickly built and because the earth's foundation made it uncertain whether first locations were well selected. Building costly embankments at the outset would have required a great many teams of horses

to move thousands of cubic feet of earth or rock, with consequent great delay in laying track. Light wooden tressels were quickly erected then, later, fills were made using work trains instead of horses, with steam shovels instead of men to load and unload the cars. These replacements were among the most costly that the C.N.R. made during the early twenties.

9 This contrast in the behaviour of gross construction and equipment expenditures would probably be more marked if proper deflators were applied. An index of equipment prices based on unit prices shows a smaller rise from 1913 to 1930 than any available indexes of construction costs. (Cf. W. H. Shaw, *The Value of Commodity Output since 1869* (New York, 1947), Appendix.) Adjustments for the implications of technology in the two fields would probably lower the former index more than the latter.

10 Canadian railway statistics were overhauled in 1907. For that reason most of the comparisons in the text are limited to the period 1907-30. The chief sources of the data used are the official sources cited in Chapter X, exhibits presented in recent cases, and W. T. Jackman, *Economic Principles of Transportation* (Toronto, 1935).

11 Exhibits 66, 67, *Thirty Per Cent Case.*

12 *Ibid.,* Exhibit 68.

13 The change in the type of equipment and the length of trains is evident in the following comparisons; average number of tons per loaded car increased from 15.37 tons in 1907 to 25.96 in 1928, the average number of tons per freight train increased 114 per cent in the same period. The change in demand over the same period is reflected in a rise of 121 per cent in tonnage carried and an increase of 256 per cent in the number of tons carried one mile. However, the peak demand in 1928 was not typical of the later period.

14 See Chapter XI for a description of accounting methods employed in this period by different Canadian railroads and Exhibit 144, *Thirty Per Cent Case,* for estimates of the average life of roads and equipment.

15 The relation of railway construction to total gross construction was shown above in Table IV. The following are the percentages that railway equipment investment comprised of all machinery and equipment investment for the seven quinquennia from 1896 to 1930: 8.7, 10.0, 15.7, 15.9, 12.9, 11.0, 9.3.

16 It is shown later that the addition of local transport facilities to this group does not alter this general pattern and, in fact, accentuates it.

17 From the official estimates of capital formation. Unpublished annual estimates were obtained from the Department of Trade and Commerce, Ottawa.

18 Interpolating 1927 and 1928 from 1926, 1929, and 1930. Total municipal expenditures, 1926-30, were $171 million. (*Public Investment and Capital Formation,* Dominion-Provincial Conference (Ottawa, 1945).

19 Cf. Appendix table M.

20 Jackman, *Economic Principles,* Chapter 21.

[21] Jacob Viner, *Canada's Balance of International Indebtedness, 1900-1913* (Cambridge, 1924), 303.

[22] Estimated on the basis of the census of occupations for 1931.

[23] Cf. Jackman, *Economic Principles*, 58. Thousands of tons hauled one mile per mile of line were 786, 810, 762, and 610 in 1913, 1920, 1924 and 1931 respectively.

[24] *Ibid.*, 70.

[25] *Ibid.*, 70.

[26] *Duff Report*, 13.

Chapter Four

[1] It should be noted that use of the term "cycle" does not imply belief in an inevitable periodic process of construction, but only the absence of stability at any level. Timing and amplitude of each cycle will vary with the character of the economic opportunities that induced it. In the absence of urban opportunities, as, for example, in the Maritimes from 1920 to 1940, there will be no cycle and the concomitant stagnation in urban residential building and real estate activity could persist indefinitely.

[2] O. J. Firestone, *The Importance of the Construction Industry in Relation to the Canadian Economy* (Ottawa, 1942), 89. This is the first of five reports prepared for the Committee on Post-War Reconstruction.

[3] It is doubtful whether even income from wheat exports – which probably has much larger leverage effects than income from other leading exports such as newsprint, base metals, and gold – gives rise to smaller leakages than construction. That both wheat exports and construction activity failed to recover in the late thirties probably explains why ratios between changes in G.N.P. and changes in exports plus investment were smaller in the late thirties than in the late twenties.

[4] Imports (plus duties) accounted for 36.4 per cent, 38.6 per cent, and 41.5 per cent of domestic disappearance of machinery and equipment at producers' prices in 1901-5, 1911-15, and 1926-30, respectively.

[5] The construction estimates from *Public Investment and Capital Formation* (Ottawa, 1945) are consistent conceptually and in coverage with the estimates from 1901 to 1930. The difference in the estimates for total construction for the five years 1926-30 in which the two series overlap is less than 1 per cent. It is remarkable that the three major components of gross construction should account for so much of the total. The level of the global estimates of total construction may be too low: it is 16.5 per cent lower than the revised official estimates for 1926-30, (Cf. *Private and Public Investment in Canada, 1926-1951* (Ottawa 1951).) The problem of reconciling the three sets of estimates is dealt with in my paper "Capital Formation in Canada," *Studies in Income and Wealth*, Volume XIX (National Bureau of Economic Research, New York, in press).

[6] The indexes are based on records of Hugh C. MacLean Publications

Ltd., Toronto. Cancellations would not invalidate the present use of the series. Cancellations relative to totals would be fairly stable except in crisis years like 1929.

[7] J. R. Riggleman, "Building Cycles in the United States, 1875-1932," *Journal of the American Statistical Association*, 1933, 179; C. D. Long, *Building Cycles and the Theory of Investment* (Princeton, New Jersey, 1940); W. H. Newman, "The Building Industry and Business Cycles," *Journal of Business Studies*, 1935; Homer Hoyt, *One Hundred Years of Land Values in Chicago* (Chicago, 1933); G. F. Warren and F. A. Pearson, *World Prices and the Building Industry* (New York, 1937).

[8] After 1885 the index is based on values of permits issued in major cities, adjusted for changes in the cost of construction. Before 1886 the index is based on numbers of permits for new buildings in Montreal. The index is described in Chapter XI.

[9] Over the years there have been changes in most cities in the types of building for which permits are required, the area within which the law applies, and the enforcement of the law. It is known that some builders understate the anticipated cost in the hope of getting a lower tax assessment, while others, speculative builders for example, may overstate the cost to dupe prospective buyers. The completion of the structures will lag behind the issue of the permits three or four months for modest dwellings and up to several years for large projects like hotels and office buildings. Also the permits are not always used and the lapse rate varies over the building cycle. Most types of public building and engineering construction are not fully covered by permits, and rural construction is not covered at all.

[10] Cf. Chapter XI.

[11] Before the mid-nineties frequent complaints about these shortcomings in the permit law appeared in early issues of *Canadian Architect and Builder* (vault records, Hugh C. MacLean Publications Ltd., Toronto).

[12] The predominance of transfers, mortgages, and discharges of mortgages in total registrations may be seen in Appendix table P, showing Toronto and York registrations.

[13] The number of mortgages discharged followed a similar pattern; the only differences being a lag in the peak during the twenties (1925) and a smaller amplitude in the cycles.

[14] The records gave values until 1924. Thereafter values were calculable for the Toronto region from tax records. The present writer compiled value series for the period 1895-1924 and secured the values for later years from a study undertaken for Central Mortgage and Housing Corporation by H. L. Buckley. (Cf. Chapter XI).

[15] M. C. MacLean, *Analysis of the Stages in the Growth of Population in Canada* (Ottawa, 1935).

[16] Persons per household were applied to total population to calculate households at each census date: Dominion Bureau of Statistics, *Eighth Census of Canada*, 1941, V, 2, and I, 5.

[17] Jerome establishes conclusively, it seems to me, that before the restrictions on international migrations became severe, movements of population into and out of the United States in the short run were induced by short-period industrial fluctuations. (Cf. H. Jerome, *Migration and Business Cycles* (New York, 1926).)

[18] This notion is accepted by C. D. Long. After a detailed examination of building permit cycles in the United States, Long is left, for explanation of the long cycles, with "the psychological feeling on the part of business men concerning the life of assets in a 'progressive business.' In a new country such as the United States 'psychological life' would be shorter and replacements would recover sooner, than would be true in old and mature countries. This may account for shorter building cycles in this country than in Europe" (Long, *Building Cycles*, 165).

[19] N. J. Silberling, *The Dynamics of Business* (New York, 1943), 176, 178, 187-9, 227.

[20] There are some parallels between the present residential building boom and that of the twenties. The impacts of war and new resource developments appear in both, and the suburban spread of larger cities reflecting changes in tastes and techniques continues. But there are new factors operating in our export market and also greater government participation in the provision of housing. Most important is the need for housing that accumulated during the thirties and during the war among the urban population. Also there has been a large movement from farms of the redundant farm labour force held back by a decade of depression. Another substantial farm movement is that of commerical grain farms into urban residence.

[21] Two population studies were used: M. C. MacLean, *Analysis of the Stages in the Growth of Population in Canada*, and Nathan Keyfitz, "The Growth of Canadian Population", *Population Studies*, IV, No. 1, 47-63.

[22] The remarkably high level of concealed unemployment on Canadian farms in the thirties was not fully recognized until the war was well under way. In spite of the movement of thousands of the agricultural population into the armed services and industrial employment, physical agricultural output was expanded to record levels.

[23] M. C. MacLean, *Analysis of the Stages in the Growth of Population in Canada*, 14-48.

[24] Some showed large declines; none increased by as much as 14 per cent, the minimum rate of expected native increase according to MacLean.

[25] In the four cities proper, 174, 542.

[26] From Macoun's *History of the North West*, written in 1882 and quoted in Bank of Nova Scotia, *Monthly Review*, November 1937.

[27] MacLean, *Analysis of the Stages in the Growth of Population in Canada*, 32.

[28] Ibid., 33.

[29] R. H. Coats, *Report of the Board of Inquiry into Cost of Living* (Ottawa, 1915), II, 956.

[30] There may well have been a series of shifts: eastern farmers going into eastern cities may have been replaced by foreign immigrants; farm

population in rural counties in the neighbourhood of cities may have absorbed labour, and so on. However, whatever the immediate background of individual movements, the cities and towns grew rapidly.

[31] Industrial production was still in the handicraft stage and was widely scattered in the small towns and villages of the rural economy. Urbanization and the factory system proceeded together after the tariff of 1879 and railways became adjuncts of industry as well as of commerce; trade had been the basis of the port cities.

[32] Calendar year figures on immigrant arrivals were available in the *Canada Year Book*. A three-year moving average has been applied to eliminate minor fluctuations.

[33] Compare Silberling, *Dynamics of Business*, 188-9.

[34] London data are those of J. C. Spensley for Metropolitan Police District, 1871-1918, reported in "Urban Housing Problems," *Journal of the Royal Statistical Society*, March 1918, taken here from Warren and Pearson, *World Prices*, 119. The Montreal data are available at the Montreal Archives and in *Annual Reports of the Building Inspector*, Montreal.

[35] A. K. Cairncross reports the number of houses built in Glasgow, 1870-1914, in *Review of Economic Studies*, October 1934. Charts of his data in Warren and Pearson, 120, show one cycle beginning in 1865, reaching a peak in the mid-seventies, dropping to a trough in the early eighties: that is, in phase with the North American cycle of that period. However, a second longer cycle got into phase with the London cycle from 1890 to 1913, except for a double peak at the turn of the century caused by a sharp, short drop in one year. The contrary movement of the Glasgow and London building fluctuations before the eighties may also be explained by internal population movements. In another interesting article in the *Manchester School* (1949), Dr. Carincross analyses internal migration in England and Wales from census data, 1841-1911. There was movement from southern towns, dominated by London, to northern towns during this period. The southern towns experienced net losses in both the seventies and eighties. Northern towns gained in the seventies, then also lost in the eighties. In the nineties the northern towns continued to lose and the movement from north to south, which had been evident since 1841, came to an end. The outflow from southern towns almost ceased. Emigration which had been very heavy in the eighties, was temporarily checked. These studies of Dr. Cairncross and also the data referred to in the following footnote are now available in more convenient form in his book *Home and Foreign Investment, 1870-1913* (Cambridge University Press, 1953).

[36] Cf. Cairncross, "Home and Foreign Investment in Great Britain, 1870-1913" (doctoral thesis, Library of the University of Cambridge), Chapter 9; also E. W. Cooney, "Capital Exports, and Investment in Building in Britain and the U.S.A.," *Economica*, November 1949, 347-54. This article treats capital flows as the prime mover. New resources – frontier opportunities in North America – attracted both labour and capital. About two-thirds of all emigrants from the British

Isles from 1870 to 1913 sailed for North America. Time series compiled by Dr. Cairncross on British and Irish passengers to the United States and English and Scottish emigrants both show long cycles like those of American building. Both came out of major troughs in the seventies and nineties two or three years before recovery from similar troughs in American building. It is significant that the flow of capital from the United Kingdom recovered from its major trough at the same time in the seventies but four years later in the nineties.

[37] The wartime trough of 1918 is the one exception.

[38] See, for example, numerous statistical studies in Hoyt, *One Hundred Years of Land Values*, 453-5. Indexes of gross rents understate the variations in the incentive to invest in both directions because operating expenses tend neither to rise nor to fall in the same proportion.

[39] These accounted for a part of the buoyancy of the index of engineering construction in Figure 5, which also rose through the recession after 1920. Highway construction to meet demands occasioned by the automobile was another important factor.

Chapter Five

[1] Maritime resistance was overcome by temporary tariff concessions, federal assumption of debts, and the Intercolonial Railway. There was no powerful agrarian export region, as in the southern states, to go to war on the questions of free land and tariffs. Since the West was unsettled, the incidence of the tariff could be discounted in advance.

[2] Cf. Chapters II and VI.

[3] V. C. Fowke, *Canadian Agricultural Policy* (Toronto, 1946).

[4] See Table XVI. Investment in railways, excluded from government totals in Table XVI, are included in Table XIX.

[5] The federal government made a contribution. The whole outlay regardless of source of funds is treated as provincial investment if the province directs the work. This point is discussed in Chapter XI.

[6] Information on Hydro has been drawn from W. R. Plewman, *Adam Beck and the Ontario Hydro* (Toronto, 1947); and *Annual Reports* of the Commission, *Ontario Sessional Papers*. Sources on T.N.O. are cited in Chapter XI. Information on finance is from S. Bates, *Financial History of Canadian Governments* (Ottawa, 1939).

[7] The province contributed one-third of the cost of construction of approved roads in the county system in southern Ontario. The work was done by the municipal authorities.

[8] In 1911 their population was 18.4 per cent of the national total.

[9] The comparison ignores utilities. Expenditures on telephone on the prairies and railways and power in Ontario were undertaken at this time; British Columbia entered the railway field at a later date.

Chapter Six

¹ Private investment excludes direct government investment but includes investment of government-owned enterprises. Deficits and surpluses from 1900 to 1930 were calculated by the writer.

The deficit or surplus for a given period is reflected in the net change in the sum of gross funded debt, less sinking funds, plus treasury bills, bank debt, and other temporary loans outstanding at the beginning and end of the period.

Complete information on municipal debt before 1920 is not available. D. C. MacGregor's study, cited below, covers the years since 1920. On the basis of an estimate for municipal debt in 1895 made by the federal Department of Agriculture, and information on Ontario from 1900, on Manitoba and Saskatchewan from 1905, on British Columbia from 1910, and on Quebec from 1915, the gaps were filled by interpolating percentages to raise the available samples to full coverage.

The following sources on public debt in Canada were consulted: D. C. MacGregor, "Statistics of Public Debt in Canada," *Contributions to Canadian Economics* (Toronto, 1933), III, 45-60; *University of Toronto Studies: History and Economics I* (1900), No. 3; K. W. Taylor and H. Michell, *Statistical Contributions to Canadian Economic History* (Toronto, 1931); *Public Accounts Inquiry,* (Ottawa, 1939) Appendix I; C. Goldenberg. *Municipal Finance in Canada* (Ottawa, 1939); S. Bates, *Financial History of Canadian Governments* (Ottawa, 1939); successive issues of the following:`Canada Year Book; Statistical Year Book of Quebec; Annual Reports,* Department of Municipal Affairs, Saskatchewan; *Annual Reports,* Bureau of Industries, Ontario; *Municipal Bulletins,* Department of Agriculture, Ontario; *British Columbia Year Book* (published irregularly); also the various *Public Accounts,* and *Submissions* of the provinces of British Columbia and Manitoba to the Royal Commission on Dominion-Provincial Relations, cited in Chapter XI.

² The estimates of the gross national product should be used with caution. See Chapter XI for the sources and methods used.

³ The question of an appropriate charge for capital replacements has not been finally settled and revision may lower it.

⁴ J. J. Deutsch, "War Finance and the Canadian Economy," *Canadian Journal of Economics and Political Science,* 1940, 538-9.

⁵ Professor Knox's estimate for 1914 was obtained by adding imports of capital to the estimate of indebtedness for 1900. Some expansion in the book value of equities may have occurred. (Cf. Jacob Viner, *Canada's Balance of International Indebtedness,* 1900-1913 (Cambridge, 1924), 99, and the appendix by Knox to Marshall, Taylor, and Southard, *Canadian-American Industry* (New Haven, 1936). D.B.S. valued bonds at par, and equities at the value of capital stock plus surplus reported in company balance sheets – which allows for reinvestment of

profits (*The Canadian Balance of International Payments, 1926 to 1948* (Ottawa, 1949), 147).

[6] Viner, *Canada's Balance*, 303.

[7] D.B.S., *The Canadian Balance* (Ottawa, 1949), 181-2.

[8] H. Marshal, K. W. Taylor, and F. A. Southard Jr., *Canadian-American Industry;* also Viner, *Canada's Balance*, Chapter 12.

[9] Viner, *Canada's Balance*, 286.

[10] D.B.S., *The Canadian Balance* (Ottawa, 1949), 84. Over 70 per cent of this direct investment was in the form of equities.

[11] Cf. D.B.S., *The Canadian Balance of International Payments* (Ottawa, 1939), Chapter 4; and *The Canadian Balance* (Ottawa, 1949), 77-81.

[12] *Report of the Special Committee on Farm Implement Prices* (Ottawa, 1937), 1254.

[13] R. W. Murchie, *Agricultural Progress on the Prairie Frontier* (Toronto, 1936), 72-3.

[14] *Ibid.*, 73.

[15] For a detailed description see D. A. MacGibbon, *The Canadian Grain Trade* (Toronto, 1932), Chapter 14.

[16] The complete account upon which this part of the note is based appears in W. T. Easterbrook, *Farm Credit in Canada* (Toronto, 1938).

[17] *Ibid.*, 43.

[18] *Ibid.*, 31.

[19] *Ibid.*, 192.

[20] The best account of the collapse of the prairie economy appears in the study of G. E. Britnell, *The Wheat Economy* (Toronto, 1939).

[21] Including agreements of sale.

[22] Mackintosh, *Economic Problems of the Prairie Provinces* (Toronto, 1935), Chapter 9.

[23] *Report of the Royal Commission on Railways and Transportation* (Ottawa, 1931) (Duff Report), 29-30.

[24] H. A. Innis, *History of the Canadian Pacific Railway* (Toronto, 1938), 107 ff.

[25] *Ibid.*

[26] See Table XXIV, from the Appendix to the *Submission of the C.P.R., to the Royal Commission on Transportation,* 1949.

[27] Par value, originally $100, was split four for one in the late twenties. (Cf. *Report on Net Investment* filed with the Board of Transport Commissioners by the C.P.R. on October 27, 1953).

[28] Chester Martin, *Dominion Lands Policy* (Toronto, 1938), 314-15.

[29] *Report of the Royal Commission to Inquire into Railways and Transportation, 1917 Drayton-Acworth Report,* p. xxxvi.

Chapter Seven

[1] O. J. Firestone, "Estimate of the Gross Value of Construction in Canada, 1940," *Canadian Journal of Economics and Political Science,* May 1943; D. C. MacGregor, "Gross and Net Investment in

Canada – Tentative Estimates," ibid., February 1941. Also the official estimates in *Public Investment and Capital Formation* (Ottawa, 1945); hereafter referred to as *P.I.C.F.;* and *Private and Public Investment in Canada, 1926-1951* (Ottawa, 1951); hereafter *P.P.I.*

[2] Cf. *P.I.C.F.,* 103.

[3] The possible discrepancies between cost of construction and costs to final users are eliminated in the present estimates by defining speculative builders as final users. Speculative builders may produce for stock, perhaps renting for a period of time, expecting to sell in a rising market. If they are regarded as final users, the consequent gains or losses after lapse of time are capital changes similar to those which occur in any kind of financial investment and transfer of existing assets.

[4] The repair work covered appears low; it was 16 per cent of the total of new and repair in 1921 and approximately the same percentage in the other years from 1919 to 1922.

[5] *Decennial Census of Canada, 1921,* IV; and D.B.S., *Census Bulletin* (1941), No. 0-6.

[6] Other skilled workers not following a construction occupation, by census definition, but employed on the site of construction projects.

[7] *Decennial Census, 1931,* V, Table 16.

[8] The percentage distribution in the census of construction was 43.21, 41.07, and 15.72 per cent for material, labour, and other costs. The value of materials added for owner-builders, farmers, etc., was $45 million, and the imputed value of labour was $15 million. Adding these to the breakdown of components derived from the construction census yielded the percentages given in the text.

[9] s This convention was followed in *P.I.C.F.*

[10] "Of the nineteen years (1921-39), fourteen showed overhead and profit ratios varying from 8 to 12 per cent, with a median of 10 per cent, while five years, in the early 'twenties and 'thirties, showed ratios from 13 to 15 per cent." O. J. Firestone, *Residential Real Estate in Canada* (Toronto, 1951), 404.

[11] The average ratio was 1.127 from 1919 to 1922. This was also the ratio in 1921. Converted to 1913 prices and wage rates, the ratio of wages to material costs was .919.

[12] Buckley, "Capital Formation in Canada," *Studies in Income and Wealth,* XIX (National Bureau of Economic Research, New York).

[13] Cf. *Labour Gazette,* publication of Department of Labour, Ottawa.

[14] *Decennial Census of Canada, 1941,* VI, 90 and 92.

[15] *Ibid.,* VII, 670; and *Census Bulletin* (1941), No. 0-6, 10-11.

[16] The files of the study are now in the Department of Trade and Commerce.

[17] *Census Bulletin* (1941) No. 0-6, 10-11. Cf. also Table 20, *Decennial Census, 1941,* VII, and Table 59, *Decennial Census, 1931,* VII.

[18] The "good roads policy" of 1921 and 1922. (Cf. *Canada Year Book, 1926,* 430.)

[19] Cf. O. J. Firestone, "Construction in Canada, 1940," *C.J.E.P.S.,* 1943, 225.

[20] The so-called "bridge companies" have reported to the census of man-

ufactures in every year of the census from 1900 to 1930. An examination of the schedules at D.B.S. revealed that less than 50 per cent of their product was bridges (for the period 1919-30), an equally large part was building construction, chiefly commercial, industrial, also some residential and institutional building.

21 Not until 1920 was a precise commodity allocation undertaken. The data are available if not in publications then in files of the D.B.S. At the end of the twenties they were published in a single bulletin, *The Manufacturing Industries of Canada, A Summary Report.*

22 *Forest Products Bulletin* (Forestry Branch, Department of the Interior, Ottawa), No. 25, 19.

23 *Statistical Year Book* (Quebec), 1915, 468.

24 Cf. *Canada Year Book,* 1942, 402.

25 The quantity of logs for lumber reported in the census for the year 1900 was measured by the "contents of the logs when sawn into lumber computed according to the following rule in census instructions viz: From ¼ of the diameter of the log in inches subtract 1, and multiply the square of the remainder by the length in feet. The product will be the content of the log in feet, b.m." (Cf. Introduction, *Decennial Census of Canada,* 1901, II, p. 1xi.)

26 R. H. Coats, *Report of the Board of Inquiry into Cost of Living* (Ottawa, 1915), 967.

27 "The American Iron and Steel Association collects and publishes annually very complete statistics of the production of iron and steel in Canada." Annual Report on the Mineral Production of Canada (Ottawa, 1908), 80. As late as 1919, John McLeish who compiled and published the official statistics made the following statement: "The record of production of finished rolled iron and steel collected and published by the American Iron and Steel Institute and the American Iron and Steel Association covers a longer period of time and is possibly more complete (than Mines Branch data)." *Annual Report of the Production of Iron and Steel* (Ottawa, 1919), 21.

28 This was the value of ties and poles sold to steam and electric railways and telephone and power companies in Canada, plus the value of ties and poles exported, reported in *Forest Products* (Ottawa, 1908).

29 According to customs officials quoted by Jacob Viner, *Canada's Balance of International Indebtedness, 1900 to 1914* (Cambridge, 1924), 26.

30 S. S. Kuznets, *National Product since 1869,* (New York, 1946), 63.

31 *P.I.C.F.,* 103.

32 The data were prepared for the computation of another index. Construction materials included: iron and steel structural materials; lumber; logs, posts, and poles; asphalt; building stone; sand and gravel; sewer pipe and drain tiles; bricks and artificial stone; lime and plaster; cement.

33 Cf. Viner, *Canada's Balance,* 245. Viner shows a change of plus 8 and minus 1.3 per cent in this period. His index is supported by comparisons made by Coats, *Cost of Living Report. 337.*

34 *P.I.C.F.,* 103.

NOTES 247

[35] *Revised Statutes of Canada*: 1920, C 71; 1921, C50; 1922, C 47; 1923, C 70; 1924, C 68; 1927, C 36; 1928, C 50; 1929, C 57; 1930, C 43.

Chapter Eight

[1] Data on many of these installations were not available for early years. The major items, telephone and telegraph equipment, have been included in the estimates of machinery and equipment in this study. They were treated as construction materials in *Public Investment and Capital Formation* (Ottawa, 1945).

[2] This convention was based on evidence in the *Decennial Census* for 1931 and 1941. Applying the same ratio to early years is a questionable procedure, but there was no basis to support any other. S. S. Kuznets used a similar flat ratio in his estimates of early capital formation in the United States *National Product since 1869* (New York, 1946), 76.

[3] The method of breaking down the series of iron and steel components and non-ferrous metal components is described in connection with the discussion of the interpolations for inter-censal years below.

[4] Jacob Viner, *Canada's Balance of International Indebtedness*, 1900 to 1914 (Cambridge, 1924), 245.

Chapter Nine

[1] The method of estimating stocks from production assumes that simple technical factors govern the relationship between stocks and output and ignores the speculative motive. In view of the parallel with the older cash-balance approach to the quantity theory of money (inventories equal some constant times output), the method is called a transactions model of inventory demand. This method was suggested by T. Barna "Valuation of Stocks and National Income," *Economica*, November 1942).

Chapter Ten

[1] Professor Knox describes his estimates in Marshall *et al.*, *Canadian-American Industry* (New Haven, 1936). His final estimates appear in his study, *Dominion Monetary Policy* (Ottawa, 1939).

[2] *The Canadian Balance of International Payments, 1926 to 1948* (Ottawa, 1949), 125.

[3] If monetary gold movements were included in the current account as in the Knox series, their effect on total investment would be merely offset by equal, opposite changes in gold stocks. The method employed in the present study was adopted in the official estimates of investment. (Cf. *Public Investment and Capital Formation* (Ottawa, 1945), 109.)

[4] I had overlooked this change in concept and am grateful to Penelope Thunberg of the National Bureau of Economic Research who brought it to my attention.

Chapter Eleven

[1] The description of procedures in Section III below is much briefer than in similar sections in earlier chapters. Although the scope of the estimates was not so great, the work involved was as great as, if not greater than, that involved in the global estimates; but in view of the inordinate share of the space already absorbed by these sections, much has been left out. In cutting down, care was taken to include all sources. It is hoped that enough of the procedure is given to establish the quality of the results.

[2] That is, "net" in the railways' use of the term.

[3] Additional data, available in exhibits and other submissions made during the railway rates cases, and during hearings of the Royal Commission on Transportation were used to check the estimates.

[4] It is this wide variation in cost per mile which precludes reliance on investment series based on changes in main-track mileage. Cost for a mile of road varied in Canada from $30,000 on the prairies to $500,000 in the Rockies and to as high as $700,000 in the Laurentian Shield.

[5] Buchanan assessed the cost of rolling stock. Swain estimated the reproduction cost of the road for the Commission.

[6] See *Public Investment and Capital Formation* (Ottawa, 1945), 12-19, for a discussion of the "public finance" and "national income" approaches to public expenditure.

[7] *Ibid.*, 116.

[8] The difficulty of making direct estimates in this field is reflected in the official estimates from 1926 to 1941, which were based on three estimates for 1933, 1937, and 1941. (Cf. *P.I.C.F.*, 117.) Since their 1926 estimate was itself an extrapolation, it was not a strong base for the present extrapolations.

[9] Jacob Viner, *Canada's Balance of International Indebtedness, 1900-1913* (Cambridge, 1924), 121.

[10] The official estimates and a detailed description of their derivation appear in O. J. Firestone's *Residential Real Estate in Canada* (Toronto, 1951).

[11] *Monthly Review*, Bank of Nova Scotia, May 1937.

[12] J. J. Deutsch, "War Finance and the Canadian Economy," *Canadian Journal of Economics and Political Science,* 1940, 538-9.

[13] These were obtained from the balance of payments study by F. A. Knox; see Appendix table G.

[14] See Chapter IV.

[15] J. W. Angell, *Investment and Business Cycles* (New York, 1941), 139.

[16] "The Problem of Price Level in Canada," *C.J.E.P.S.*, May 1947, 157-196.

Index

254

256

THE CARLETON LIBRARY